Social Studies through
Children's Literature

Social Studies through Children's Literature
An Integrated Approach

Anthony D. Fredericks
Assistant Professor of Education
York College
York, Pennsylvania

Illustrated by
Rebecca N. Fredericks

1991
TEACHER IDEAS PRESS
A Division of
Libraries Unlimited, Inc.
Englewood, Colorado

TEACHER IDEAS PRESS
A Division of Libraries Unlimited, Inc.
P.O. Box 6633
Englewood, CO 80155-6633
1-800-237-6124
www.lu.com/tip

Library of Congress Cataloging-in-Publication Data

Fredericks, Anthony D.
    Social studies through children's literature : an integrated
approach / Anthony D. Fredericks ; illustrated by Rebecca N.
Fredericks.
    xvii, 191 p. 22x28 cm.
    Includes bibliographical references and index.
    ISBN 0-87287-970-4
    1. Social studies--Study and teaching (Elementary)--United States.
2. Language experience approach in education--United States.
3. Children's literature--United States.   I. Title.
LB1584.F66   1991
372.83'044'0973--dc20   91-32627
                                                 CIP

*To all my students at York College—
each of whom has enriched my life
with a plethora of possibilities.*

Contents

Preface

As a writer, I constantly find myself asking lots of questions. Queries that begin with "What if ...?" "Why can't ...?" "What's another way of ...?" and "How does ...?" are typical of those that greet me each morning as I face my computer screen. As a teacher, I also find myself asking students innumerable questions such as "Why do you believe ...?" "Can you elaborate ...?" "What do you think about ...?" and "What if ...?" I suspect that this inquisitive nature is a natural consequence of both professions. In a sense, writers and teachers are constantly seeking new dimensions for exploration, stretching those already in existence, or attempting to expand the parameters of creative thought. To use a "Star Trek" phrase, it could be said that all of us who educate are continually trying "to boldly go where no one has gone before."

Indeed, what I find most intriguing about the educative process is that there are *always* new possibilities just down the street or around the next corner. I often tell my students that "the best teachers are those who have as much to learn as they do to teach." So it is with children, who need to be provided with constant and frequent opportunities to stretch their imaginations and expand their perceptions of the world outside the classroom. The subject we refer to as *social studies* offers an arena where that can happen, not just for a few minutes each day, but for each and every minute of the entire school year.

Social Studies through Children's Literature was born of a perceived need to infuse the use of children's literature into the *entire* elementary curriculum. It also grew out of conversations with educators around the country who were seeking to expand social studies and make it part of a truly integrated curriculum. If one subscribes to the notion that books and reading are vehicles by which students can explore every dimension of their world (and beyond), then we should also believe that we can facilitate those discoveries through an active, process-oriented, and literature-based social studies program. This book is designed to offer teachers, librarians, administrators, parents, and anyone else who works with children a participatory approach to social studies education — an approach that says that when students are provided opportunities to make an investment of self in their education, that education will become both meaningful and relevant.

During research for *Social Studies through Children's Literature*, it became evident that many teachers were frustrated by a lack of sufficient social studies materials as well as requirements to use outdated or lackluster texts. Yet I also discovered classrooms in California, Georgia, New York, Ohio, Nevada, and Pennsylvania where teachers were casting aside traditional methods of social studies instruction and where the *social studies plus literature* connection was as much a part of the regular curriculum as were silent reading time and math homework. These were exciting classrooms that demonstrated the overwhelming power of a holistic approach to education.

The projects and activities offered in these pages have come from several sources: my own fifteen years of public and private school teaching, conversations and visits with educators from throughout the country, a thorough investigation of, and a belief in, the dynamics of the whole language classroom, and the creativity and energy of my teacher education students at York College. The emphasis here is on the *processes* of learning, not the *products*. The suggestions in this book are designed to provide a structure for, and an enhancement of, the teaching of social studies. Novice as well as experienced teachers will find a host of intriguing opportunities that can be used throughout the social studies program, across the curriculum, and with all levels and abilities of students.

As you use this book, you are encouraged to modify, alter, or elaborate on any of the activities as you see fit. You know your students best—their needs, interests, and inclinations should be the springboard for any extensions or modifications of these ideas. It is also important to encourage your students to create their own learning activities for selected pieces of literature. By providing students with real opportunities to create and develop activities that are meaningful to them, you can provide them with the motivation and inspiration to take an active role in the entire social studies/literature program.

It is my hope that you will discover within these pages a plethora of learning possibilities for your classroom and that your students will discover an exciting array of mind-expanding and consciousness-raising experiences. Undoubtedly, this approach involves some risk taking, not only for you, but for your students as well. But if you believe as I do that "nothing ventured, nothing gained" is an appropriate maxim for the holistic classroom, this book will provide both support and encouragement to make your social studies program one in which students continually ask questions, not to find right answers or simple solutions, but rather to discover a host of new and divergent questions and an infinite variety of possibilities.

Anthony D. Fredericks

Acknowledgments

This book would not have been possible without the support and encouragement of many individuals.

A special note of appreciation is due all my students at York College who have provided me with inspiration, creativity, and imagination. Their ideas are liberally sprinkled throughout the pages of this book and reflect their enormous energy and enthusiasm for the teaching profession. May their future classrooms be filled with laughter, love, and loads of literature!

I am indebted to the many elementary school and public librarians throughout York County who led me to new discoveries among the shelves of their libraries. A special note of recognition goes to Carol Hurst of *TEACHING K-8* magazine, who provided me with an invaluable bibliography of literature possibilities.

To my friend, colleague, and editor Suzanne Barchers, who gives me constant support and that necessary pat on the back all writers need now and then, thanks a million.

My daughter Rebecca merits extra recognition and appreciation for her dynamic and creative illustrations. My son Jonathan gets a generous helping of additional affection for his patience in enduring the travels of an itinerant father. And my wife Phyllis deserves special commendation for handling the idiosyncrasies and strange work habits of a writer-teacher-husband with love and patient understanding.

Our department secretary, Bev Snyder, earns a special note of admiration for making our office an efficient and exciting place to work and learn. Our work/study student, Michalene Dauplaise, receives incalculable accolades for her humor and helpfulness on numerous projects.

A special prize deservedly goes to the National Geographic Society for producing the finest and most creative collection of audiovisual materials for the elementary social studies curriculum.

My undying appreciation goes to the WordPerfect Corporation for creating a word processing program that faithfully recorded and preserved all my thoughts and musings despite my frequent inadvertent efforts to do otherwise. Much gratitude is also extended the General Foods Corporation for manufacturing the essential elixir of all writers—rich Colombian coffee.

Perhaps my cats, Norton and Zeb, deserve the highest award of all. They were my constant companions during early morning typing and late night editing. Requiring only an occasional belly scratch and a comfortable place under the computer table, they made sure I was always on the job.

1—Introduction

—Inspiration—

The teacher said to the students, "Come to the edge."
They replied, "We might fall."
The teacher again said, "Come to the edge,"
And they responded, "It's too high."
"COME TO THE EDGE," the teacher commanded.
And they came,
    And she pushed them—
        And they flew!
           —Author unknown

Tell me,
    and I forget.
Show me,
    and I remember.
Involve me,
    and I understand.
        —Chinese proverb

Mrs. McDonald was my sixth-grade teacher at St. Matthew's School in Pacific Palisades, CA. One day I asked her, "How many different uses did the Indians have for the buffalo?" She replied, "I don't know, but let's find out together." And we did.
        —A.D.F.

After more than twenty years of teaching I have discovered three basic teacher behaviors that contribute to the academic success of students. While this may be a simplistic stance on educational excellence, I believe that we make a difference in children's live when we embrace the following triad of factors:

Commitment. Our students succeed because we expect them to succeed. This model of self-efficacy is based on the idea that we, as teachers, make a positive difference in the lives of our students. That we believe our students will grow—educationally, socially, and emotionally—has a significant impact on their success in the outside world.

1

Engagement. The concepts and "learnings" that are most meaningful to our students are those in which students are actively involved. "Hands-on, minds-on" activities are those in which students actively participate, actively make decisions, and actively learn from first-hand experiences. When students can manipulate information, instead of simply digesting data, learning blossoms tremendously.

Teacher as Learner. Becoming a teacher is much more than taking the requisite number of college courses, passing an exam, and being issued a certificate. It is a constant process of growth and regrowth, during which new discoveries about learning, students, and the art of teaching are made every day. It is my fundamental belief that *the best teachers are those who have as much to learn as they do to teach.*

Whether you have been teaching for twenty years or this is your first year of classroom experience, you must agree that this is an exciting time to be in the education profession. We are discovering new and different things about learning and learners. We are discovering that learning is much more than committing a collection of facts and figures to memory—it should be an active processing of information that has personal meaning for individual students. Indeed, when students are provided with opportunities to process and manipulate data, they are able to develop conceptual understandings that extend far beyond the textbook or the four walls of the classroom.

This is no more evident than in the social studies program. Traditional methods of teaching social studies have promoted the memorization of names, places, and dates. Unfortunately, students may not be able to understand the relationships that exist between those pieces of information or how that data relates to their own lives. However, when students are provided with activities that allow them to assume an active role in processing important social studies concepts, then learning mushrooms.

This book is based on the premise that the social studies curriculum can be enriched through the use of quality children's literature in concert with a variety of meaningful "hands-on, minds-on" activities, many of which can occur in the school library. By so doing, teachers and librarians can offer their students a plethora of learning possibilities that extend and enhance the social studies program as well as the entire elementary curriculum. Teachers using literature infuse social studies concepts into every corner of children's lives, sharing with them experiences and precepts that are relevant, purposeful, and interesting.

This book is also oriented to the premise that *you* can significantly enhance the social studies curriculum, that *students* can take an active role in learning social studies, and that *you* AND *your* students can explore new and fascinating dimensions of social studies together as partners in learning. When literature becomes the vehicle for animating the social studies curriculum, your students become the pilots for journeys and destinations which may only be mentioned in the regular textbooks.

In short, this book is not only an alternative approach to the teaching of social studies but can also be an enhancement of your entire classroom program. The use of fiction, nonfiction, narrative, and expository books throughout grades K-3 provides new dimensions and new possibilities for clarifying concepts, motivating students, and expanding all facets of your curriculum. This integrated approach to social studies is built on a foundation of children's literature and the developmental needs of young learners—elements that transcend any and all curricular boundaries. This orientation, I believe, can make your entire social studies curriculum and your whole classroom program exciting, not because students *have to* participate, but because they *want to*!

Views of Social Studies

In my "Teaching Elementary Social Studies" courses each year, I frequently ask prospective teachers to list their recollections of or reactions to the social studies classes they had when they were elementary students. Following are samples of comments that are typically presented by students:

"It was dull and boring."

"I hated it!"

"All we did was read from the textbook and answer questions at the end of each chapter."

"It was always done at the end of the day for about twenty minutes or so."

"I hated it!"

"The teacher wasn't very excited about teaching it."

"The textbook was out of date and wasn't very interesting."

"I hated it!"

These comments are probably indicative of many students' experiences with social studies. Social studies may be seen by most students as an unmotivating and uninspirational part of the elementary curriculum. Often relegated to the end of the day, it is frequently squeezed in whenever time allows or when teachers are required to do so. As a result, students often get the impression that social studies is the least important subject in the curriculum simply because (1) it is given the least amount of time in comparison with subjects such as reading and math, (2) teachers are required to use out-of-date and uninspiring textbooks, (3) there is a dearth of supplemental materials and projects available in social studies, and (4) it is often ursurped by assemblies, field trips, and other special programs. As a result, students may get the idea that social studies is a "filler" subject that can be pulled in and out of the curriculum at will according to the demands of other subjects or the inclinations of the teacher.

In conversations with teachers around the country, I also discover that they, too, frequently have a less-than-enthusiastic response to the social studies program. Perhaps their experiences with social studies when they were students were the result of an overburdened curriculum that allotted less and less time to more and more subjects. As a result, social studies frequently gets short shrift — inserted here and there whenever possible or taught somewhat less enthusiastically than subjects such as reading and language arts. Teachers, just like their students, may feel that social studies textbooks are significantly less stimulating than other texts, but they are required to use them whether they like to or not. As a result, the social studies program may be given the least amount of attention in comparison with other subjects, resulting in decreased enthusiasm on the part of both teachers and students.

Indeed, social studies may be the least favorite subject of both teachers and students alike. A major reason may be that it is viewed as a book-bound topic — that is, the information, knowledge, and skills to be taught and learned come mainly from textbooks. There are few opportunities for students to take an active role in their own learning and appreciation of social studies, nor are there many opportunities for teachers to provide projects and activities that enhance social studies and make it come alive for their classes. In short, social studies is often treated as a passive subject, in which large amounts of factual information are given to children with few opportunities to actively process that data. On the other hand, I believe that social studies can and should be *active, interactive*, and *reactive*.

Active. Students should have a plethora of opportunities to engage in hands-on experiences with social studies. They can manipulate, design, structure, and handle a variety of learning projects.

Interactive. Social studies is not an isolated subject. It can be integrated into all phases of the elementary curriculum, becoming part of each and every subject.

Reactive. Students should be provided with opportunities to engage in active decision making, direct their own courses of study, generate their own queries for exploration, and arrive at individual conclusions as a result of self-directed investigations.

Trying to do all this in an overactive and overburdened curriculum may seem daunting to many teachers, yet my own classroom experiences, as well as those of several colleagues, suggest that it need not be so. We have discovered that when good children's literature is integrated fully into the social studies curriculum, children have learning opportunities that extend far beyond the pages of the text, enhancing their attitudes and aptitudes—not just in social studies, but across the curriculum.

The integration of literature into the social studies curriculum is timely in that there is a wealth of new and exciting children's books now being published that enhance social studies in intriguing and interesting ways. A variety of trade books that have been around for some time can add immeasurably to the entire social studies program. Also, the integration of children's literature into the social studies program is supported by recent curricular changes in states such as Arizona, California, New York, and Wisconsin, each of which has implemented guidelines that underscore a strong relationship between literature and social studies teaching. Even more interesting is that many textbook publishers are now rushing to include literature selections as part of the lessons in their new text series. Although there is increasing interest in and emphasis on making the "literature connection" in social studies, teachers often do not take advantage of these supplemental materials. Instead, they rely on the textbook as their primary source of information.

Social Studies through Children's Literature is based on the idea that incorporating trade books into the elementary social studies program provides students with extended learning opportunities going far beyond the facts and figures of social studies. New worlds of discovery and exploration open up for students through the magic of literature, worlds that expand the curriculum and enlarge students' appreciation of their environment and their place in it.

In the sections to follow, I will share with you not only the value of a literature-based social studies curriculum but also ways in which literature can make your effectiveness as a teacher of social studies more positive and dynamic. Students, too, will gain a new appreciation of social studies through varied literature selections and will be allowed to process information in meaningful contexts.

Social Studies Teaching and Learning

One great fortune of my current job is the many opportunities I have to visit elementary classrooms in my own area and around the country as well. Not too long ago I was invited into several classrooms in an elementary school in upstate New York to share some books and literature with the students. At the conclusion of a storytelling session in one second-grade room, one young man came up to me and said, "You know, Mr. Professor, learning with books sure seems like a lot of fun!" The student's comments were totally unsolicited and may have been part of the impetus for this book, and they send a strong signal that infusing literature and trade books throughout the curriculum can add power to learning and help children appreciate and value the world outside the classroom.

With that in mind, I will share with you some ideas, biases, and beliefs I have about teaching in general and about teaching social studies specifically. I ask you to review these particularly in terms of how literature can and should be part of the teaching/learning cycle in social studies. It is not important that you agree with all of these statements but that you evaluate them in terms of your own philosophy of how to teach social studies and how children can learn social studies.

1. The textbook should not be the entire social studies program. Instead, the program should be broad-based, including a variety of materials and learning options.

2. Students have different learning styles, interests, and ability levels. A well-rounded curriculum will provide learning opportunities for each student rather than stay geared to the so-called average student (if in fact there is such a creature).

3. Integrating social studies into the rest of the curriculum can be a positive experience for children. Students should be able to experience a broad definition of social studies as a positive dimension of all the other subject areas.

4. A child-centered curriculum is more meaningful and relevant than a teacher-directed one. In other words, when students are provided with opportunities to make their own decisions and select learning activities in keeping with their needs and interests, learning becomes much more productive.

5. Inquiry-based learning has powerful implications in any classroom. Allowing students to chart their own paths of discovery and investigation through in-class and library experiences can lead to the inculcation of valuable concepts.

6. Social studies instruction relying on the memorization of dates, names, places, facts, and figures is boring! Placing this information in a context that has meaning for students helps them appreciate significant data as it relates to their lives.

7. Social studies should be taught all day, every day. This statement may be difficult to accept for most teachers, yet it is possible to integrate social studies into every aspect of the elementary curriculum without limiting other subjects or running out of time.

8. Teachers do not need to be repositories of all there is to know about social studies. When teachers work with their students to investigate and learn about areas of mutual interest, children are given a powerful message that a person does not need to know every fact and figure to be competent in social studies. Instead, individuals can share knowledge and information in mutually supportive ways.

9. Social studies is just as important as reading, math, science, and language arts. Social studies becomes important in children's lives when it is integrated into their life experiences and used to extend those experiences.

10. Social studies is fun! Social studies can be one of the most dynamic, exciting, stimulating, and invigorating elements of any school day—particularly when it is taught by an enthusiastic teacher!

Given these precepts, let us look at the composition of the elementary social studies program in terms of teacher responsibilities and student engagement. First, a definition. The National Council for the Social Studies defines *social studies* as follows:

Social studies is a basic subject of the K-12 curriculum that (1) derives its goals from the nature of citizenship in a democratic society that is closely linked to other nations and peoples of the world; (2) draws its content primarily from history, the social sciences, and, in some respects, from the humanities and science; and (3) is taught in ways that reflect an awareness of the personal, social, and cultural experiences and developmental levels of learners (National Council 1984).

The implication is that social studies is a broad-based exploration of people, how they live, and how people get along with one another. To that end, social studies encompasses all of the other disciplines of the elementary curriculum. For example, reading provides the tools to study and learn about humankind; science gives opportunities to understand people and their interactions with the environment; language arts allows people to communicate with one another; and mathematics provides the quantitative tools to measure and evaluate our world. In short, social studies is not an isolated subject but rather one that can and should be integrated throughout all the academic experiences of children.

The scope and sequence of most social studies programs is based on tradition as well as on suggestions from the National Council for the Social Studies (NCSS). Typically, most elementary programs are designed according to the following hierarchy:

Child/Self. At this stage, usually initiated at the kindergarten level, students are given opportunities to investigate topics most familiar to them, including their persons, going to school, rules for safe living, and working together.

Families. Here children are exposed to aspects of what families do, as well as the world beyond their own families. Topics at this level may include the relationship of the individual to the family, families and their needs, how families work, and families in neighborhoods.

Communities/Neighborhoods. At this stage of the social studies program, students are introduced to neighborhoods and communities. Typical topics include transportation and communication, community services, celebrating holidays, how neighborhoods change, and rural and urban communities.

Cities/Country. At this level, students are exposed to information on larger community concepts. Usually comparisons are made between communities and cities in terms of the parts of a city, life in early cities, local government, comparative cultures, country versus rural living, and locations of cities.

States/Regions. This level of the social studies curriculum includes information on different sections of the United States as well as various geographical characteristics of selected states. Emphasis includes comparative studies on desert, mountain, plains, and forest regions of the United States and other selected areas within our country.

Nation/United States. The primary emphasis at this level is on the United States, although it may include references to Canada and/or Latin America. Topics include the founding of our country, historical facts, geographical data, chronology, and our cultural and ethnic heritage.

World. This level often includes a large number of topics dealing with either the western or eastern hemispheres or both. Areas covered include ancient civilizations, Asia, Europe, Africa, and the Middle East. At this level the curriculum is very crowded and diverse.

This type of curriculum is usually referred to as the *widening horizons* or *expanding environments* curriculum. It is based on the idea that children first need to deal with concepts that are relative to their immediate environments (self) and systematically progress to concepts that move in concentric circles out and beyond that environment, as depicted in figure 1.1.

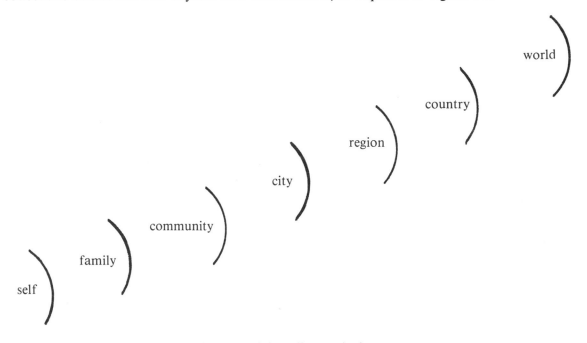

Fig. 1.1. Systematic progression in the social studies curriculum.

As students become more familiar with each component of their environment, they then develop the capacity to deal with larger elements of the world environment. Although this is the dominant plan of action for most elementary programs, a note of caution is in order. That is, the media are providing children with more and more exposure to events that occur far beyond their immediate environments. The conflict in the Persian Gulf from August 1990 through March 1991 is testament to that. During those months, schoolchildren of all ages were exposed, on a daily basis, to events that far exceeded the concepts in their classroom social studies textbooks. What that means for teachers is that the social studies program must not be restrictive—it must not assume that second-grade children, for example, can only deal with events occurring in their local communities. As second-grade students around the country wrote letters to the troops in the Persian Gulf, they were getting valuable social studies lessons that far exceeded anything presented in their textbooks or the ubiquitous workbooks.

The organization of the social studies curriculum illustrated in figure 1.1 is typical. However, many experts also advocate a spiral approach to social studies. In this method of presentation, students are introduced to concepts (such as landforms, cultures, political systems) and a host of processes (such as inferring, predicting, observing) that allow them to manipulate conceptual data. The significance of a spiral approach is not that it eliminates the expanding environments plan but that it offers students opportunities to engage in hands-on learning activities rather than simply committing facts to memory. Also, teachers do not need to overemphasize obvious information that children may already know (themselves, their family) simply because it is in the textbook. Instead, that foundational data serves as a focal point for other related and interwoven information. This style of learning, often referred to as *inquiry learning*, is based on three understandings (Ellis 1991):

1. Students can engage in learning opportunities with a greater degree of self-direction.

2. Students can develop improved attitudes toward learning.

3. Students can retain and utilize information for longer periods of time.

This approach can easily be woven into the traditional social studies curriculum. When students are given opportunities to use their knowledge in ways that are meaningful to them, social studies education becomes more realistic and relevant. Thus, while most social studies curricula are predicated on the expanding environments idea, teachers need to be cognizant of the interests, needs, and abilities of their students if they are to present a constantly evolving and dynamic social studies program. In short, good social studies programs allow for modification of the expanding environments plan; they begin with what children know, but they also include content that allows students to venture beyond their immediate environment (Hennings, Hennings, and Banich 1989).

Social Studies as Process

Many social studies programs are designed to *give* children lots of information, have them *memorize* that data, and then ask them to *recall* the information on various assessment instruments. As discussed earlier, that may be a significant reason for students' less-than-enthusiastic response to social studies, because that type of instruction does not allow for the active involvement of students in their own learning, nor does it allow children opportunities to think critically about what they are learning.

My own experiences as a teacher have taught me that when students, no matter what their abilities or interests, are provided with opportunities to manipulate information in productive ways, learning becomes much more meaningful. I refer to this as a *process approach to learning*, which provides students with an abundance of projects, activities, and instructional designs that allow them to make decisions and solve problems. In so doing, students get a sense that learning is much more than the commission of facts to memory. Rather, it is what children do with that knowledge that determines its impact on their attitudes and aptitudes.

A process approach to social studies is one in which children *do* something with the concepts and generalizations they learn. It implies that students can manipulate, decide, solve, predict, and structure the knowledge of social studies in ways that are meaningful to them. When teachers provide opportunities for students to actively process information, learning becomes more child-centered and less text-based. This results in a social studies program that is expansive, integrated, and dynamic.

A review of any social studies text reveals a great deal of "stuff" for children to learn. However, asking students to memorize data simply because it is in the book may do more harm than good. Yet, when pupils can *process* the information, they have opportunities to make the knowledge relevant. In figure 1.2 are two social studies concepts typically found in many texts. However, instead of asking students to commit information to memory, teachers can provide a selection of processes that involve problem-solving and decision-making in a meaningful context.

Name Different Means of Transportation in Cities and Suburbs

---

1. Brainstorm for different types of transportation.

2. Cut pictures out of a magazine depicting modes of transportation, past and present.

3. Create a city out of boxes illustrating restaurants, movies, roads, etc. Discuss the forms of transportation to put in the city. Do the same for a suburban area.

4. Use a telephone book's Yellow Pages to come up with a list of transportation-associated services.

5. Invite an elderly person into the classroom to discuss the differences in transportation when he or she was a child and transportation today.

6. Do a collage of bicycle pictures depicting the changes in bicycles over the years.

7. Create a pie chart illustrating the number of cars in a city versus the number of cars in a suburban area.

8. Obtain a local transit map (bus, train, etc.) and discuss its importance to commuters.

9. Write a journal entry on "A typical day in the life of a [car, taxi, bus, subway]."

10. Create a simulation of a traffic jam using students waiting in line for lunch. Discuss students' feelings about the crowding and noise.

11. Create a poster on the benefits of carpooling.

12. Take a walk around the school and discuss the health benefits of walking.

13. Write a letter to the editor of the local newspaper asking people to carpool, walk, or take the bus to work.

14. Have students organize a bike-a-thon to promote bicycle riding.

15. Have students plan an imaginary trip to a distant location. Direct them to consider four different forms of transportation that could be used on the trip.

Fig. 1.2. Examples of activity processes for social studies concepts.

(Fig. 1.2 continues on page 10.)

Know That July 4th Is the
Birthday of Our Country

---

1. Make birthday announcements for the United States. Include information such as "Mother" (England), where, and when.

2. Have students plan for the first birthday party for the country. Make up invitations and plan the ideal celebration.

3. Write a play using several historical figures (such as George Washington, Paul Revere, and so on).

4. Give students an opportunity to write with a quill and ink (use a feather and some crushed berries).

5. Make a newspaper for July 5th. What would the headlines say?

6. Recreate a calendar for the year 1776. Mark and identify important dates.

7. Create imaginary diary entries for one of the historical figures.

8. Divide the class into the thirteen colonies and ask each to conduct research on their identified state.

9. Sing songs such as "My Country 'Tis of Thee" and "Yankee Doodle Dandy."

10. Design a crossword puzzle incorporating historical events.

11. Create a classroom "Declaration of Independence."

12. Have students make a collage of life in 1776 and another collage of life in the current year. Discuss similarities and differences.

13. Select several children to be reporters and others to take on the roles of historical figures. Conduct mock interviews.

14. Design several different birthday cards for the 25th, 50th, 100th, and 200th birthdays of the country.

15. Have students write an imaginary letter from the future (the current year) to a child in 1776.

What should become evident is the fact that when children are given a plethora of hands-on experiences within all dimensions of the social studies program, their appreciation and interest in social studies increase accordingly. At the same time, their knowledge of social studies concepts and generalizations is made personal and relevant. Quite simply, the inquiry-based social studies program gives students some control over what they are learning and why they learn it. It allows for the integration of all the social sciences (anthropology, history, economics, geography, political science, and sociology) in a multicurricular environment that is supportive and encouraging rather than dogmatic and static. In summary, when students are provided with multiple opportunities to take an *active* role in the social studies curriculum, social studies will be meaningful, exciting, and productive.

Reference List

Ellis, Arthur K. 1991. *Teaching and Learning Elementary Social Studies*. Boston: Allyn and Bacon.

Hennings, Dorothy, George Hennings, and Serafina Banich. 1989. *Today's Elementary Social Studies*. New York: Harper & Row.

National Council for the Social Studies Task Force on Scope and Sequence. 1984. "In Search of a Scope and Sequence for Social Studies." *Social Education* 48 (April): 251.

2—Whole Language and Social Studies, and More

Early in my teaching career, I often felt as though I was being consumed by the system. Trying to juggle lunch counts, teacher manuals, behavioral objectives, workbooks, standardized tests, skill sheets, absence slips, "Meet the Teacher" nights, and a plethora of other responsibilities, rules, and regulations often left me frazzled and dazed. Now that I am older (and supposedly somewhat wiser), I have begun to see that I was doing too much *directing* in my classroom and not enough *facilitating*. In short, I was taking on *all* the instructional responsibilities in the room and not providing my students with opportunities to direct or monitor their own learning. I can now see that although I was in control, I did not provide students with sufficient mechanisms to initiate their own discoveries or pursue their own self-directed queries.

There is now a generation of *irresponsible learners*. This term is not meant negatively; rather, it signifies that students have not been given sufficient choices or opportunities to make their own instructional decisions. They have been told what to do, but not necessarily why. That fact comes home to roost at the beginning of each semester when I go over the syllabus for each of my college courses. Typically, I am bombarded with questions such as "How long should this paper be?" "How many books will I have to read?" or "Is attendance required?" It appears that my college students are products of a system that has all the answers neatly lined up in plan books and teachers' manuals. What my college students are really telling me is that they have not been given sufficient opportunities to chart their own educational courses or make their own decisions about what can or should be learned. That is certainly not their fault, but it may be indicative of how we have taught students in elementary and/or secondary school. In other words, teachers tend to have all their behavioral objectives carefully arranged for students and, at the same time, ask the students to memorize facts and figures and regurgitate data on workbook pages or standardized tests—without necessarily understanding the reasons for doing it.

What we are now discovering is that learning that provides students with opportunities to make personal decisions on the dynamics of their own education is meaningful, relevant, and positive. It underscores the need for teachers to relinquish some of their control and give students active opportunities to take on some responsibility for what can be learned. It says that learning that is process-oriented, rather than product-oriented, is geared to the needs, interests, and individual abilities of students rather than to some artificial standards dictated by the teachers' manual or curriculum guide. In short, it means a student-based educational program that integrates all aspects of the elementary curriculum into all aspects of children's lives.

For those reasons, I am a strong advocate of a whole language philosophy of instruction. I define *whole language* as the integration of reading, writing, speaking, and listening into a context that is meaningful to the child. Whole language offers students a framework for learning in which self-initiated goals can be established, literature abounds, skills are taught in a meaningful context, and purposeful activities are interwoven into all dimensions of the curriculum. Thus, whole language is not a program but a philosophy of teaching and learning that is child-centered and contextually based.

Whole language implies that there are no artificial barriers between the typical subjects of the elementary curriculum. We often find that children have a concept of reading, for example, as a subject that occurs only between 9:00 a.m. and 10:00 a.m. on Mondays through Fridays or is relegated to the pages of a basal textbook. The arbitrary barriers we often create between subjects tend to circumscribe the learning possibilities for children rather than enhance them. A whole language perspective on learning breaks down those barriers and provides students with limitless opportunities to investigate, discover, and explore learning for its own sake, and not because it is 2:30 p.m. and that is the only time we can teach social studies.

The whole language philosophy of teaching is also based on the successful integration of children's literature throughout the curriculum. Literature provides the vehicle by which children can travel to all sectors of the elementary curriculum, observing and appreciating the scenery along the way. In short, children are given choices (as is the teacher) to actively participate according to their abilities and interests. Obviously, this means the relinquishing of some typical teacher responsibilities and the transfer of some of those responsibilities to children, giving them more freedom to process learning rather than just memorize data. In the long run, whole language helps children develop their creative and critical thinking abilities in a meaningful and relevant context. Filling in worksheets from a commercial publisher does not necessarily develop critical thinking; deciding on the format for a skit on a particular historical event does.

A whole language approach allows children to create personal responses to learning. For that reason, whole language cannot be mandated or dictated by a school or principal. It is clear from the research that whole language succeeds because teachers believe it will succeed, not because they have to do it. How much you embrace the whole language philosophy determines, to a great extent, how well it will succeed in your classroom. This does not mean that whole language is for everyone, but it does mean that whole language must be subscribed to by teachers who are willing to learn and discover along with their students. As in more traditional forms of teaching, we know where we would like to go, but now there are so many new, exciting, and as yet uncharted roads to explore along the way.

Social Studies through Children's Literature provides whole language options to integrate into your social studies curriculum. It is not a whole language manual but a compendium of whole language possibilities, explorations, and inquiries that can expand the social studies program into new worlds of discovery. It echoes my philosophy that a literature-based curriculum knows no curricular boundaries, time limits, or limitations of skills. It is an experiential approach to education that says that when children get "down and dirty" with learning, attitudes escalate and instruction blossoms! In short, this book has been written with the idea that when students are allowed to make an investment of self in learning, they become more responsible learners.

Whole Language Activities

The list in figure 2.1 contains a number of whole language activities, any of which can be easily integrated into your social studies program. I am not suggesting that you try all of these, nor that all are appropriate for every student in your classroom. They are simply offered as examples of the diversity and variety of hands-on learning opportunities available to you as part of your social studies program.

(Text continues on page 19.)

Social Studies and Language Arts and Reading

Read a new book (or part of a book) each day.

Write a letter to a friend about what is being learned.

Read fiction and nonfiction books on the same topic.

Read several books by the same author.

Keep a journal or diary.

Invent a newspaper from a past date.

Create a fictional journal about a historical figure.

Write an original adaptation of an event.

Set up a "Reading Corner" filled with periodicals, books, and other printed materials.

Record part of a book on cassette tape.

Collect recipes and write a cookbook.

Design a wordless picture book.

"Publish" an original book.

Share a story with a classmate or partner.

Design and write a newspaper article.

"Publish" a classroom newspaper.

Locate and read a relevant magazine article.

Write an original play.

Write poetry.

Write a letter to a character or historical figure.

Write a sequel or prequel to an incident or event.

Adapt a story into a news report or television program.

Create multiple endings for a story.

Write a description of a book in twenty-five words or less; in fifty words or less; in seventy-five words or less.

Create interview questions for a guest speaker.

Rewrite a portion of a story with students as major figures.

Create a glossary or dictionary of important words in the story.

Create word puzzles or crossword puzzles of events or characters.

Create a rebus story for younger students.

Write riddles about events or circumstances in a story.

Design a "Question Box" containing questions and answers about specific books.

Keep a card file of all the books read.

Fig. 2.1. Whole language social studies activities.

Create a rating system for books read (Terrific, Good, O.K., So-So, Rotten).

Print important phrases or quotations on construction paper and post throughout the room.

Create a calendar of important events.

Pretend you are a historical figure and write a letter to someone in the future.

Write a "Declaration of Independence" for the class.

Create a fictional autobiography of a historical person.

Write a travel guide.

Create a want ad for something in a book.

Write a horoscope for a historical figure.

Write a travel itinerary for visiting selected countries.

Create a scrapbook about important places, people, and events.

Write a ten-question quiz for a book.

Learn some simple phrases in a foreign language.

Write a poem about a historical event.

Research your family name.

Create a word bank of words from different countries or different time periods.

Write a picture book (or wordless picture book) about a significant event.

Play a game of "Twenty Questions."

Conduct a debate or panel discussion.

Interview outside experts in the local community.

Create a new title for a book.

Make up a list of information you would still like to learn.

Make a story map.

Design a trivia game.

Social Studies and Mathematics

Create a scale model of a particular location.

Make a time line.

Build a sundial.

Calculate the number of years between various historical events.

Create bar-graph representations of sizes of states, rivers, mountains, etc.

Investigate different monetary systems.

Learn to count to 10 in a foreign language.

Measure distances on a map or globe.

Design an imaginary blueprint of a building.

Calculate distances between places.

Graph or chart the rainfall or population in different countries.

(Fig. 2.1 continues on page 16.)

Divide the classroom into different time zones.

Create word problems using distances between cities, states, or other geographical areas.

Create a scale model of a city.

Conduct a poll of favorite countries and graph the results.

Study the history of the abacus.

Study the history of numerals (Roman, Arabic, etc.).

Plan travel itineraries to different countries.

Create a budget for travel to another state or country.

Set up a trading post in the classroom.

Create flash cards using illustrations from a book.

Count the number of characters, settings, or specific objects in a story.

Design a pictograph.

Create a graph or chart to record data.

Calculate the heights of mountains or the depth of lakes.

Use a calendar to keep track of important dates.

Create a recipe.

Social Studies and Science and Health

Investigate ancient cultures.

Identify foods associated with different ethnic groups.

Create an environmental guide to your community.

Make a climate map.

Trace the lives of certain scientists.

Create a display of different forms of medicine (e.g., comparing medicines of the twentieth century with those of the seventeenth century).

List important scientific discoveries in the last fifty years.

Build a volcano.

Study different healing methods through history (leeches, bloodletting, etc.).

Create a montage of different shelters from around the world.

Create a display on animals specific to different regions of the United States or world.

Create a replica of a historical invention.

Study sanitary methods in various countries and across various times.

Compare the living conditions in different areas of the United States.

Chart the environmental changes that have taken place over a period of years.

Investigate the history of space exploration.

Identify the animal or plant species that have become extinct over the last twenty-five years; the last fifty years; the last hundred years.

Create a display of different landforms in different countries.

Create a "Bill of Rights" for scientists.

Make a list of nature's laws. Make a list of manmade laws.

Identify ecological concerns in your community.

Create a chart of weather patterns in different lands.

Write a logbook on the climate of an area.

Social Studies and Art

Turn part of a book into a series of cartoons.

Create a political cartoon about a significant event.

Illustrate portions of a book.

Make an advertisement about the book or story.

Draw illustrations of each character in a book.

Create a historical fashion magazine.

Put together time capsules for different historical periods.

Establish a historical museum in one corner of the classroom.

Create a pop-up book about a historical event.

Make puppets of historical figures.

Draw or paint the outline of a country on the playground.

Make masks from different countries.

Make crafts from different time periods.

Create an original slide show.

Draw map keys.

Study paintings, past and present.

Make a papier-mâché head of a famous person.

Design a new book cover.

Make a flip book about selected events.

Create a collage from old magazines.

Design an original flannel board.

Create a commercial to get others to read the book.

Paint a large wall poster.

Design and create a diorama of a significant scene.

Create a three-dimensional display of artifacts associated with a story.

Give a chalk talk about the book.

Take photographs of similar scenes from the local community and arrange them into an attractive display.

Make movie rolls using shoeboxes, adding machine tape, and pencils as the rollers.

Assemble a collage of pictures.

(Fig. 2.1 continues on page 18.)

Plan a bulletin board of pictures cut out of old magazines.

Design clay models of important characters.

Locate paintings that relate to scenes mentioned in the book.

Create a scrapbook.

Design a transparency about an important event and show it to the class.

Create a salt map of a specific location.

Social Studies and Physical Education

Simulate and run the route of an explorer on the playground.

Develop an exercise program for a historical figure.

List the physical skills needed to climb a mountain, conquer a distant land, or navigate an ocean.

Play "Around the World" basketball.

Have a classroom Olympics.

Play a variation of "Pin the Tail on the Donkey" using flags and countries instead.

Play "Geography Hopscotch."

Invent a game of "Geography Capture the Flag."

Study games (cricket, bocci ball, etc.) from different countries.

Invent other games (for example, "Continent Twister").

Study dances from different countries.

Reenact a battle.

Play games from different parts of the world.

Create a Question-and-Answer relay using specific social studies facts.

Social Studies and Music and Drama

Create a radio show about a book.

Act out events in a story and videotape them.

Design costumes for characters in a story.

Pantomime selected events in a story.

Write an original play.

Create a cultural concert.

Sing folk songs.

Schedule a "Culture Day."

Role play a recent presidential election.

Schedule a "Renaissance Fair."

Create a commercial for a historical artifact.

Invent a new national anthem.

Create songs about a person or event.

Collect examples of ethnic or cultural dances.

Present examples of music from different ethnic groups.

Learn a song in another language.

Create replicas of original instruments from different lands.

Take a popular song and rewrite the lyrics using words or phrases from a story.

Role play selected characters from a book.

Design a filmstrip for a book (special filmstrip kits can be obtained from education dealers).

Give dramatic readings of a book.

Select and include appropriate musical selections for an oral reading of the book.

Create cassette recordings of selected stories.

Dramatize a section of the book for another class.

Produce a puppet show about part of a book.

As you examine these lists, it will become apparent that the approach to social studies is multidisciplinary. It presupposes that children can take on many instructional responsibilities themselves and that they can become active processors of information within any facet of the curriculum. This is certainly not the only way to teach social studies, but it offers you and your students a cornucopia of possibilities that will diminish the negative feelings and lessen the uncomplimentary remarks about social studies that have dominated this subject in the past.

Please look over these possibilities and adopt or modify them according to the needs of your students. No single activity is appropriate for all students in your classroom. Children should be given opportunities to select and choose activities in keeping with their needs, wishes, and interests, not forced to do them simply because they were written in a teacher's lesson plans. Obviously, giving students choices will mean that some students may select activities that are too difficult for them, while others will select activities that are too easy. That is all right! Your primary responsibility will be to guide students to make appropriate choices, not to make the choices for them. Plan some regular discussion time during which you and a student or group of students can talk about activities and projects appropriate to skills and ability levels and how those choices will help students acquire both competence and interest in all sectors of the social studies program.

The activities you or your students select should be inspired by the content or context of your social studies program. Do not select an activity or series of activities just because they sound good or will fill up some time in your schedule. It is important that the activities be driven by the curriculum and that they be aimed at developing or enhancing specific concepts at a specific time. For instance, if your social studies program focuses on the life of George Washington, it would be appropriate to use one or more of the following whole language activities:

1. Have students write a letter to George Washington asking him questions about some of the decisions he made during the Revolutionary War.

2. Direct students to create a time line of some of the important events in the life of George Washington.

3. Encourage students to create a scale model of the encampment at Valley Forge. Library resources may be consulted to obtain the necessary measurements.

4. Have students create a political cartoon about an event during Washington's presidency.

5. Using the music from a familiar song, have students create new lyrics about an event in George Washington's life (chopping down the cherry tree, crossing the Potomac, making his inauguration speech, etc.).

The activities in figure 2.1 are listed according to a union between social studies and the other elementary subjects. Understandably, these are not perfect bonds; many activities can be used in several different curricular areas, and you are certainly encouraged to do so. More important is that students be given opportunities to extend, expand, and enhance their mastery of social studies objectives in a variety of formats within all dimensions of learning. By so doing, you can give them a broad-based approach to social studies. Over time, students will begin to appreciate social studies as a viable and important element of their entire lives because they experienced it rather than memorized it.

3—Making Connections: Integrating Social Studies and Children's Literature

The inclusion of children's literature within the social studies curriculum should be a natural and normal part of students' experiences with social studies. Doing so provides youngsters with valuable opportunities to extend and expand their knowledge of the world around them as well as to develop a rich appreciation for the social studies concepts, values, and generalizations contained within good literature. By infusing books and literature into your social studies program, you are helping students understand that social studies is much more than a dry accumulation of facts and dates. Instead, you are helping your students explore and investigate their immediate and far-flung world in an arena that knows no limits.

The use of literature within social studies is based on several precepts:

1. Literature provides an ever-expanding array of information in a welcome and familiar format to students.

2. Literature extends the social studies curriculum beyond any textbook constraints.

3. Literature relates to children's lives in diverse and divergent ways.

4. Literature, both fiction and nonfiction, helps children understand their cultural, ethnic, and religious heritage.

5. Literature assists children in developing positive attitudes towards themselves, persons in their immediate environment, and peoples from around the world.

6. Literature provides vicarious *and* firsthand experiences with all social studies disciplines.

7. Literature provides students with new information and knowledge unobtainable in any other format.

8. Literature stimulates creative thinking and problem-solving abilities in a variety of contexts.

9. Literature opens up the world and draws students in to make self-initiated discoveries.

10. Literature is fun!

These precepts, although couched in terms of the social studies curriculum, serve as motivators for all parts of the elementary program as well. While this book is concerned with the integration of literature into the social studies program, literature has a powerful influence on the development of skills and attitudes in any subject area (see *Science through Children's Literature: An Integrated Approach*, by Carol M. Butzow and John W. Butzow [Englewood, Colo.: 1989]).

The Literature Connection

When quality literature is made a significant part of the social studies program, children can become involved in activities and gain experiences that they may not be exposed to within a text-based program. Therefore, I suggest two whole language approaches for the integration of literature into your social studies curriculum: *bookwebbing* and *thematic units*. It should be understood that these two approaches are not the only ones at your disposal. Both of them are appropriate for any elementary grade, skill or ability level, grouping strategy, or social studies series. You are encouraged to try either one of these methods (or modifications thereof) or both in your classroom. They are offered as proof that social studies and literature are compatible elements in children's academic experiences.

Teaching Social Studies via Bookwebbing

Bookwebbing is a process that extends a specific piece of social studies literature into all areas of the elementary curriculum. It provides students with opportunities to work on projects and activities that have a social studies base yet also relate to other elements of their academic experiences. Its value lies in the fact that children are offered extended opportunities to move beyond the textbook, taking social studies skills and attitudes and applying them in other curricular areas.

The process is initiated by selecting a single book that relates to a particular concept in your social studies program (see the annotated bibliography at the end of this book for suggestions). You may choose either a fiction or nonfiction book, although initially a nonfiction book may be preferred. Be sure you are familiar with the book before sharing it with your students. The sharing process can encompass one or more of the following strategies:

1. Read the book to the entire class.

2. Obtain multiple copies and have students read the book on their own.

3. Have students read the book to each other.

4. Record the book on cassette tape for students to listen to during their free time.

5. Have a guest speaker (principal, parent, librarian) read the book to the class.

After your students have had an opportunity to read and discuss the book, the class will have to brainstorm for potential extending activities. These activities are categorized according to the other areas of the curriculum and are primarily generated by students. This process allows children the opportunity to take responsibility for some of their own learning and to expand their levels of consciousness about the utility of the book. During this brainstorming process, you may wish to construct a "web" on the chalkboard, as in figure 3.1.

Allow students to brainstorm for possible subject-related activities that could be used to extend and expand the concepts presented in the book. (Note: initially, you may wish to do this yourself and model the process for students several times before they undertake it on their own.) After completion of the brainstorming session, you can begin to develop lessons based on the ideas suggested by students. As students engage in their self-selected activities, be sure to provide them with opportunities to refer to the book and draw relationships between the projects they are engaged

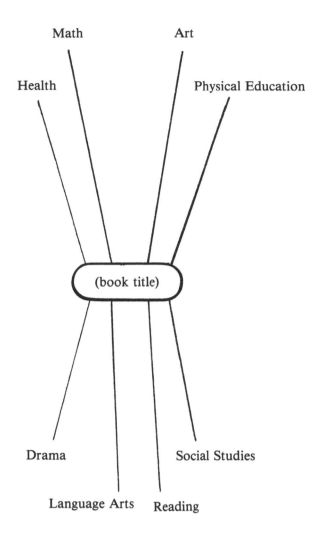

Fig. 3.1. An initial book web.

in and the ideas, themes, or concepts presented in the literature selection. In this way, you will ensure that students understand the interrelationships that exist between literature, social studies, and other subject areas.

Figure 3.2 is an example of how one book, *A Visit to the Fire Station* by Dotti Hannum (Chicago: Children's Press, 1985), was developed into a multidisciplinary unit using the bookwebbing strategy.

A Visit to the Fire Station

Math

1. Create fire-engine flash cards for math facts.

2. Collect data on the sizes, dimensions, and weights of different fire engines.

3. Calculate the amount of water used to put out a house fire.

4. Create word problems on the speed needed to reach a burning house from a fire station in a certain amount of time.

Health

1. Review fire safety rules with your parents.

2. Develop a list of rules for safety at home, at work, and at school.

3. Discuss the treatment for minor burns.

Drama

1. Create a skit about a day in the life of a fire fighter.

2. Write a play about a famous fire.

3. Create a puppet show about the training fire fighters must undergo.

Language Arts

1. Prepare an invitation for a local fire fighter to visit your classroom.

2. Create a quiz show on fire facts and fiction.

3. Design a brochure on home fire safety.

Art

1. Design fire safety posters.

2. Create a collage of flammable materials found in your home.

3. Construct a fire engine from clean milk cartons.

4. Create and illustrate the ideal fire engine.

Physical Education

1. Design an obstacle course on the playground and imitate fire fighters as you go through the course.

2. Put on a series of old clothes, run to a destination, and take off the clothes. Time each other.

Social Studies

1. Investigate the history of fire fighting in this country.

2. Look into the evolution of fire engines.

3. Visit a local fire station and ask questions on the fire fighters' importance to the community.

Reading

Read and enjoy the following books:

a. *Poinsettia and the Firefighters* by Felicia Bond (New York: Crowell, 1984)

b. *Blue Bug's Safety Book* by Virginia Poulet (Chicago: Children's Press, 1973)

c. *The Big Book of Real Fire Trucks and Fire Fighting* by Teddy Slater (New York: Grosset & Dunlap, 1987)

Fig. 3.2. Multidisciplinary activities developed from a book web.

Teaching Social Studies via Thematic Units

It was Karen who first taught me about thematic units. Karen was one of my third-grade students several years ago. And Karen loved horses! She prodded and cajoled me to bring in every conceivable book about horses I knew of or could collect from the library. We talked about horses, made horse collages of pictures cut from old magazines, created posters filled with all sorts of horse facts, constructed scrapbooks about famous horses in history, discussed the care and feeding of horses, and viewed films and filmstrips of horses from around the world.

During that time my family and I lived on a farm in southeastern Pennsylvania where we raised some animals. Included in our menagerie of dogs, cats, chickens, geese, rabbits, and ducks was a pony named Cinnamon, who was a never-ending source of delight for my own children. During that year I had to provide Karen with a running account of Cinnamon's activities and bring in photographs of her for Karen to add to one of the scrapbooks. Karen wrote stories about Cinnamon, created replicas of Cinnamon from modeling clay, developed a chart on the differences and similarities between ponies and horses, and collected data from the local county extension agent on the nutritional needs and diseases of horses and ponies.

It soon became evident that Karen knew more about horses than I did. Her interest became the impetus for the creation of a self-initiated thematic unit in which literature and an assortment of cross-curricular activities were combined into a series of learning opportunities that made education fun for Karen. Math, science, social studies, health, language arts, reading, and even physical education were all part of the lessons and activities Karen and I shared that year. What was even more amazing was the fact that Karen had been diagnosed as a nonreader by her previous teacher in another school. Her records noted that she lacked the aptitude or attitude to succeed in reading or any other subject. What Karen and I discovered was that when she was given an opportunity to expand on her interests through literature and a variety of hands-on activities, anything was possible. By the end of that year Karen had read twenty-seven books, twenty-five of which dealt with horses. Before that she had never completed a book. With her own self-initiated theme, however, she pursued learning with a vengeance and taught me a most valuable lesson in the process.

Thematic units can be described as an interrelated collection of books and activities which expand the learning opportunities for children within a designated area of the elementary curriculum. Thematic units are valuable because they demonstrate for children how literature can be integrated into all aspects of a subject (such as social studies) and how that subject thereby becomes more meaningful to their own lives. Thematic units provide teachers with a chance to enhance any aspect of the curriculum via literature and to open up new worlds of discovery for their students. These units provide teachers and students with processes that move learning beyond the textbook, making learning realistic and relevant. The integration of a variety of literature within a designated topic emphasizes the value of that topic and the unlimited possibilities for exploration and discovery.

Thematic units can be as simple or as complex as you wish. Initially, you may wish to start with selected topics from your social studies text. Later, you may want to design units based on the needs and interests of your students. Above all, it is important that you consider the focus of the thematic unit; that is, what understandings will be examined or explored via the thematic unit? In other words, a unit is not just a bunch of books and a bunch of activities. They must tie together as a purposeful, cohesive unit.

You should also give some thought to the materials you have available (including literature selections from the classroom, community, or school library). In addition, you will need to consider the potential activities for each literature selection as well as the unit as a whole. It may be valuable to work with colleagues or even your own students to brainstorm for potential activities for each of the literature selections designated for a particular unit. Of course, you are encouraged to utilize any and all of the ideas and activities in this book as "starters" for your own units. Indeed, with a little modification and adjustment, you will be able to create exciting and dynamic units simply by combining two or more pieces of literature from this book into your own thematic unit.

When developing a unit, it is important to consider some initiating activities, literature-related activities, and culminating activities. The careful selection of several cross-curricular activities prior to, during, and at the conclusion of a thematic unit will provide your students with a plethora of learning opportunities and extensions that enhance the literature and make the unit relevant and meaningful.

Figure 3.3 is a sample thematic unit called "Communities." It is designed around four literature selections and includes several initiating activities, activities specific to each of the selected books, and a series of culminating activities built around a "Community Festival Day." Consider it a proto-type for the development of your own thematic units within your social studies curriculum. You will discover that the design and inclusion of several thematic units stimulates and encourages students to take an active role in processing and understanding more about the world around them.

Thematic Unit: Communities

General Activities

1. (Art) Provide students with several old magazines that can be cut up. Have students search for pictures pertaining to urban or rural life. Students can make two collages, one on urban living, the other on rural living.

2. (Language Arts) Divide the class in half and challenge one group to create an urban newspaper and the other group to create a rural newspaper. Provide students with copies of the local newspaper, *USA Today*, or a newsmagazine. Ask them to select certain stories and rewrite each one with either an urban or rural slant.

3. (Math, Social Studies) Obtain a detailed map of the school district. Have students plot the route they take to school each day, using the map as a guide. Have students compute the distances they travel in terms of miles, kilometers, yards, or meters. Have students determine the shortest route to school, the longest, or the most difficult.

4. (Language Arts) Read to the class Lorinda B. Cauley's book *Country Mouse, Town Mouse* (New York: Putnam, 1984). Afterwards, have the class create an original puppet show based on the book. Puppets can be created from paper bags or paper plates. Students may wish to share their production with another class.

5. (Social Studies) Using a large sheet of oaktag, have students create a community calendar of events. Students can record community and school activities for an entire month. The calendar should be hung in a prominent place in the classroom and referred to regularly. Each month a new calendar can be prepared. Sources for community activities can include the local newspaper, school calendar of activities, community group newsletters, and various bulletins posted around town.

Fig. 3.3. Sample thematic unit.

6. (Language Arts/Art) Have students make an "Occupation Tree." Put a medium-size branch in a weighted container in a corner of the classroom. Provide students with index cards, each with a different letter of the alphabet. Challenge students to identify a community worker for each letter and to write the name of the worker on the corresponding card (A = animal pound worker; B = baker; C = carpenter). Hang each of these cards on the Occupation Tree.

7. (Social Studies) Display a map of the United States or of your state. Show students where they live in relation to other communities around the country or around the state. Your community can be designated with a red star. If students were born in other cities, these can be identified on the map, too. Connect each of the different communities with lengths of yarn.

8. (Language Arts) Encourage students to write riddles about community helpers. These riddles can contain several lines, but only one line at a time should be read to the class. Students can try to guess who the helper is after a line of the riddle has been read. If the answer is not guessed correctly, the next line of the riddle can be read. For example:

> I drive a bright red vehicle. (first clue)
> I wear heavy rubber boots. (second clue)
> I rescue people and animals. (third clue)
> I put out fires. (fourth clue)
> Who am I? (A fire fighter)

9. (Language Arts/Art) Have a fashion show of community helpers. Children can design their own costumes from old material, curtains, clothing, hats, wigs, or grocery bags decorated with markers or crayons.

Book Activities

Title: *Town and Country*
Authors: Alice Provensen and Martin Provensen
Publisher: New York: Crown, 1984

---

1. (Language Arts) Using all the information learned about the town and the country from this book, have children create travel brochures promoting both geographical areas. The brochures should contain a written and detailed summary promoting the town and/or country. The brochure should also contain a drawing or illustration of the designated area(s).

2. (Math) Show students the difference in the number of people in the city illustrations versus the country illustrations. Discuss population density in the city and the country. Contact local officials to obtain a population density count of the school district and have students create a corresponding map.

3. (Art) Divide the class in half and have students in one half create a diorama of a country scene and students in the other half create a diorama of scenes from a city. Post these illustrations on two sides of the classroom.

(Fig. 3.3 continues on page 28.)

4. (Language Arts) Have students write about a proposed trip to a big city. Their entries can focus on real or imaginary events, places, or people. Students may also wish to write about a simulated trip to the country, too. Be sure to provide opportunities for students to share their stories orally.

5. (Science) Discuss the importance of weather conditions for crop survival. Bring in weather reports from the newspaper and have students do the same. Have students discover what types of climate, soil, etc., are in their general area.

6. (Art) Have each student cut out a barn shape from construction paper and fill it with farm words and farm animals (cut out of old magazines). Then have each student cut a skyscraper shape from construction paper and fill it with city words and pictures (cut from old magazines). Post these along one wall of the classroom.

7. (Language Arts) Have students make picture dictionaries using vocabulary words from the book. Cut sheets of drawing paper in half and punch two holes in each page. Join the pages with a piece of colorful yarn and make an attractive cover from construction paper. Each page will feature a letter, word, picture, and a short sentence that explains the designated word. Once completed, students can refer to their dictionaries whenever they need a city or country word for writing.

Discussion Questions

a. What do you like most about the city? What do you like least? Explain your answers.

b. What do you like most about the country? What do you like least? Explain your answers.

c. Pretend you are a skyscraper. Tell what you see and hear.

d. What types of chores are necessary on the farm? Which ones would you enjoy doing?

e. If you could be a farm animal for a day, which one would you choose? Why?

f. If you could choose, would you live in the city or in the country? Why?

Title: *The Little House*
Author: Virginia Lee Burton
Publisher: Boston: Houghton Mifflin, 1969

1. (Social Studies) Design a bulletin board for the book. Start with cutout shapes in a country atmosphere. Each day have students add items to the bulletin board to illustrate the changes and growth taking place as a country area develops into a city area. Be sure to discuss these changes with students periodically.

2. (Science) Introduce the four seasons to students. Have students identify characteristics of each season, as described in the book. Then have students divide a sheet of drawing paper into four sections and in each section draw a picture depicting the characteristics of a specific season. Encourage students to add descriptors using sentence stems such as "Summer is the time of year when ..." "Spring brings out many beautiful ..." or "Winter is a wonderful season because ...."

3. (Social Studies) Have students study the changes in transportation as portrayed in the story, beginning with early transportation (horse and buggy, trolley cars) and progressing to present-day transportation vehicles. Have students create a time line with illustrations of each form of transportation mentioned in the story.

4. (Language Arts) Have selected students pretend that they are the little house. Ask each of these students to give a short talk about all the adventures that happened during the course of the story. Direct other students to ask questions of "the house" during the presentation.

5. (Social Studies/Language Arts) Have students make a master list of all the dwellings people live in (igloos, huts, castles, farmhouses, tepees, etc.). Allow each student to select one of the listed dwellings and describe how it would feel to live in such an abode instead of his or her present home. Students may wish to write descriptions of their selected dwellings, including illustrations, for posting on a bulletin board.

6. (Physical Education, Math) Have students play a game of "Streets and Alleys." Take children out to the playground and spread them out, making sure they are facing in different directions. Begin by yelling "streets." Students then walk, jog, or run in a forward direction until you yell "alleys," at which time they must each turn 90 degrees in either direction and continue moving. When "streets" is called again, students must each make another ninety-degree turn and continue moving. The game proceeds like this until one student touches the caller. The game continues with that student taking on the role of caller.

7. (Math) Invite a construction foreman or architect into your classroom. Ask the guest speaker to describe some of the steps taken in house construction. A blueprint can be used to illustrate how homes are planned before construction. Later, students may wish to create blueprints for their own homes.

Discussion Questions

a. What predictions did the man who built the little house make at the beginning of the story? Did they come true?

b. The little house experienced disappointment when the city evolved around her. What are some things that have disappointed you recently? What have you been able to do about them?

c. Could the little house have done anything to improve her situation? Why or why not?

d. If you could talk to the little house, what would you say?

e. What changes occurred for the little house as time passed? How did she feel about those changes?

Title: *A Visit to the Post Office*
Author: Sandra Ziegler
Publisher: Chicago: Children's Press, 1989

---

1. (Language Arts) After a visit to your local post office, have children pretend they are a letter, card, or package. Ask them to tell of their experiences as they travel through the postal system to reach their final destinations. Encourage them to draw several illustrations of the journeys they take.

(Fig. 3.3 continues on page 30.)

2. (Language Arts) Set up a replica of the post office in the drama center of the classroom. Furnish it with props such as stamps, envelopes, paper, pens, stamp pad and stamper, file folders for sorting mail, old laundry hamper, mail satchel, hats and uniforms, etc. Construct and paint a mailbox from a cardboard box for students to mail letters to classmates. Set up an individual mailbox center in the classroom (clean milk cartons glued together) for students to receive mail. This is a perfect opportunity for you to write regular letters to each child, noting something special about his or her academic or social performance. Be sure to provide opportunities for students to take on the roles of letter carrier, postmaster, etc.

3. (Art/Science) Have students design their own lickable stamps. Use pieces of white drawing paper, each of which has been divided into sixteen square sections. Cut each sheet into four strips. Provide each child with a strip consisting of four blocks. Instruct students to draw a design or illustration in each block. After the drawings are completed, make glue by combining the following ingredients and warming over a low heat:

> 1 package of unflavored gelatin
> 2 tablespoons of fruit juice
> 1 teaspoon sugar
>
> (Makes enough for two sheets of stamps.)

Cool the mixture slightly and paint the back of the sheets with it. Allow to dry overnight. Cut the strips apart and notch the edges with scissors to make the blocks resemble real stamps. Students can lick these stamps and use them for delivery of their classroom letters. A potato cut in half can be used as a stamp cancelling tool. Use a fork to create wavy lines in the potato face. Press the potato on an inked stamp pad and "cancel" students' letters.

4. (Social Studies) You and your students may wish to start a collection of stamps. Have students bring in used stamps from mail received at home. Mount these on a large sheet of cardboard or on sheets of paper fastened together into a scrapbook. Provide a notation next to each stamp on the country of origin as well as corresponding data about the country, individual, or event depicted on the stamp. Be sure to include some reference to the collected stamps as you present information about areas of the United States or other countries to the class. You may want to visit a variety store and obtain starter kits of stamps to initiate this project (this will be particularly appropriate if you need stamps from foreign countries).

5. (Math) Using play money to purchase stamps, weighing packages and letters on a scale, and putting mail into the properly numbered slots are all appropriate reinforcers of math skills. If desired, shoeboxes with slots can be arranged to represent houses. Print math problems on the fronts of several envelopes ($3 + 5 = ?$). Students can solve the problems by putting the problem envelope into the box with the corresponding address (8 Main Street).

6. (Physical Education) Introduce a relay race game wherein students pass a letter. The first player runs to collect a letter from box number 1. The player runs back with the letter in hand and passes it to the next player. The new runner takes the letter and drops it into box number 2. Then the runner takes a new letter from the first box. This procedure continues until all the letters from the first box are delivered to the second box. The first team to finish is the winner. All participants can receive "Good Mail Carrier" ribbons.

7. (Social Studies) Have students research the history of past and present postal service. Create a time line depicting the changes beginning with the pony express and stagecoaches up to present-day airmail delivery. Discuss the many obstacles that had to be overcome, such as poor roads, weather conditions, and travel time. Also, other ways of sending messages can be researched and discussed, for example, smoke signals, drum beats, carrier pigeons, Inca runners, etc.

8. (Language Arts) Encourage students to make up riddles about mail service. Here are some to get you started:

> What are the best letters to read in hot weather?
> (Fan mail)
> Who are the best letter writers?
> (Fishermen, because they'll always drop you a line)
> What person delivers mail for cats?
> (A litter carrier)
> What caused a riot at the post office?
> (A stamp-ede)
> What did the stamp say to the envelope?
> ("I'm stuck on you")

Discussion Questions

a. What are some of the steps involved in mailing a letter?

b. Why is the postal service so important to us?

c. If you could receive a letter from anyone in the world, who would it be? What would you write in response?

d. Why does the postal service use zip codes? Can you invent another way of speeding up mail delivery? If so, what would it be?

e. How has mail delivery changed over the years?

f. What would you find most enjoyable about working as a mail carrier? Least enjoyable?

Title: *Farm Morning*
Author: David McPhail
Publisher: New York: Harcourt Brace, 1985

---

1. (Music) Sing "Old McDonald Had a Farm" and sing the animals in the same order as they appear in the story. Afterwards, have students create new verses that pertain to where animals live and what they eat.

2. (Science) Contact your local county extension agent and ask about the availability of an incubator and some fertilized eggs for the classroom. Have the agent make a presentation on the growth and development of chicks. During the twenty-one-day incubation cycle, provide students with responsibilities for turning the eggs and keeping track of the temperature within the incubator. When the eggs hatch, have students chart the activities and eating habits of the chicks for about one week.

3. (Health) The book describes what the animals ate in the morning. Ask students to speculate on what the daughter and farmer ate for breakfast. Discuss the need for a good breakfast each morning and what foods should be considered for breakfast. Students may wish to construct charts of typical American breakfast foods (eggs, pancakes, juice, bacon, milk, etc.), listing the nutritional aspects of each food (vitamins, protein, etc.) along with some of the less desirable elements (cholesterol, fats, etc.).

(Fig. 3.3 continues on page 32.)

4. (Social Studies) Have students investigate what a typical breakfast might be like in different countries. For example, what do children in England typically have for breakfast? How about children in Brazil? In Israel? In Japan? In Italy? Students may wish to make up a large chart that describes and compares the different breakfasts.

5. (Language Arts) Direct each student to select one of the farm animals mentioned in the story. Ask the student to take on the role of that animal and write about some of his or her feelings about living on the farm. What do they like about farm life? What displeases them? What would they like to change? Do they feel they are being adequately taken care of on the farm? Do they enjoy their daily routines?

6. (Math, Health) Schedule a pancake breakfast at school one morning for all your students. Provide students with opportunities to calculate the quantities of ingredients and supplies needed as well as the necessary equipment (you may need to make prior arrangements with the cafeteria manager or building principal). Take students on a shopping trip to the local market to purchase the necessary supplies. On the day of the breakfast, provide opportunities for students to mix ingredients for the pancakes, calculate amounts of juice or milk to pour into individual glasses, discuss oven or stove temperatures, number of strips of bacon per person, and similar mathematical calculations. Later, provide some discussion on the elements of a nutritional breakfast.

Discussion Questions

a. If you could be any animal, what would you be? Why?

b. Would you like to spend some time on a farm? What do you think you would like most? What would you like least?

c. What are some of the responsibilities of the daughter in this story? What are some of the responsibilities you have at home? Are there any similarities?

d. If you lived on a farm, what animals would you have? Why did you choose those?

e. Would you enjoy getting up early every morning to feed animals before you went to school? Why do you think farm animals must be taken care of so early in the day?

f. Which part of the story is most like what you do at home?

Culminating Activity

The culminating activity for this thematic unit is a "Community Festival Day." This day could include some of the following activities:

1. Encourage students to wear costumes or clothing that represents their cultural background or heritage.

2. Have students create salt maps of urban and/or rural scenery.

3. Have students write stories about their lives as farmers or mail carriers.

4. Have students draw outlines of their bodies on separate sheets of butcher paper. Direct students to clothe their silhouettes in the dress of a city or country dweller. Post these around the room.

5. Encourage students and their parents to bring in samples of cultural or ethnic foods representative of their backgrounds or neighborhoods. Have parents write recipes on sheets of paper for later collection and assembly into a class recipe book.

6. Have students research and present examples of folklore and/or literature from their families' cultures or countries of origin.

7. Provide students with modeling clay and ask them to design dwellings from different areas of their local community. How many different dwellings are there (apartments, single-family homes, condominiums, etc.)?

8. Play a game of "Jeopardy" with the class responding with questions matching the supplied answers on rural and urban life.

9. Have students work in groups to design the ideal community. What buildings would it have? What services? What features would make it distinctive from other communities? Why would people want to live in this community?

10. Ask students to bring in photographs of different areas of the local community. Create a community scrapbook with one- or two-sentence descriptions of each photo.

11. Have students gather items for a time capsule. Challenge the students to collect twenty items that would be most representative of their community and that would provide future generations with a realistic picture of the community.

12. Students may wish to create crossword puzzles or word-search puzzles, each of which includes data relevant to the local community.

13. Encourage students to create a song about their community. Use the music from a popular song and have students provide their own lyrics. Students may wish to create a video or cassette tape of their song for presentation to other classes.

14. Students may wish to create a "big book" of urban life and a "big book" of city life. These books can be shared with youngsters in lower grades.

15. Turn the classroom into a replica of any community. Using different sizes of appliance boxes, students can create buildings, houses, and other edifices. These can be painted and set up in the classroom as a miniature village. Streets can be created with strips of masking tape, cars from small cardboard boxes, traffic lights with flashlights, and telephone poles from pencils. Challenge students to create additional community items from common objects already available in the classroom.

Although you will probably not want to use all the suggestions in this sample unit, they should provide you with some possibilities and some stimulation for the classroom and for your own community festival. It is strongly suggested that you involve your students as much as possible in the design and selection of potential activities. Such a procedure will ensure the success of the festival as well as the entire thematic unit.

4—Introduction

The following seven chapters contain activities and processes designed for each of thirty-two books. These books have been selected because of their appropriateness to the social studies curriculum, their adaptability to all grades (K-6) and ability ranges (high-low), and their usefulness in promoting social studies concepts within a whole language environment. Included are Caldecott Award winners and Caldecott Honor Books, Reading Rainbow selections, American Book Award medalists, and classics recommended by teachers and children's librarians from throughout the country. There is something for everyone! Although I would have liked to have included more book selections, space limitations precluded that option. The reader will discover, however, a potpourri of additional literary resources, musical selections, audiovisual materials, and whole language activities, all of which can be used to extend and expand these books, as well as any others the teacher may care to use, throughout the social studies curriculum.

The books used in these chapters have been organized around the seven major areas of the elementary social studies curriculum: self/child, family, community/neighborhood, city/country, states/regions, nation/country, and world. It is important to recognize that the placement of a book within one of those categories is arbitrary at best. The intent was to demonstrate the wide variety of children's literature available for every aspect of the social studies program, not to designate a particular book exclusively for a single division. Teachers will discover that many of these books can be used across the length and breadth of the curriculum. The important point is not that a designated book be used only in "nation/country," for example, but rather that it has the potential for extending and expanding global concepts and universal precepts no matter where it is used. Thus, teachers will discover that most books can be used across the grades and throughout the curriculum in a holistic and purposeful manner.

The listing of books within any division is alphabetical (by author) and not by level of difficulty. Teachers should feel free to select literature that best meets the needs and abilities of their students as well as books that promote universal ideals of the social studies curriculum. The emphasis here is that a fully integrated curriculum will include literature selections throughout. Teachers will discover innumerable opportunities for developing thematic units based on the books presented here and their own favorites. In that regard, remember that the readability or difficulty level of a single book should not determine if or how it should be used; rather, the emphasis should be on whether children are interested and motivated to pursue literature-related activities that promote learning in a supportive and holistic curriculum.

Teachers are provided with a host of potential activities and processes for each book. You are not expected to use all those activities nor all parts of any one activity. Instead, you and your students should decide on those activities that best serve the needs of the program and of students themselves. Teachers will discover activities that can be used individually, in small groups, in large groups, or as a whole class. Providing students with opportunities to make activity selections within the context of a work of literature can be a powerful and energizing element for the entire social studies program. When youngsters are given those opportunities, their appreciation of social studies and their interest in incorporating literature as a natural and normal part of the school day and their daily lives grow tremendously.

Teachers will also discover a wealth of extending activities that can be incorporated into all areas of the elementary curriculum. Science, language arts, music and visual art, health, physical education, math, and reading are all included in the activities listed for each book. While you may wish to match some of these books and procedures with specific elements of your social studies program, you are also encouraged to consider selected activities as extensions of other portions of students' classroom work, too. Indeed, when children begin to see the relationships that exist between social studies and other areas of their educational program, they begin to discover the universality of social studies and its implications for daily living. In fact, of all the curricular areas, social studies has the potential for expanding concepts and widening scholastic horizons as does no other subject area, particularly when accomplished in a literature-based context. This book has been designed to help you help your students to see the impact and significance of social studies throughout each and every aspect of the curriculum and their lives.

5—Child and Self

Once There Were Giants
Martin Waddell
(New York: Delacorte, 1989)

SUMMARY

A newborn baby girl realizes that all the adults in her life are like giants. As she grows up, they become less like giants but are still an important part of her development. Soon she marries, has a baby girl of her own, and becomes one of the giants for her child.

SOCIAL STUDIES TOPIC AREAS

Anthropology, sociology

CONTENT-RELATED WORDS

oatmeal, married, bride

CURRICULAR PERSPECTIVES

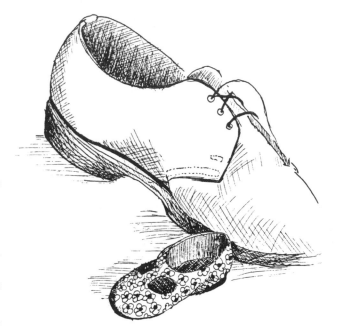

The process of growth. Magical. Mysterious. Magnificent. Most children take their growth and development for granted. All children expect to grow up into adults, have lots of friends, have a job, get married, and all the other usual happenings of life. It is expected. It is part of the plan.

This story, however, looks at the growth process from another perspective. Told from the viewpoint of a young child as she begins her development, it continues throughout her life, describing her perceptions and observations of the world around her—a world that expands as she grows up. Although "giants" are something many children fear, the narrator of this tale slowly realizes that perceptions can change, viewpoints can be modified, and size becomes a relative issue.

Through this simply crafted story, children become aware of their own growth and the fact that it is a naturally occurring process experienced by all humans. They become aware of their own unique sense of individuality; that they are singularly distinctive individuals yet part of the larger category of humans. The message is clear and well told: we are all part of a cycle of living that, for the most part, remains unchanged from generation to generation.

This book can be an important part of the social studies curriculum. Not only does it focus on the developing child, but it also demonstrates the relationships we all experience with our own families. Children will find much to enjoy here, for the book deals with a universal set of background experiences we all go through. In many ways, children will find a host of experiences with which they can identify and relate to their own lives. They will begin to see how their growth is similar to the development of each of their peers—a process that is important in a physical, cognitive, and affective sense.

CRITICAL-THINKING QUESTIONS

1. Why do you think the baby thought of her parents as giants in the beginning of the story?

2. Why do you think Uncle Tom is mentioned throughout this book?

3. Do the narrator and her brother have a typical brother/sister relationship? How is their relationship similar to the one you have with your brother(s) or sister(s)?

4. What experiences will the narrator's child have that might be similar to those the narrator had?

5. In the end, why does the narrator now consider herself a giant?

6. Does the narrator feel she had a happy or unhappy childhood? What clues in the story lead you to that decision?

7. Are there disadvantages to being smaller than those around you? Advantages?

RELATED BOOKS AND REFERENCES

Carlson, Nancy. *I Like Me*. New York: Viking, 1988.

De Regniers, Beatrice Schenk. *Everyone Is Good for Something*. Boston: Houghton Mifflin, 1980.

Hallinan, Patrick. *I'm Glad to Be Me*. Chicago: Children's Press, 1968.

Hines, Anna Grossnickle. *All by Myself*. New York: Clarion, 1985.

Sesame Street: I'm Glad to Be Me (30-minute video). New York: Random House, 1986.

Titherington, Jeanne. *Big World, Small World*. New York: Greenwillow, 1985.

Watanabe, Shigeo. *It's My Birthday*. New York: G. P. Putnam's Sons, 1988.

ACTIVITIES

1. Direct students to interview their parents and other relatives on some of their recollections of memorable events in the student's life. Students may be interested in obtaining more than one retelling about a single event to determine if different people remember it in the same way. When completed, students may wish to combine their data into an indexed directory of important events in their lives.

2. Have students record important events from their own lives, one event on each of several index cards. Hang some strings along one wall of your classroom or overhead. Provide students with several clothespins and ask each one to select a string and hang their cards along the string in the proper sequential order. Provide opportunities for each student to describe his or her personal time line.

3. For each student, tape a sheet of newsprint on one wall of the classroom. Place a child between the paper and the light from an overhead projector so that a silhouette of the child's head is projected on the newsprint. Have another student trace the silhouette on the paper. Do this for each student in the class. Have students cut out their individual silhouettes and write important events from their lives on the papers. Each silhouette can be highlighted with a watercolor wash and hung in an appropriate place in the classroom. Students should be encouraged to add additional events to their silhouettes as they occur during the year.

4. Have each student create a personal newspaper. For example, under the heading of "Sports," a child could write about some of the physical activities he or she participates in regularly. Under "Horoscopes," children could write personal predictions; under "Fashion," describe the clothes they like to wear; under "Music," list their favorite songs. Have children decide on the headlines or categories they would like to include in their personal newspapers. Make sure these are published and shared with all students.

5. Students may wish to create personal time lines using photographs brought from home. Students can be encouraged to bring in several photos of themselves. The series of photos can be posted on an appropriate bulletin board in sequential order. Students can also write a short caption for each picture describing what the picture portrays, the approximate date, and what it means to the individual child.

6. Have students interview friends, family, and other acquaintances. Direct each student to ask each person for a list of single adjectives that best describe the child. After students have collected an adequate sampling of adjectives, direct them to sort the adjectives into several categories, for example, adjectives related to size, adjectives related to personality, adjectives related to sports. Another set of categories could include adjectives from family, adjectives from friends, and adjectives from self. Provide students with an opportunity to decide on the categories they would like to use. Each student's list can be included in a large class scrapbook decorated with photos of all the children.

7. Pair each student with another student. Direct each student to interview the partner with a standard set of interview questions (these can be brainstormed by the class beforehand). Provide opportunities for each student to record the results of the interview. Later, put students into new pairs to conduct identical interviews, once again recording the results. Provide an opportunity for students to compare the two interviews and compare the perceptions of the two classmates who interviewed them.

8. Have students create family alphabet books. Provide each student with twenty-six sheets of paper. Ask students to write one letter of the alphabet on each sheet of paper. For each letter, have students choose a word or phrase that describes something about themselves or their family and record it on the appropriate sheet. When completed, students may wish to bind their sheets between two sheets of cardboard to create a complete family alphabet book.

9. Direct students to create a series of true/false questions about themselves. Print these statements on sheets of paper and duplicate. Pass out one or more of the sheets each day and ask students to see how much they know about their classmates. When a sheet is completed, a designated person can stand and explain each of the statements on his or her sheet to the entire class.

10. Have each child lie down on a sheet of butcher paper or newsprint. Ask another child to trace the subject's outline on the paper. Have children cut out their individual outlines and post them on a wall of the classroom. During the course of several weeks, have all the children write within the outlines of their classmates, recording positive phrases or observations about that specific individual. Keep these up throughout the year and encourage children to continually add comments in the outlines of their classmates. You should also put up an outline of yourself within which students can record their observations of you.

11. Encourage students to write a sequel to *Once There Were Giants*. The sequel could be told from the perspective of the original narrator as she watches her own child grow up. The sequel could also be written from the perspective of the new baby girl and her observations of the world around her.

12. Have children imagine that they are newborn babies in a hospital nursery. What would they like to say to the other infants in the nursery? What kinds of things or people do they see? What kinds of experiences do they have?

13. Students may enjoy imagining that they are born as giants and progressively get smaller as they get older. Ask students to write several diary entries from that perspective. How do their lives change? How do other people react? What kinds of experiences happen to them? How does that perspective compare with the perspective of the narrator in the book?

14. Share several newspaper ads with your students. Then ask students to create original ads about themselves (as though they were items for sale). What qualities would they want to emphasize in a limited amount of space? What special features do they have that others would enjoy? Students may wish to emphasize physical characteristics, personality characteristics, or both. Post the ads in a prominent location in the room.

15. Have each child make a hand or foot casting at the beginning of the year. Here is a recipe for flour dough (makes approximately 2 cups):

> 2 cups self-rising flour
> 2 tablespoons alum (available at large drug stores)
> 2 tablespoons salt
> 2 tablespoons cooking oil
> 1 cup plus 2 tablespoons boiling water

> Carefully mix all the ingredients in a large bowl. Knead until mixture attains a doughy consistency. Provide a portion for each child (you may need to make larger quantities of the original recipe). Ask each child to press his or her hand or foot into the dough. Air dry each cast outside or in a slow oven (250 degrees) for several hours.

Keep these casts in a safe place. At the end of the year, repeat the process and have students compare the differences between their two casts. Discuss the amount of physical growth each student has undergone during the year.

People

Peter Spier
(New York: Doubleday, 1980)

SUMMARY

This book investigates the similarities and differences among the four billion people on the earth. Although we are all unique individuals, we also share many common features. The book emphasizes the commonalities among people more than their differences.

SOCIAL STUDIES TOPIC AREAS

Geography, history, sociology, anthropology

CONTENT-RELATED WORDS

unique, delicacy, dialects, culture, imaginable

CURRICULAR PERSPECTIVES

The theme of this book is perhaps one of the most important children will be exposed to throughout the social studies curriculum, and certainly throughout the entire elementary curriculum. That is, while people are different in terms of eye color, shape and size, hair style, or country of origin, we are all essentially the same—people. Peter Spier weaves a rich tapestry of people from around the world, highlighting their distinctive qualities and distinquishing characteristics, yet truly emphasizing the commonalities that we all have as members of the human race.

The book examines humans' shapes and sizes, skin colors, eye configurations, facial features, types of hair, and clothing worn in different parts of the world. Readers are introduced to the games other children play around the world, the hobbies people pursue, the feasts and holidays they celebrate, and the wide variety of foods they consume. Attention is given to the many religions of the world's peoples and how individuals try to earn a living. Several pages are devoted to the different ways people communicate with each other through language and other devices.

The book's emphasis is on diversity and commonality. Although people may eat different foods, have distinguishing physical characteristics, or pursue different lifestyles, we all embrace common dreams and hopes. This book stresses the importance of the common person and the philosophy that, while we may believe different things or look different, we are all human beings—all four billion of us!

CRITICAL-THINKING QUESTIONS

1. How would your life be different if you were born in China? In Brazil? In France?

2. What do you think when you see someone who looks different from you?

3. Why is it important to keep an open mind when meeting new people for the first time?

4. If everyone looked the same, how would life be different?

5. If you moved to a new country, what new things would you have to learn?

6. Why is it important to learn about different cultures?

7. What are some of the different ways in which people communicate?

8. What if everyone in our class spoke a different language?

9. What about your physical body would you most want to change? Why?

RELATED BOOKS AND REFERENCES

Adoff, Arnold. *Black Is Brown Is Tan*. New York: Harper, 1973.

Allen, Thomas B. *Where Children Live*. New York: Prentice Hall, 1980.

Anno, Mitsumasa. *All in a Day*. New York: Putnam, 1986.

Balestrino, Philip. *Fat and Skinny*. New York: Crowell, 1975.

Bendick, Jeanne. *All around You*. New York: McGraw-Hill, 1951.

Florian, Douglas. *People Working*. New York: Harper, 1983.

Goldin, Augusta. *Straight Hair, Curly Hair*. New York: Crowell, 1966.

Hautzig, Esther. *At Home: A Visit in Four Languages*. New York: Macmillan, 1969.

Quinsey, Mary Beth. *Why Does That Man Have Such a Big Nose?* New York: Prentice Hall, 1986.

Rice, M., and C. Rice. *All about Things People Do*. New York: Doubleday, 1989.

ACTIVITIES

1. Direct students to begin corresponding with a pen pal from another country. Information about international pen pals can be obtained from: International Pen Pals, P.O. Box 2900065, Brooklyn, NY 11229-0001.

2. Have students create a list of interview questions and ask family members or friends to describe a country they have lived in or visited. Have students tape record the interviews. Students may also wish to create a slide show by taking slides of pictures from several travel magazines. The tape recordings and slides can be combined into a most interesting show.

3. Have each student trace his or her roots back to another country. Flags can be placed on a large wall map of the world indicating countries of origin of students. Students may wish to write make-believe accounts of their relatives' travels to the United States with reference to the social conditions, travel difficulties, and time period.

4. Students may wish to collect examples of recipes from as many different types of ethnic groups as are represented in the classroom. Recipes from other students in the school may also be added to the class cookbook. Students may wish to look at examples of other cookbooks and then create their own. You may hold an international food bazaar with parents submitting favorite foods and delicacies for everyone to enjoy.

5. Have a "Same Day." Tell students that during a selected day everyone in the class must come to school dressed in identical clothes, eat the same foods for lunch, sit in their chairs the same way, answer the same questions, talk the same way, etc. At the end of the day, ask students to discuss their feelings about "Same Day" and how it compares with real life.

6. Invite a linguist from a local college to visit your class. Ask this individual to explain the nature of his or her work. Ask the linguist to translate students' names into another language and help them pronounce those names phonetically.

7. Have students design and create a travel guide to a foreign country. Direct them to write the guide outlining the similarities and differences of that land to their own culture. Students may also wish to include an itinerary, distances from selected sites, and points of interest. Invite a travel agent to the classroom to explain the details of foreign travel.

8. Assign each student a partner and have the partners learn as much as possible about each other. Then have each compare himself or herself to the other in categories such as foods eaten, hobbies, family size and origin, clothes, friends, body features, etc. Students can then prepare illustrative posters about their partners for classroom display.

9. Obtain several books in the *Count Your Way* series (e.g., *Count Your Way through Italy*). These books introduce students to countries by using that country's language to count from 1 to 10. Later, students may want to create their own Count Your Way book of local significance to share with a class in another part of the country (potential correspondents can be obtained from the "Reader Exchange" section of *Learning Magazine*).

10. Encourage each student to select a skill, talent, or specialty that he or she is best at doing (interviewing individuals beforehand will ensure that each student can focus on one particular strength). Put together a "Guiness Book of Classroom Records" with each student listing his or her specialty. The book could deal with the obvious (one who can jump the highest, one with the curliest hair, etc.) to the not-so-obvious (one with the longest thumb, one who knows all the verses of "Yankee Doodle Dandy," etc.).

11. Discuss diet as a function of climate. Have students research the climates and diets of selected foreign countries and lead them toward conclusions concerning famine and surplus.

12. According to the book, approximately 750 babies are born in the world every minute. Have students calculate various math problems such as the following:

    a. How many babies are born in an hour?
    b. How many babies are born during our social studies class?
    c. How many babies are born during a typical school day?
    d. How many babies will be born between the end of school today and the beginning of school tomorrow?

13. Challenge students to bring in as many different types of communication as they can (telephones, drums, records, signal flags, etc.). Encourage students to create a classroom display of all the forms of communication possible. Ask them to note similarities and differences.

14. Have students create a classroom display of items, objects, or pictures cut from old magazines of common things we use that are manufactured in other countries [coffee (Colombia), electronic devices (Japan), Saab cars (Sweden), etc.].

15. Direct students to take photographs of many different people in the school, in the neighborhood, or in the local shopping mall. Have students put together a bulletin-board collage of all the different nationalities and/or ethnic groups.

16. Have students create a scrapbook of pets. Encourage them to bring in pictures of all their pets and to write individual descriptions of those pets. What similarities do the pets have? What differences do the pets have?

17. Get a copy of *The Whole Earth Holiday Book* by Linda Polon and Aileen Cantwell (Glenview, Ill.: Scott, Foresman, 1983). Investigate several holidays and national celebrations and hold one or more of them in your classroom.

18. Students may wish to create a calendar of various ethnic holidays and celebrations. They can collect data from the school library and add it to a large wall calendar. Be sure to refer to the calendar on a regular basis and celebrate a different holiday or two every month.

19. Students may be interested in learning some sign language. Invite an instructor from a local social agency or the local college to teach your students a few basic hand signs. Have students discuss the difficulties they have with sign language in comparison with their usual means of communication.

20. Discuss with students the various monuments, postage stamps, buildings, rooms, etc., that bear the pictures or names of people (such as the Washington Monument, Lincoln Room, Martin Luther King Jr. stamp, etc.). Students may wish to create a display of various memorials to share with other classes. Ask students how they would like to be remembered after they die.

21. The National Geographic Society (Washington, D.C. 20036) produces a series of filmstrips titled People and the Places Where They Live (No. 04333; 1981). This series of three sound filmstrips includes *People in Mountains, People in Deserts*, and *People Near the Water*. These filmstrips would be an excellent adjunct to the study of people around the world.

Sarah Morton's Day
Kate Waters
(New York: Scholastic, 1989)

SUMMARY

This is the story of a day in the life of Sarah Morton, a typical nine-year-old girl living at Plimouth Plantation, Massachusetts, in 1627. Her life is both different from and similar to that of nine-year-old girls today.

SOCIAL STUDIES TOPIC AREAS

Geography, sociology, history

CONTENT-RELATED WORDS

cockerel, coif, waistcoat, garters, hasty pudding, much, perchance, Sabbath, petticoat, bounty, knickers, pottage, thee

CURRICULAR PERSPECTIVES

The year is 1627, and life is not easy for the early settlers of Plimouth Colony. There is land to till, animals to take care of, and a host of other chores and jobs necessary to ensure the economic and social survival of the colony. There are many struggles, both personal and political, and the colonists are faced with numerous decisions and challenges every day of their lives.

This story tells the tale of one young girl as she begins her day in Plimouth Colony. It describes the chores, tasks, and daily activities of a nine-year-old girl from the start of her day until she retires at night. We see her tend to her chores, meet with her friends, attend school, and work at a variety of tasks. The day is filled with a neverending stream of jobs and responsibilities, many of which are repeated each day.

Sarah's story is told through photographs taken at the outdoor living museum of seventeenth-century Plymouth, Massachusetts. At the museum the year is always 1627. The costumes, events, and village are accurately portrayed, down to the minutest detail. The visitor, whether in person or through the descriptive photographs of this book, is transported to a time and place that are long ago but not forgotten.

Included in this book are notes about the actual Plimouth Plantation, the life of the real Sarah Morton (who actually lived at Plimouth Plantation), and about the young girl who portrays Sarah Morton in the book. Children will find this book to be an accurate and wonderful introduction to this time period and an exploration of an important time in this country's history.

CRITICAL-THINKING QUESTIONS

1. How difficult would it have been to live in the 1600s as compared to today?

2. Would you like to trade places with Sarah, even for one day?

3. What do you think a trip across the Atlantic would have been like in the early 1600s?

4. If you did not have television or radio (or even electricity), what kinds of hobbies or activities would you participate in?

5. What are some of the chores you do at home that are similar to those done by Sarah Morton?

6. What would be the hardest thing to get used to if you had to live during the 1600s?

7. What would the colonists have done if they had not been able to get a sufficient supply of crops for one year?

RELATED BOOKS AND REFERENCES

Colloms, Brenda. *The Mayflower Pilgrims*. New York: St. Martin's Press, 1973.

Fritz, Jean. *Who's That Stepping on Plymouth Rock?* New York: Coward, McCann & Geoghegan, 1975.

Goode's World Atlas. 17th ed. Chicago: Rand McNally, 1982.

Haslam, Cliff, and John Miller. *Colonial and Revolutionary War Seasongs and Chanteys*. Folkway Records, 1975.

McGovern, Ann. *If You Sailed on the Mayflower*. New York: Scholastic, 1969.

Plymouth Plantation. Glastonbury, Conn.: Video Tours, 1989.

Siegel, Beatrice. *New Look at the Pilgrims*. New York: Walker, 1977.

ACTIVITIES

1. Direct each student to keep a personal diary of a day's activities (as was done with Sarah Morton). If possible, select one or two students and photograph them in various activities. Later, when the photos are developed, post them on the bulletin board and attach the corresponding entries from the students' journals. Other students may wish to create personal scrapbooks of journal entries and selected photographs.

2. Have students create a menu of foods served during the time of the Pilgrims. A good resource is Suzanne Barchers and Patricia Marden, *Cooking Up U.S. History* (Englewood, Colo.: Libraries Unlimited, 1991). Direct students to prepare a meal using original foods or recipes. Invite parents and other classes to participate.

3. One of the customs the Pilgrims had was that children spoke only when spoken to. Structure a classroom simulation in which students may speak only when you tell them to or ask them a question. Do this in the morning and in the afternoon discuss with students their feelings about this custom.

4. Ask a group of students to plan and create a new form of government for the classroom. What would make their government different from or similar to their current form of government. Ask the group to create a charter or constitution for their government and present it to the rest of the class.

5. Have students work in groups to create a travel brochure for the New World. What aspects should be emphasized? What features of the New World should be depicted in the brochure? What elements should not be included in the brochure? The inclusion of photographs would be a valuable part of these brochures.

6. Sailing across the Atlantic took a long time in the 1600s. Invite students to research the games and other activities ship passengers might have played during their voyage. What games or activities would students take with them if they were to embark on a long and perilous journey across the ocean?

7. One of the chores young girls had to do during the time of Sarah Morton was to make butter. Students may enjoy making their own homemade butter, too. Here's a set of simple directions:

   > Pour heavy cream into jars with tight-fitting lids. Shake the jars until the cream separates into a solid and a liquid. Allow the solid to drain in a strainer for a few minutes. Stir in a little salt and spread on bread or muffins.

8. Direct students to research the various types of sailing ships used during the book's time period. They may wish to create a scrapbook or bulletin-board display of their findings. Obtain some models from a local hobby store and ask students to construct them.

9. Since the Pilgrims did not have any type of refrigeration, foods had to be preserved in a variety of ways. Ask students to research the different ways of preserving food. They may wish to bring in several types of fruits and allow them to dry in the sun for a few days to create fruit jerky.

   > Cut fruit into thin strips. Lay the strips on pieces of cardboard and cover with cheesecloth. Be sure to take the fruit in each evening and put it out each morning until it is dried.

   Have students experiment with different types of fruit to see which one dries best and tastes best.

10. Invite a local furniture maker into your classroom to describe the differences between furniture created during the early days of the country and furniture built today. You may be able to borrow a piece of antique furniture from the parents or grandparents of one of the students for display purposes.

11. Have students calculate the distance from Plimouth Plantation to the following locations:
    a. Their home town
    b. Washington, D.C.
    c. London, England
    d. A non-North American site where their relatives grew up.

    Have students plot those distances on a map of the world. Put the map on a bulletin board and use pieces of string to represent the various distances and locations.

12. Students may wish to create their own version of "Jeopardy." Have one group of students create various answers from the book and present them to another group. The other group must then create the corresponding questions for those answers.

13. Have students create their own candles using the following directions:
    a. Melt some paraffin over a double boiler.
    b. Get some small (half-pint) milk cartons and punch a small hole in the bottom of each. Thread a piece of wicking (available at hobby stores) through each hole and tie a knot in the end, or attach a paper clip to the end of the wick for weight and center the clip in the bottom of an unpunched carton.
    c. Place a pencil on the top of each carton and wrap the loose end of the wick around the pencil, making sure the wick is centered in the carton.
    d. Slowly pour melted wax into each carton (for color, crayon shavings may be added before pouring). Allow to solidify and tear the milk carton away from the outside of each candle.

14. Have students divide a large sheet of posterboard in half. On one side ask students to list all the ways in which the Pilgrims recycled materials or conserved energy. On the other side have students record all the ways in which their families recycle and conserve. What similarities or differences do students note? Were the Pilgrims more conscious of preserving their natural resources?

15. Provide each student with a long rectangular piece of black or brown felt (2" x 14", for example). Put a squash seed at one end of each piece of felt, fold it over, and wet it down. Add a new squash seed every two or three days, fold over the felt, and wet it down. Keep these seed packets in a dark area. After a week or so, have students check the growth of their seeds. Later, some of the seeds may be transplanted to a growing area on the school grounds.

16. Obtain a large sheet of newsprint. Have individual students stand between the sheet and an overhead projector. Turn on the projector and ask each student to assume one of the poses Sarah took in the story. Have other students trace the outline of each silhouette on the newsprint. Create several silhouettes and ask students to color them and post them around the room.

17. Some students may wish to participate in a game of charades. They can illustrate one or more of Sarah Morton's actions for other students to guess.

18. Borrow some costumes from your local high school or college drama department. Ask students to create an original skit about a day in the life of a Pilgrim boy. What activities or chores would the Pilgrim boy do that would be similar to or different from those of Sarah Morton?

19. Students may wish to initiate secret pen-pal journals with other students in the school or at another school. Ask each student to write to an individual and share parts of his or her day; they need not reveal the names of their pen pals. You can act as the messenger (or mail carrier) and deliver those messages from one school or classroom to yours.

20. Have students write to the following address to obtain information and/or brochures about Plimouth Plantation: Plimouth Plantation, Dept. 189, P.O. Box 1620, Plymouth, MA 02360.

21. Students may enjoy making corn bread in much the same manner as the Native Americans did:
    Boil 3 cups of water and stir in 1 cup of cornmeal grits. Simmer until all the water is absorbed. Allow to cool and turn onto a work surface which has been floured with a cup of fine cornmeal flour. Work the mixture into 2 round flat cakes. Bake on a floured cookie sheet at 400 degrees for about 45 minutes.

6—Family

Always Gramma
Vaunda Micheaux Nelson
(New York: G. P. Putnam's Sons, 1988)

SUMMARY

A little girl remembers the good times she had with her Gramma. But Gramma has gotten older and has changed—she doesn't even live with Grandpa any more. The little girl tries to remember Gramma just as she was before.

SOCIAL STUDIES TOPIC AREAS

Sociology, history

CONTENT-RELATED WORDS

nursing home

CURRICULAR PERSPECTIVES

Growing old is not always easy. Along with a loss of physical capabilities, there is often a loss of mental capacity. Older people tend to forget names, lose objects, or suffer from other problems associated with memory loss. Many of these occurrences are just a normal and natural part of growing old. In some instances, this diminished capacity may be due to Alzheimer's disease, a reduction in mental facilities typically associated with the aging process.

This book presents a sensitive and compassionate look at Alzheimer's disease told from the perspective of a little girl who does not understand. Wishing for the good times she and her grandmother had before, the girl finds it difficult to believe that her beloved relative has forgotten things that were special to both of them. Confused, hurt, and bewildered, the youngster searches in vain for some way to explain her grandmother's altered behavior, but is unable to do so.

Students will enjoy this book because of its realistic and insightful portrayal of believable characters. Teachers will relish this book because it tackles a subject that is often avoided with young children. The author's handling of a traumatic topic provides a host of opportunities for youngsters to share similar experiences and discuss the dynamics of growing old. Students are exposed to a basic fact of life, namely, that growing old is both natural and perilous.

Sharing this book with students will provide teachers with many chances to integrate the study of aging into the curriculum and to present aging not as something we traditionally fear or ridicule but as a normal part of living. There may be facets of the aging process that are still mysterious to young children, but this book provides a wonderful window into an aspect of aging that needs to be shared by all, no matter what their ages.

CRITICAL-THINKING QUESTIONS

1. Would you have continued to visit Gramma in the nursing home even though she could not talk with you? Why?

2. What were some of the emotions you felt as you read the story? Did it remind you of anyone you knew?

3. Why do you think this is a good book to share with children your age?

4. How do you think Grandpa felt when he had to put Gramma in the nursing home?

5. What do you think Gramma would like to say to her granddaughter at the end of the story?

6. How do you think Grandpa's life has changed since he had to put Gramma in a nursing home?

7. What kinds of activities would you like to do with your grandmother if you could?

8. Would you want to have Gramma as your grandmother? Why?

9. Have you ever gotten lost in a public place? How did you feel? Was it the same feeling the little girl had when her Gramma got lost? Why?

RELATED BOOKS AND REFERENCES

Aliki. *The Two of Them*. New York: Greenwillow, 1979.

Farber, Norma. *How Does It Feel to Be Old?* New York: Dutton, 1979.

Frank, Julia. *Alzheimer's Disease: The Silent Epidemic*. Minneapolis, Minn.: Lerner, 1985.

Guthrie, Donna. *Grandpa Doesn't Know It's Me*. New York: Human Sciences Press, 1986.

Maclachlan, Patricia. *Through Grandpa's Eyes*. New York: Harper & Row, 1983.

Oxenbury, Helen. *Grandma and Grandpa*. New York: Dial, 1984.

Pellowski, Anne. *Betsy's Up-and-Down Year*. New York: Philomel, 1983.

Tapp, Kathy Kennedy. *Smoke from the Chimney*. New York: Atheneum, 1986.

ACTIVITIES

1. Have students create an original book discussing activities that they and their grandparents have done together. If students have not had contact with their grandparents, have them create a book discussing the activities that they would like to do with their grandparents.

2. Have students create a map of the route from Gramma's house to the creek. Students should create a map that could easily be used by Gramma so that she would not get lost on her walks.

3. Encourage students to create a sequel to the story. What happens to Gramma and the little girl? Does Gramma have any more adventures? Will the little girl have different feelings about Gramma?

4. Just for fun, lead the class in a round of "When the Red Red Robin Comes Bob, Bob, Bobbin' Along," a song mentioned in the book.

5. Have students write to Heraldic Center—"1776" House, 260 Massachusetts Avenue, Boston, MA 02115. Direct them to request information on creating coats of arms for their family names. When the information is received, provide students with an opportunity to create personal coats of arms for their families.

6. Discuss how Gramma got angry and threw a dish. Have the students brainstorm two lists, one for positive, good ways of expressing anger and the other indicating negative, bad ways of showing anger. Post master lists in the classroom and have students periodically put check marks beside one way they handled their anger during a particular incident.

7. Purchase some violet seeds from a local garden center. Locate several areas around the school or in the local community to plant the seeds. Be sure students weed and water the seeds according to directions. Indicate that these plants are in honor of Ophelia or any other elderly person.

8. Arrange for the students to "adopt" a grandparent through a local nursing home. When students are paired with their adopted grandparents, provide them with several opportunities throughout the year to write letters and send cards. Encourage students to discuss how it feels to be an adopted grandchild. Arrange a field trip to the nursing home near the end of the year (or during selected holiday times) so that adoptees can meet each other and spend some time together.

9. Challenge students to create a set of aerobic exercises that can be done by elderly people. Invite the physical education teacher to explain how older people often have a limited range of motion and/or weakened muscles. Students may wish to put together a guidebook on appropriate activities and exercises.

10. Gramma thought that her granddaughter might change the world. Have students write their own books entitled, *I Can Change the World*. Have students base their books on the one thing they would do to change the world and make it a better place.

11. Invite a doctor or other health care worker into your classroom to discuss Alzheimer's disease. Have the doctor discuss both the physical and emotional ramifications of the disease. Students may wish to create a poster illustrating some of the facts and details about Alzheimer's disease.

12. Encourage students to compose a letter to their parents thanking them for all the wonderful things they have done for their children. These letters can be posted in the classroom or sent to students' parents.

13. Discuss with students the different types of families that exist today, for example, single-parent families, nuclear families, extended families, foster-parent families, etc. Have students create a bar graph representing the types of family structures represented in the classroom. Later, have students take a survey of other students at their grade level or throughout the school and graph those results, too. Compare the various groups.

14. Set up a "Family of the Week" bulletin board. Designate one student each week to be the honored representative of his or her family. Ask the featured student (prior to the designated week) to bring in photographs, artifacts, and memorabilia of his or her family to set up and display to the class. Students may also wish to include lists of books family members enjoy reading, titles of favorite songs, or favorite pieces of clothing. At the end of each student's week, take a photograph of his or her display and collect all the photos into a yearbook for sharing at the end of the year.

15. Read to the class *My Grammy* by Marsha Kibbey (Minneapolis, Minn.: Carolrhoda, 1988). Have students compare and contrast how Amy (the girl from *My Grammy*) and the girl from *Always Gramma* handle their grandmothers' diseases.

16. Discuss how Gramma burned herself because she forgot about the cigarette Grandpa was smoking. Discuss with students the negative effects of smoking. Have students design and create posters on the dangers of smoking to display in the local community.

17. Provide students with a simple recipe to make a birthday cake; however, do not list the measurements in their lowest terms. Students will have to reduce the measurements to their lowest terms before they can make the cake. Here is a quick and easy recipe (note the "expanded" measurements):

> 9/3 cups sifted cake flour
> 5/5 teaspoon baking soda
> 12/16 teaspoon salt
> 6/8 cup shortening
> 12/8 cups sugar
> 6/2 eggs, unbeaten
> 12/16 cup milk
> 5/20 cup distilled vinegar
> 9/6 teaspoons vanilla

    Sift the flour, soda, and salt together. Cream the shortening and add the sugar gradually. Cream until light and fluffy. Add the eggs, one at a time, and beat thoroughly after each addition. Combine the milk, vinegar, and vanilla and add alternately with the flour, about a third at a time. Beat until smooth after each addition.

    Turn into three greased, 9-inch layer cake pans. Bake in a moderate oven (375 degrees) 25 to 30 minutes. When cool, frost with frosting (canned or packaged).

18. Take the students out for a bird-watching tour. Have them list or draw illustrations of some of the birds they see. Upon your return to the classroom, have small groups of students research the birds they saw and prepare short descriptions of each one. A bulletin board can be set up with drawings and accompanying names of all birds.

19. Discuss with students the necessity of knowing the local emergency phone number (911). Have students act out skits or simulations dealing with emergency situations. Each skit will result in one child calling 911 and giving the operator the appropriate information (toy phones or disconnected push button phones can be used). Stress to students that 911 is not a number to play with—it is for emergency situations only!

Granpa

John Burningham
(New York: Crown, 1985)

SUMMARY

The author describes the special love that exists between a little girl and her grandfather. In a seemingly disjointed conversation, the two of them grow to appreciate one another in a most unusual way.

SOCIAL STUDIES TOPIC AREAS

Sociology

CONTENT-RELATED WORDS

Florence, Africa, Noah's Ark, olive branch

CURRICULAR PERSPECTIVES

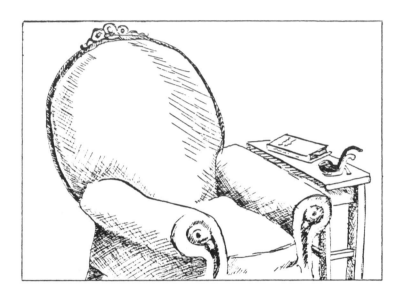

There is often a magical kind of relationship between children and their grandparents. Even though they may speak different languages, see the world from different perspectives, and have wildly different life experiences, there is always a special bond that holds them together. Watching a mother bird take care of its young, seeing patterns in the clouds overhead, or even skipping a stone across the surface of a lake are events that may hold great meaning for children and grandparents.

There is a special fascination in watching the interaction of children and their grandparents. Although years may separate them, they have a wonderful type of communication that is both simple and complex at the same time. They can talk about things that may seem relatively unimportant to the rest of us, yet are powerfully important in their lives. Those conversations and discussions are filled with magic and mystery and help cement a relationship that transcends years and underscores more similarities than differences.

This book is about one of those special relationships. The casual reader may have difficulty at first sorting out the interaction between the little girl and her grandfather, but it becomes apparent after a while that they are alike in many ways. In fact, this book becomes a celebration of similarities rather than a description of differences; therein lies its strength.

Young readers will grow to appreciate the particular relationship that often exists between old people and young people. Teachers will find this book to be a fantastic aid in any discussion of families and all the relationships that can exist within a family. Indeed, this book is a celebration of life as well as a celebration of families. Teachers and children will find many special moments to share within the pages of this book as well as in their own lives.

CRITICAL-THINKING QUESTIONS

1. What is a special experience you have had with one or both of your grandparents?

2. What did you like most about the grandfather in the story? Was he similar in any way to your grandfather?

3. What kinds of activities would you like to do with your grandchildren when you are a grandparent?

4. Is the little girl similar to anyone you know?

5. What kinds of activities do you like to do by yourself? What kinds of activities do you like to do with friends? What kinds of activities do you like to do with adults?

6. What will you look forward to when you are older?

7. What is difficult about growing old?

8. Why do some grandparents enjoy playing with children while other grandparents do not enjoy children?

RELATED BOOKS AND REFERENCES

Cole, Babette. *The Trouble with Gran*. New York: Putnam, 1987.

Farber, Norma. *How Does It Feel to Be Old?* New York: Dutton, 1979.

Hammond, Winifred. *The Riddle of Seeds*. New York: Coward, McCann & Geoghegan, 1965.

Hines, Anna Grossnickle. *Grandma Gets Grumpy*. New York: Clarion, 1988.

Kibbey, Marsha. *My Grammy*. Minneapolis, Minn.: Carolrhoda, 1988.

Nelson, Vaunda Micheaux. *Always Gramma*. New York: Putnam, 1988.

Pringle, Lawrence. *Death Is Natural*. New York: Four Winds, 1977.

ACTIVITIES

1. Have students conduct interviews of their grandparents. Work with them beforehand to design a series of appropriate questions. Students may elect to tape record their interviews or record the information on questionnaire sheets. Later, some of the information can be assembled into scrapbooks entitled "What We Learned from Our Grandparents."

2. Schedule a "Grandparents Day" for your classroom. Have students draft and send out invitations to all the grandparents who live in the local area. Grandparents who live some distance away may be able to tape record messages to be played for the entire class. Activities scheduled for the day could include a read-along session, story-telling hour, a special lunch, and other activities as decided by the students.

3. The National Geographic Society (Washington, D.C. 20036) produces a series of five sound filmstrips entitled The World of Plants (No. 03785). These thirteen-minute filmstrips introduce students to parts of the plant, how plants grow, kinds of plants, where plants grow, and the relationship between plants and people. This series is a wonderful introduction to plant life.

4. Have students bring in empty egg cartons. Place potting soil in each of the compartments of an egg carton and distribute a variety of seeds to each student. Have each student dampen the potting soil and plant one or two seeds in each compartment (about ¼" to ½" below the surface). Label the compartments with the type of seed in each and place the cartons in a sunny location. Have students watch for signs of growth and record in a diary the different growth patterns of each compartment.

5. Share some spring poetry with your students. You may wish to include "Ode to Spring" by Walter R. Brooks, "Pussy Willows" by Aileen Fisher, "Smells" by Kathryn Worth, "Spring" by Karla Kuskin, and "Spring Is" by Bobbi Katz.

6. Have students do a survey of their grandparents on children's songs that were popular when they were growing up. Direct students to put together lists of songs that were popular in their grandparents' day as well as a list of songs students sing or know about today. Do any songs appear on both lists?

7. Students may enjoy creating nature crafts from plants and other objects in and around their homes. Refer to any of the following books for ideas and suggestions: *From Petals to Pinecones: A Nature Art and Craft Book* by Katherine N. Cutler (New York: Lothrop, Lee and Shepard, 1969), *Nature Crafts and Projects* by Beverly Frazier (Los Angeles, Calif.: Price/Stern/Sloan, 1987), or *Snips and Snails and Walnut Whales* by Phyllis Fiarotta (New York: Workman, 1975).

8. Introduce your students to different kinds of tea. Most larger supermarkets carry of variety of flavored, herbal, and spiced teas. Brew several kinds in your classroom and invite students to sample them. Have students record their impressions of the different teas. Which was the strongest? Which was the most flavorful? Which was the most unusual? Provide students with a variety of sweeteners to test as well. Sugar, honey, syrup, and artificial sweeteners can all be tried. Have students establish a rating scale for the effect of various sweeteners on different types of tea.

9. Students may enjoy listening to some winter poetry, too. Poems can include "I Heard a Bird Sing" by Oliver Herford, "Winter" by Jack Prelutsky, "First Snow" by Marie Louise Allen, "It Fell in the City" by Eve Merriam, and "Winter Clothes" by Karla Kuskin.

10. Many winter activities and projects can be found in the following books: *Exploring Winter* by Sandra Markle (New York: Macmillan, 1984), *Into Winter: Discovering a Season* by William P. Nestor (Boston: Houghton Mifflin, 1982), or *Winter Book* by Harriet Webster (New York: Macmillan, 1988).

11. Students may enjoy making their own ice cream. Here is a recipe to try with them (makes approximately four small servings):

> 2 pounds of ripe peaches (peeled)
> 3 tablespoons lemon juice
> 1½ cups granulated sugar
> 2 eggs, separated
> 2 tablespoons confectioner's sugar
> 1 cup heavy cream

Cut peaches in half and remove pits. Place peach halves in a mixing bowl with lemon juice and crush with a potato masher. Stir in granulated sugar. In medium bowl with rotary beater, beat egg whites with confectioner's sugar until soft peaks form. In a small bowl, beat egg yolks well. Fold yolks gently into whites, using wire whisk. Whip cream until it holds soft peaks and then fold it into the egg mixture. Fold in peaches. Pour into one-quart ice cube tray (without compartments). Freeze until slightly firm. Transfer to bowl; beat with rotary beater until creamy. Freeze again until firm.

12. Direct students to interview their grandparents, parents, and other adults in their neighborhoods. Have students put together various lists of toys that were popular 100 years ago, 75 years ago, 50 years ago, 25 years ago, and 10 years ago. What similarities or differences do students note in their lists?

13. Students may enjoy some poetry about the ocean. Poems such as "Driving to the Beach" by Joanna Cole, "Sea Shell" by Amy Lowell, "Until I Saw the Sea" by Lillian Moore, and "The Sandpiper" by Frances Frost would all be appropriate.

14. Students can create their own waves in a wave bottle. Collect several plastic two-liter soda bottles. Fill each one about a third full with salad oil. Fill the rest of each bottle (all the way to the top) with water. Put a few drops of blue food coloring in each bottle and cap tightly. Direct students to put each bottle on its side and tip back and forth gently to create miniature sets of waves. Obtain a recording of Claude Debussy's "La Mer" (*The Sea*) and play it as students create their waves. Ask students to write or discuss their feelings or emotions.

15. Obtain a box of popsicle sticks (most hobby stores sell them) or a box of tongue depressors (available from the school nurse). Invite students to work together to create several buildings or other objects pictured in the book.

16. *Fish* (No. 51073) is a sixteen-minute color videotape available from the National Geographic Society (Washington, D.C. 20036). It demonstrates in close-up and slow-motion photography the movement and anatomy of a fish. Show the film to your students and invite them to describe any similarities between the movements a fish makes and movements children make. The information from that discussion can be transferred to a poster.

17. Ask students to find the birthdates of as many of their grandparents as possible. Have students make up a "Guinness Book of World Records" scrapbook that includes some of the following data: the oldest grandparent, the youngest grandparent, the grandparent who lives farthest away, the grandparent and child with the largest number of years between them, or the longest-married grandparents.

Ox-Cart Man
Donald Hall
(New York: Viking, 1979)

SUMMARY

It is fall, and the ox-cart man packs his cart with wool, mittens, candles, linen, shingles, brooms, and all the things he and his family have made during the past year. He sets off for Portsmouth Market where he sells everything, including the ox and cart. Returning home, he and his family begin the process of making candles, whittling brooms, carving a yoke, and creating other items all over again.

SOCIAL STUDIES TOPIC AREAS

Sociology, economics, history

CONTENT-RELATED WORDS

sheared, linen, shawl, harness, embroidery

CURRICULAR PERSPECTIVES

This is a story in the best oral tradition. Its lyrical tone and simple style reflect a time when the entire family participated in its own economic survival.

The reader is easily led through the manufacturing, processing, and selling of goods that were necessary to a family's existence in eighteenth-century New England.

What makes this a particularly good book for use in the classroom is that it demonstrates the wide variety of events that must be taken care of annually by all members of the family. Children will see several relationships between the daily or weekly chores they do around their homes and the tasks required for economic subsistence by the members of the ox-cart man's family.

The chronology of the story achieves an important purpose—that is, children become aware of the importance of many single events to the welfare of the entire family. Readers also learn of the variety of activities, chores, and jobs that families had to engage in to maintain an adequate standard of living. Teachers will find this book to be an ideal introduction to the concept of economics, which, more than just money matters, encompasses all the ways resources are used and distributed.

The illustrations (which garnered a Caldecott Medal for the book) realistically depict lifestyles, architecture, furnishings, and the geography of early New England. Wonderfully simple, they offer readers a valuable insight into a way of life that, though long past, is still very much a part of our historical heritage and culture.

CRITICAL-THINKING QUESTIONS

1. What are some chores or jobs you do around the house that are similar to those done by the children in this story?

2. Would you enjoy living on a farm a long way from the city? Why?

3. What items made by the ox-cart man's family do you have in your home? How were they manufactured?

4. Why did all members of the family have to make things to be sold in Portsmouth Market?

5. How would you feel about living in eighteenth-century New England? What difficulties would you have? What would you enjoy most?

6. Do you think your friends would enjoy this story? Why?

7. Would you enjoy doing the same jobs year after year? Why?

8. If you were the author of this story, what new events would you want to add?

9. How is this family similar to your family? How are they different?

10. Which of the events of the story was the most interesting?

RELATED BOOKS AND REFERENCES

Graff, N. P. *The Strength of the Hills: A Portrait of a Family Farm*. Boston: Little, Brown, 1989.

Larrick, Nancy. *Piping Down the Valleys Wild: Poetry for the Young of All Ages*. New York: Delacorte, 1985.

Livingston, Myra. *A Circle of Seasons*. New York: Holiday House, 1982.

National Geographic World. Washington, D.C.: National Geographic Society. Published monthly.

New Hampshire Vacation Center, Box 856, Concord, N.H. 03301.

Precek, K. W. *Penny in the Road*. New York: Macmillan, 1989.

Rappaport, D. *The Boston Coffee Party*. New York: Harper, 1988.

Waters, K. *Sarah Morton's Day: A Day in the Life of a Pilgrim Girl*. New York: Scholastic, 1989.

ACTIVITIES

1. Have students create a model of an ox cart. Using oatmeal boxes cut in half lengthwise, rubber wheels, wire, and pieces of fabric, students can assemble carts similar to that in the story.

2. Provide students with a map of New Hampshire and ask them to locate Portsmouth. Have them plot an imaginary route that the ox-cart man would have taken to get to Portsmouth.

3. Give students several old magazines or travel brochures on New Hampshire. Ask them to create an original collage of scenes and locations that would be similar to those depicted in the book.

4. Have students create original advertisements for one or more of the goods the ox-cart man sold in Portsmouth. What modern-day advertising techniques should be included in their ads to ensure a sale?

5. Many people today still wash, dye, card, spin, and weave their own wool. Locate an individual who has a spinning wheel and can demonstrate for youngsters the various steps used in turning raw wool into a finished product. If a local person is not available, obtain a film or video (the National Geographic Society has several) and show it to students. Encourage them to discuss any similarities or differences in the way fabric is created today as compared with two hundred years ago.

6. Students may enjoy creating candles as their ancestors did. For directions, see activity 13 in chapter 5 (page 47).

7. Have students prepare stories that include many of the events or activities they do annually. What similarities are there between their events and any in the story?

8. Provide each student with a potato and a cup of water. Ask students to push toothpicks around the middle of their potatoes and suspend them halfway in the cups. Direct them to monitor any growth in the potatoes and record it on an appropriate graph. Be sure each student keeps sufficient water in each cup.

9. Have students prepare an imaginary journal of the ox-cart man's travels into Portsmouth, his activities while in the town, and his journey homeward.

10. Students may enjoy setting up a classroom store similar to that in the story. Ask them to decide what goods they could manufacture on their own for sale in the store. Encourage them to develop a barter system for the exchange of those goods.

11. Most students have never tasted *real* maple syrup. You may wish to get some and treat students to a pancake lunch.

12. Have students create an original book about life on a farm. They may wish to create one book about farm life in the 1700s or 1800s and another book about farm life today.

13. Have students interview their grandparents or several residents in a local nursing home on some of the family traditions they remember most from their childhoods.

14. Here is a recipe for soft pretzels, a favorite snack of children for many, many years:

> 1 package dry yeast
> ¾ cup warm water
> 1 teaspoon salt
> 1 tablespoon sugar
> 2 cups sifted flour
> coarse salt (kosher salt)
> 2 tablespoons milk or water

Preheat oven to 425 degrees. Dissolve yeast in warm water in a large bowl. Add salt and sugar and mix well. Beat in flour and knead dough in bowl until smooth. Turn dough out on floured board. Pinch off 2-inch sections of dough and roll them into ropes. Form into pretzel shapes. Place on greased baking sheet. Brush with milk or water. Sprinkle with coarse salt. Bake immediately, 12 to 15 minutes, until nicely browned.

15. Have students pretend they are going to sell the items the ox-cart man sold. Direct them to create magazine advertisements or television commercials for selected items.

16. Divide the class into four groups, one for each season. Direct each group to create a diorama of one of the four seasons. Have each group make three-dimensional figures of the ox-cart man and his family for placement in each diorama.

The Wednesday Surprise

Eve Bunting

(New York: Clarion, 1989)

SUMMARY

Wednesday nights are special for Anna, because that is when Grandma comes over with a big, lumpy bag filled with books. Together they read story after story. All the time they are also planning a surprise for Dad's birthday.

SOCIAL STUDIES TOPIC AREAS

Anthropology, sociology

CONTENT-RELATED WORDS

(none)

CURRICULAR PERSPECTIVES

Imagine going through life without ever having learned to read. Think about all the great books you would have missed, the letters shared between friends, even the newspaper accounts of events and happenings in your own home town. We sometimes take literacy for granted, never really appreciating the gift we have and the ability we can use to discover and participate in the world around. Yet, for some 26 million Americans literacy is a real problem. That is the number of individuals in this country who cannot read or write, people often referred to as *functional illiterates*. They are people for whom reading the daily newspaper or enjoying the latest best seller are impossible dreams.

Despite these statistics, much is being done to help nonreaders. Organizations such as Literacy Volunteers of America and the International Reading Association are making concerted efforts at helping people of all ages learn to read. Obviously, one of the difficulties in the quest to help people read is the fact that those who have been nonreaders for many years—older citizens—are often too proud or too ashamed to admit their lack of literacy skills.

This book is an important book for students because it approaches literacy as a concern of all individuals, not just teachers. It demonstrates for children that literacy is not just something learned in school, nor is it something we should take for granted. Rather, it is an important part of our everyday lives—a part we can share with each other. In this book, the author tells a poignant tale of how one youngster helps her grandmother learn to read. The tone is light and fresh, but the message is strong. We see the strength of a familial relationship and also how that relationship can be used to promote a common goal.

Through this book, children will begin to understand that children can be teachers for adults just as much as adults are teachers for children. This mutuality reinforces family ties and strengthens bonds of understanding between generations. Though this is a book about families, it is also a book about working together and sharing dreams.

CRITICAL-THINKING QUESTIONS

1. Why do you think Anna's grandmother wanted to learn to read?

2. Why do you think Anna's grandmother was unable to read? Do you think she went to school?

3. Why was Anna's father so happy?

4. How do you think adults feel when they are unable to read?

5. If Anna's grandmother could relive her life, what do you think she would do differently?

6. What are some things people do when they are not able to read?

7. What are some of your favorite family moments?

8. If you had to, could you teach your grandparents to read like Anna did? Describe in detail what you would do.

9. What is the best present or gift you have ever given your grandparents? Any family member?

10. What are some of your favorite birthday memories?

RELATED BOOKS AND REFERENCES

Adler, Carol S. *One Sister Too Many*. New York: Macmillan, 1989.

Aliki. *The Two of Them*. New York: Morrow, 1987.

Bates, Betty. *Bugs in Your Eyes*. New York: Archway, 1979.

Beatty, Patricia. *Behave Yourself, Bethany Brant*. New York: Morrow, 1986.

Gordon, Shirley. *The Boy Who Wanted a Family*. New York: Harper, 1980.

Hautzig, Esther. *A Gift for Mama*. New York: Penguin, 1987.

Oxenbury, Helen. *Grandma and Grandpa*. New York: Dial, 1984.

ACTIVITIES

1. Invite a member of the local literacy council or reading council to visit your classroom and discuss the nature of illiteracy. Encourage your students to ask questions about the extent of the problem and what efforts are being made to overcome the problem.

2. Have students create a large class scrapbook of the activities they enjoy doing with their grandparents. The scrapbook could include photographs with accompanying captions as well as illustrations of holidays or family gatherings.

3. Have students write to the International Reading Association (800 Barksdale Road, P.O. Box 8139, Newark, DE 19714-8139) and request single copies of the following brochures (they are free for the asking):

Good Books Make Reading Fun for Your Child

Your Home Is Your Child's First School

You Can Use Television to Stimulate Your Child's Reading Habits

Studying: A Key to Success ... Ways Parents Can Help

You Can Encourage Your Child to Read

You Can Help Your Child in Reading by Using the Newspaper

Summer Reading Is Important

Be sure to include a stamped, self-addressed envelope. After the brochures arrive, discuss with students how the information in them can be used to promote good reading habits. How could the information in the brochures be used to help adults learn to read?

4. Have students create posters on the importance of reading for all individuals, children *and* adults. Get permission from several local businesses to post the posters in store windows or near the cash registers. Periodically create new posters and rotate them every so often.

5. Have students create an oath in which they agree to read with their parents or guardians for at least fifteen minutes each day. Students may wish to design a contract to be signed by you, their parents, and themselves vowing to support the oath.

6. Schedule a family "read-in." Invite parents, grandparents, and other adults to visit the classroom at a scheduled time (during the school day, immediately after school, or in the evening). Direct each person to bring a collection of favorite books and a pillow or two. Schedule a block of time (about one hour or so) for everyone to gather in a central location and just read silently. Afterwards, individuals may wish to share some of their thoughts or things learned via their reading.

7. Encourage students to select the oldest living relative in their families and conduct an interview. The interview can be done in person, by telephone, or by mail. Ask students to inquire about some of the most memorable events for their relatives as well as some of the reading materials they used when they were children. Provide opportunities for students to share their discoveries in writing or orally.

8. All families celebrate holidays differently. Set up a bulletin board for students to post explanations of family celebrations and special events. Descriptions and photographs should also be included.

9. Students may enjoy creating a family newspaper. Assign each student the role of reporter and ask him or her to interview family members about their opinions of current issues, selected hobbies and free-time activities, and vacation spots, for example. The information on each family can be assembled into a sheet of news and all the sheets collected into a large class newspaper on families.

10. Have students create a fictional journal about a relative living one hundred years ago. These journals can include events of the time or the thoughts of the relatives in reaction to the events.

11. Set up a special spot in the classroom where all sorts of books about families are included (see the annotated bibliography). Encourage students to read a variety of these books.

12. Provide students with modeling clay and ask each one to create a bust of a favorite family member. Discuss the reasons why a particular person was selected as the designated individual. After all the busts are completed, set up a gallery of busts in the classroom.

13. Ask students to bring in photographs of various family members. Have students put push pins into a large world map indicating the countries of origin of members of their families. Post the pictures next to the countries of origin.

14. Students may be interested in creating a family time line. Have them ask their parents about the marriage dates, birth dates, and deaths of various family members. Have students record these dates on a time line to be put up on one wall of the classroom. To make a time line, record each date on an index card. Hang lengths of string across one wall of the room. Clip the index cards to the string in the correct order with clothespins.

15. Have students write imaginary letters to "Dear Abby" about a real or fictional family problem or situation. You can have an anonymous student respond to the letters received or you can do it yourself.

16. Have students create a collage (pictures and words cut from old magazines and glued to a sheet of poster board) of all the important things that are necessary for a family, such as love, sharing, conversation, listening, caring, etc.

17. Do you remember baking cookies with your grandmother? Here is a recipe for no-bake cookies your students may enjoy preparing on their own or with your guidance.

> 2 cups granulated sugar
> ½ cup water
> ½ cup cocoa
> 4 tablespoons butter
> 1 teaspoon salt
> ½ cup peanut butter
> 1 teaspoon vanilla
> 3 cups oats

Combine sugar, water, cocoa, butter, and salt in a saucepan. Boil for 1 minute. Add peanut butter, vanilla, and oats. Cool slightly. Drop by spoonfuls onto wax paper and allow to set. This can also be prepared in a microwave oven with a plastic or glass bowl.

When I Was Young in the Mountains

Cynthia Rylant

(New York: Dutton, 1982)

SUMMARY

This is a young girl's story about growing up in a rural mountain region of America. The story details the life of mountain people, the relationships of friends and family, and the impact rural living had on the author.

SOCIAL STUDIES TOPIC AREAS

Sociology, anthropology, geography

CONTENT-RELATED WORDS

okra, jonny-house, congregation, baptism, cowbells, bobwhite

CURRICULAR PERSPECTIVES

The simple pleasures of life. Swimming in a swimming hole. Sitting on a porch swing just to watch the stars at night. Eating homemade cornbread. Simple pleasures in the fast-paced, fast-food, fast-track world of today. Yet, they are also part of the special memories and heritage of so many people, a memory that is preserved in books such as this.

This book is a tribute to the generations of people for whom the simple life is the only life they know. It is a celebration of an uncluttered existence filled with hard-working days and bright summer nights. It is a return to a time when families created their own pleasures and scratched out a living without all the conveniences we often take for granted today. It is an endearing look at the life and times of people who were satisfied with the way they lived—people who were content to make do rather than trying to get ahead.

In a wonderfully told tale, this book outlines some of the activities and pastimes of a young girl as she grows up in a mountain region of the United States. Her recollections are fondly recounted so that the reader realizes they are not only an important part of her past, they are also a significant element of who she is today. In a sense, her past is her present, as it is for each of us.

Children will delight in this story. Its evocative illustrations and patterned text give readers an opportunity to become truly involved with the memories and activities of a youngster not much different from themselves. Students will get a sense of an era that may be considerably different from theirs, but which is filled with special memories and special times. The book is both a sociological study of a rich element of the American culture and a historical flashback to a time and place as distant as long ago or as recent as yesterday.

CRITICAL-THINKING QUESTIONS

1. Would you enjoy living in the mountains? Why?

2. How would your daily life be different if you had no running water or indoor plumbing?

3. Why do you think the author wrote the book?

4. How is the store mentioned in the story different from the store in your town or neighborhood?

5. Why was the boy baptized in the pond?

6. Where are the parents of the young girl?

7. How would living in the mountains be different from living near the ocean?

8. What are some things you do every day that you would not be able to do if you lived where the girl did?

RELATED BOOKS AND REFERENCES

Burch, Robert. *Ida Early Comes over the Mountain*. New York: Viking, 1980.

Dragonwagon, Cresent. *The Itch Book*. New York: Macmillan, 1990.

Hendershot, Judith. *In Coal Country*. New York: Knopf, 1987.

ACTIVITIES

1. Students may wish to create an original play about the book. Some students can rewrite scenes from the book, others can act as scenery artists, and others as the actors and actresses. Video-tape the production and share with other classes.

2. Students may wish to create a papier-mâché model of a mountain. This can be done by forming a piece of chicken wire into the shape of a mountain (about three feet high). Take several newspapers and tear them into strips. Dip the strips into a thick mixture of flour and water and layer them over the chicken wire. Make three or four layers of newspaper. When the mountain is dry, have students paint it with tempera paints in appropriate colors. Students may wish to use plant clippings and toothpicks to recreate the flora and buildings of mountain life.

3. Have each student create his or her own book entitled *When I Was Young*. Ask students to recollect the events of early childhood and describe them in their individual books. When completed, students should set up a special display for all the books.

4. Have students create and send invitations to residents of a local senior citizen center to visit your classroom. Set up a panel discussion in which the senior citizens describe their childhood experiences for students.

5. Students may wish to create their own mountain posters. Provide each student with an array of different sizes of sponges and different colors of poster paint. The sponges can be dipped in the paint and pressed against newsprint or oaktag to create colorful mountains. Display these around the classroom.

6. Challenge students to create wordless picture books about the events and scenes in the story. What kinds of illustrations can they create that provide an accurate depiction of story scenery?

7. Have each student create an imaginary pen pal who lives in the mountains. What kinds of things would students like to learn about their pen pals? How do students' lives compare with the pen pals'?

8. Students may enjoy making (and certainly eating) their own cornbread. Here is a simple recipe:

   Mix and sift 1 cup of enriched flour, 3 teaspoons of baking powder, ½ teaspoon of salt, and ½ cup of sugar. Stir in ½ cup of yellow corn meal. Add 1 cup of milk to one well-beaten egg and stir into first mixture. Add 1 tablespoon of melted shortening and blend. Pour mixture into a greased 8-inch pan and bake in a hot oven (400 degrees) for about 20 minutes. Cut into squares and serve.

9. Have students create a topological map of the major mountain regions in the United States. What similarities do students observe in the different areas? What differences?

10. Have students discuss how their lives are different from that of the narrator in this story.

11. Most students have probably never tasted, much less seen, okra. They may be interested in planting some okra in a small garden plot somewhere on the school grounds or in their gardens at home. If this is not possible, you may want to obtain some fresh okra at a major supermarket (it also comes canned). Wash it and cut it into bite-sized pieces. It can be fried in a small amount of cooking oil (stir frequently so it does not burn) for about 10 minutes.

12. Have students discuss and/or write about a peaceful place they like to go to in order to get away from everyone. Be sure students understand that this is a natural behavior of humans.

13. Have students make a list of some of the physical skills they would need to climb a mountain. What exercises can they suggest that would build up the necessary muscles for that task?

14. Students may wish to start personal or classroom rock collections. You may want to begin by having students collect rocks found in and around the school grounds or in their own neighborhoods. Starter kits of various rocks can be obtained from Edmund Scientific (101 E. Gloucester Pike, Barrington, NJ 08007) and Hubbard Scientific Company (P.O. Box 104, Northbrook, IL 60065).

15. Use school stationery and write to the Geologic Inquiries Group (907 National Center, Reston, VA 22092). They will send, free of charge, an extensive packet of teaching materials, geologic and topographic maps, and earth science bibliographies related to your state.

16. "A Study in Time" is a 17" x 22" poster featuring geologic activity in the Precambrian, Paleozoic, Mesozoic, and Cenozoic eras. It is available for a small charge from the American Geological Institute (4220 King St., Alexandria, VA 22302).

17. Invite a woodcarver into your classroom to describe and illustrate his or her craft. Contact your local art association or craft store for the names of potential invitees.

7—Community and Neighborhood

In Coal Country
Judith Hendershot
(New York: Knopf, 1987)

SUMMARY

A child growing up in a coal-mining community finds both excitement and hard work in a life deeply affected by the local industry.

SOCIAL STUDIES TOPIC AREAS

Geography, sociology, history, economics

CONTENT-RELATED WORDS

coal, tipple, gob pile, red dog, mumblety peg

CURRICULAR PERSPECTIVES

Coal mining is an occupation not many of us would relish, but for the coal-producing regions of Ohio, Pennsylvania, and West Virginia, it is an all-consuming way of life. Coal dust tends to settle on anything and everything and it pervades every nook and cranny of coal miners' lives as well as the lives of their families.

The life of a coal miner is not easy. Beset by all sorts of dangers down in the mines, the rest of a miner's life is just as rugged and harsh. Low wages and long hours keep many coal-mining families at the subsistence level. Eking out an existence and dealing with the daily dangers of the mines is part and parcel of family life in and around the mines. Families are often held together with prayers, hopes, and an inner strength that wards off adversity but never eliminates it.

Although there are many negative features of this lifestyle, there are several positive ones, too. Families have to work together and contribute to the welfare of the entire unit. In so doing, bonds are forged that are not possible in other occupations where the job is completely divorced from the family. So, too, are bonds established between families. Whenever an accident occurs or a family is in desperate financial straits, those around rally to help in whatever ways they can. A sense of community, in which everyone takes care of everyone, is built and maintained among mining families. Coal-mining families combine the inner strength of family members working together and the community strength of other families to help themselves through the heartaches, agonies, and disappointments of a lifestyle that is frequently passed down from father to son.

This book offers a unique sociological look into one family. But it is more than just a paean to family life—it is also a testament to a way of life that is unique in American culture. It demonstrates to children that no matter what our job or station in life, the strength of our family can see us through the pitfalls and hardships of daily living. If coal miners have a resilience, then that resilience comes from the strength of their families more than from the dangers of their job.

CRITICAL-THINKING QUESTIONS

1. Would you like to live in a coal camp? Why?

2. Do you think the family in this story was rich or poor, happy or sad? What clues tell you that?

3. What part of the story was most like your own childhood? Which part was most unlike your childhood?

4. Should everyone be proud to do their work? Explain what you mean.

5. Tell about some of the ways Mama made her home as pretty as it could be. How is your home as pretty as it could be?

6. What other questions would you like to ask the author of this story?

7. After reading this story, would you like to live without television for a while? Why?

8. Would you have liked to live in the 1930s? Why?

9. How would you feel if you went to a creek to swim and the water was black? What would you do about it?

RELATED BOOKS AND REFERENCES

Coal: The Rock That Burns (fourteen-minute film). Lawrence, Kans.: Centron Educational Films, 1976.

Cranfield, John. *Where Are You Going with That Coal?* New York: Doubleday, 1977.

Davis, Bertha. *The Coal Question*. New York: Watts, 1982.

Gunston, Bill. *Coal*. New York: Watts, 1981.

Kraft, Betsy Harvey. *Coal*. New York: Watts, 1982.

Lenski, Lois. *Coal Camp Girl*. New York: Lippincott, 1959.

Map of Coal Areas in the U.S. Washington, D.C.: National Coal Association, 1977.

"The Story of Coal" (booklet). New York: Bethlehem Steel, n.d.

ACTIVITIES

1. Obtain pieces of coal to bring in and show students (contact Edmund Scientific, 101 E. Gloucester Pike, Barrington, NJ 08007 or Hubbard Scientific Company, P.O. Box 104, Northbrook, IL 60065). Have students break the coal samples apart carefully with hammers and discuss how coal mining can be a dusty, dirty job.

2. Check with a local high school science teacher and obtain maps of coal-producing regions in the United States. Post these for students and discuss reasons why coal is found in particular areas of the country.

3. Students may wish to create a scale model of Willow Grove using small boxes, toy building blocks, Legos™, or Lincoln Logs™.

4. Invite a parent or grandparent of one or more students into the classroom to describe the process of canning various foods. Students may want to try canning different food items (be sure all safety rules are followed closely!).

5. Obtain or borrow a tub and washboard from a local antique shop or neighbor. Have students try washing clothes using these items. Ask them to describe the difficulties they had.

6. Students may wish to visit a local nursing home or senior citizen center and interview residents about the "good old days." What conveniences do they have now that were not available when they were growing up? How has life changed in the last fifty or seventy-five years? What elements of their youth do they miss the most? The results of the interviews can be combined into a journal or scrapbook with photos.

7. Students may enjoy creating a country store in the classroom. Have them bring inexpensive items or food from home to be bought, sold, or traded at the store with their classmates.

8. Coal is only one of the natural resources we get from the earth. Students may enjoy learning about other fossil fuels such as oil and natural gas. Show the filmstrip *What We Get from the Earth* (No. 04418) (Washington, D.C.: National Geographic Society, 1981) (sixteen minutes, with sound).

9. Have students write journal entries using the following sentence stems as starters:

   "If my father was a coal miner, I would...."
   "If my family did not have a washing machine we would...."
   "If I didn't have a television I would...."

10. Discuss the term *company town*. What would be some of the disadvantages of living in a company town? What might be some advantages?

11. In the story, the father went to work while the mother stayed home. Discuss with your students this traditional view of family roles. Survey the class to see how many students' families are traditional like the one in the story. What other kinds of families are represented in the class?

12. Encourage students to do some library research on the different uses of coal. They may wish to combine their findings into a large mobile from which important facts and information can be suspended. The mobile can be hung in the center of the room.

13. Have students consult the local Yellow Pages to see whether coal is sold in your community. If it is not, you can obtain copies of telephone books from many metropolitan areas throughout the country at your local public library. Borrow one or more and conduct a search through the Yellow Pages for coal suppliers and distributors. Discuss with students reasons why it may be difficult to locate a supplier of coal in your area.

14. Encourage students to create their own coal-mining songs using music from some popular songs and writing their own lyrics. Point out to students that miners created their songs in order to keep a good, steady pace as they worked and have your students create songs that do likewise.

15. Some students may be interested in rewriting portions of the story from the mother's or father's point of view. This can be done as an individual activity or as a group project. Be sure the stories are shared with all class members.

16. Obtain some charcoal pencils or sticks from the art teacher and have students create their own original illustrations for the book.

17. Students may enjoy creating some rock candy. Here is a recipe:

    Bring ½ cup of water to a boil. Add about one cup of sugar to the water by teaspoonfuls, stirring so that the sugar dissolves completely. When all the sugar has been added, stirring should continue until the mixture is clear and syrupy. Allow the mixture to cool for about 10 to 15 minutes.

    Tie a piece of clean string to the middle of a pencil. Tie a paper clip to the end of the string as a weight. Lay the pencil over the top of a glass so that the clip is suspended just above the bottom of the glass. Pour the cool sugar-water mixture into the glass and watch crystals begin to form along the string (this process will take about a week). If a film develops on the top of the syrupy mixture, remove it very carefully so that the liquid can evaporate.

18. Have students locate Neffs, Ohio, on a map of the United States. This town is near the town of Willow Grove, where the author lived as a young girl. Have students plot the distance from their home town to Neffs. Have them convert that distance into other units of measurement (inches, feet, yards, miles, etc.) and draw an appropriate graph.

19. An excellent video on coal mining is *Portrait of a Coal Miner* (No. 51175) (Washington, D.C.: National Geographic Society, 1980). This fifteen-minute film portrays the life of a coal-mining family, how coal is mined, and what life is like both inside and outside a coal mine.

Miss Rumphius
Barbara Cooney
(New York: Viking/Penguin, 1982)

SUMMARY

Like her grandfather, Alice Rumphius longs to travel around the world and live by the sea. Her grandfather advises her that she must also do one other thing: make the world more beautiful.

SOCIAL STUDIES TOPIC AREAS

Different cultures, geography, history, anthropology

CONTENT-RELATED WORDS

figureheads, conservatory, tropical

CURRICULAR PERSPECTIVES

This book is an ideal supplement to the social studies curriculum for many reasons. It provides youngsters with a wonderful introduction to small-town and rural living and also introduces them to a believable character in a very believable time. Told from the perspective of Miss Rumphius's great-niece, it is a delightfully woven tale of one woman's determination to accomplish the goals she has set for herself during her lifetime.

The story begins in a small New England town and then takes the reader on a journey through tropical islands, mountainous terrain, and desert scenery. The narration is sparse but precise and evokes a mystical quality to the story, to which children can relate quite well. The main character is easily identified and readers come to appreciate the strength of her will and her resolve to accomplish her goals.

Through this story, children become aware of the infinite variety of lifestyles in places both near and far away. They become sensitized to the variety of peoples and places in the world and how our knowledge of those cultures can help make us all more well rounded. The fact that the main character is a woman is a positive assurance that individuals, no matter what their gender, can accomplish what they wish in life. Thus, Miss Rumphius can be an important role model for girls.

Teachers will discover that this book can and should be part of not only the social studies curriculum, but also the science, language arts, and reading programs. Its beautiful illustrations and descriptive vocabulary (for which it won the American Book Award) will be an appropriate addition to the entire elementary curriculum.

CRITICAL-THINKING QUESTIONS

1. Would you want to have Miss Rumphius as a relative? Why?

2. Why is Miss Rumphius an interesting character?

3. If you were the author of this story, would you want to change the ending? How would you change it?

4. How is Miss Rumphius different from other elderly people that you know?

5. What kinds of adventures away from home would you like to have during your lifetime?

6. Why do people enjoy traveling?

7. Would your friends enjoy this story? Why?

8. Why do you think Miss Rumphius never married?

9. Where would you like to live when you retire? What makes that place so special to you?

RELATED BOOKS AND REFERENCES

Atlas of the World. 6th ed. Washington, D.C.: National Geographic Society, 1990.

dePaola, Tomie. *Now One Foot, Now the Other*. New York: G. P. Putnam's Sons, 1981.

MacDonald, Golden. *The Little Island*. Garden City, N.Y.: Doubleday, 1946.

Songs and Sounds of the Sea. Washington, D.C.: National Geographic Society, 1973.

Vivaldi, Antonio. *The Four Seasons* (recording). (E.g., Israel Philharmonic Orchestra, Zubin Mehta conducting, Deutsche Gramophon.)

Willard, Nancy. *The Voyage of the Ludgate Hill*. San Diego, Calif.: Harcourt Brace Jovanovich, 1987.

ACTIVITIES

1. Have students create an original book on the history of sailing ships. They may wish to do some library research or create a model (store-bought or original) to use as a three-dimensional illustration.

2. Have students make a collage or poster of one of the countries hinted at in the book. This may include, but not be limited to, Switzerland, Kenya, Morocco, Tahiti, Australia, or any other countries which could have kangaroos, mountains, deserts, tropical environments, or lions.

3. Students may wish to make a tape recording of the book and loan it to the school library. Some sound effects (lions roaring, waves on a shore, winter winds) could be added to the recording.

4. Have several students keep an ongoing daily journal of some of Miss Rumphius's journeys into distant lands. You may wish to divide the class into several groups, with each group responsible for creating journal entries about a particular part of Miss Rumphius's travels.

5. Using a map of the world, have students put push pins into all of the places Miss Rumphius could have visited during her travels.

6. Have students investigate the various ways seeds are dispersed. Ask them to determine if wind, water, or animal dispersal is the most efficient. Show *Seeds and How They Travel*, a sixteen-minute filmstrip with cassette, from the National Geographic Society (No. 04655). Invite a botanist or college professor from a local college to explain the various ways seeds are dispersed.

7. Have students investigate some of the major deserts of the world. What makes some of the deserts unique? How are deserts in the United States different from or similar to deserts in other parts of the world? (Students may be interested in learning that each year the world's deserts grow by as much as sixteen thousand square miles.)

8. Make a bulletin-board display on how different types of mountains are created. Ask students to speculate on why some mountains are easier to climb than others.

9. Bring in several different types of flower seeds, including lupines. Ask students to grow the seeds (either outside or indoors using a "grow lamp"). Direct them to chart the different germination rates of the seeds as well as differences in the shape, color, and size of the resultant flowers. What makes lupines different from other types of flowers?

10. Have students create an imaginary dialogue between their grandparents and Miss Rumphius. What kinds of things would they talk about? What differences would there be in their child-hood experiences?

11. Direct students to write a prequel or sequel to the story. What other events could have taken place after the story or before the story began?

12. Have students check the Yellow Pages of the local phone book and compile a list of all the services related to elderly people (nursing homes, special equipment, social groups, etc.).

13. Have students put together a scrapbook of different types of seashells. If some students have been to the ocean or lived by the sea, they may be able to provide some shells for others to enjoy.

14. Direct students to read *50 Simple Things Kids Can Do to Save the Earth* (Kansas City, Kans.: Andrews & McMeel, 1990). Ask them to develop a plan of action on how they want to make the world or their local neighborhoods more beautiful. Be sure to encourage some healthy discussion on their proposals.

15. Have small groups of students create salt maps of their favorite place in the book. Use the following recipe:

    > 4 cups flour
    > 1 cup salt
    > 1½ cups warm water

    Knead all the ingredients about 10 minutes. The mixture should be stiff but pliable. Spread the mixture out on a cookie sheet or piece of aluminum foil, forming it into various landform and ocean areas. Cook at 325 degrees for about 1 hour or more, depending on size. Brush with egg yolk mixed with 1 tablespoon of water and bake until very dry. Seal with two or three coats of polyurethane. Paint various areas with tempera paints and label.

16. Have students pretend that they are visiting one of the countries mentioned in the book. Ask them to create postcards that they would send back to their families at home. Post these cards on the bulletin board.

17. Have students pretend that they are news reporters for a local television station. Have them make up a series of questions they would like to ask Miss Rumphius. One student may wish to take on the role of Miss Rumphius to answer the questions.

18. Ask students to interview their parents, grandparents, or relatives about family stories, folktales, or legends that they learned as children. If some of these adults have immigrated from other countries, you may wish to invite them to visit your classroom to share some stories and legends from their country of origin.

19. Have students write to the consulate or foreign embassy of some of the countries suggested in the book. Students can ask for travel details and other pertinent information that would be useful in planning a trip to those countries. Students can also prepare a travel plan for selected countries (length of stay, required documents/inoculations, necessary clothing, etc.).

20. Have students create a sailing-ship mobile by tying pieces of yarn to a coat hanger and pictures of different types of sailing ships to the yarn. Some students may wish to create their own drawings of ships, which can also be part of the mobile.

21. Small groups of students may wish to create a shoebox diorama of a favorite scene from the story. Using construction paper, glue, toothpicks, cotton balls, clay, and other similar art materials, a wide variety of dioramas can be created.

22. Have students collect several types of seed catalogs. What differences and similarities exist between the various catalogs? Are prices for similar seeds comparable?

23. Students may wish to visit a local nursing home to talk with the residents about some of the adventures they had as children. Prepare children beforehand for some of the things they can expect to see as well as some of the questions they should ask the residents.

24. Provide several groups of students with small balloons and ask them to blow up the balloons. Mix equal parts of liquid starch and water together until the starch is dissolved. Then soak newspaper strips in the mixture and layer them over the balloons. When dry, direct students to use tempera paints to outline areas of these balloon globes and identify countries Miss Rumphius may have visited.

25. Have students create an imaginary route for Miss Rumphius's travels. Have them plot this route on a map and calculate the distances between selected sites.

26. Have students create a poster or advertisement for a particular place mentioned in the story. What facts, figures, data, or illustrations need to be included in the advertisement in order to stimulate tourists to visit a particular destination?

27. Introduce students to songs about the sea or old sailing songs. Check with the school's music teacher or the local public library for recordings of appropriate tunes.

28. Have students create an exercise book for older adults. What activities could be included? Which should be eliminated? Students may wish to consult a physical therapist or the physical education teacher.

29. Provide students with bars of soap and dull knives (table knives work best). Ask them to design and carve figureheads that could be used if the classroom were a sailing ship.

30. Have students create costumes illustrating those worn by people mentioned in the story. What differences do they note in the costumes appropriate for warm countries as opposed to those appropriate for colder climates?

31. Have students create imaginary driver's licenses for some of the forms of transportation mentioned in the story. For example, what would a license to drive a camel look like? What about a license for a sailing ship?

32. Ask students to collect several copies of travel magazines and prepare a collage of pictures clipped from those magazines. Each collage could focus on one of the countries Miss Rumphius visited during her journeys or could depict all possible countries.

33. Ask students to look in the telephone Yellow Pages and create a list of all the services Miss Rumphius might have needed prior to her journeys. For example, a travel agent, a clothing store, a doctor, and a bookstore are possibilities. Students may wish to create their own special Yellow Pages specifically for Miss Rumphius.

Mr. Griggs' Work
Cynthia Rylant
(New York: Orchard, 1989)

SUMMARY

Mr. Griggs has worked in the post office for many years. He loves his job so much that it is all he can think about. The story deals with the events that happen when he gets sick one day and cannot work.

SOCIAL STUDIES TOPIC AREAS

Sociology, economics, anthropology, history

CONTENT-RELATED WORDS

post office, parcel post

CURRICULAR PERSPECTIVES

Why do people work? For love, for money, for personal satisfaction, or for enjoyment? Although we may all have different reasons for working, we can all agree that the world of work is very much a part of who we are and what we believe. Work provides us with a means of economic survival, but it is also much more than that. We may hate it, love it, or be ambivalent about it, but it is still an important part of our lives, shaping our attitudes and perceptions of ourselves and the world we live in.

This story deals with work in its most positive sense. It is a story about a man who dearly enjoys what he does to make a living and the effect his love of work has on those around him. It is, however, much more than a paean to work, for it emphasizes the value of doing one's job to the best of one's ability. It is a tale about making a positive contribution to the lives of other people, a contribution made through the daily tasks we sometimes take for granted.

Children will learn that when one enjoys one's work, a tremendous amount of fulfillment can ensue. They discover that the greatest accomplishment of all may be making a contribution to other people through work.

Although we may take postal carriers for granted, the book makes a case that we should not necessarily take our own jobs for granted. Our work may be more than a series of paychecks—it may help make someone else's life easier, more worthwhile, or more enjoyable. In short, this book offers an important introduction to the world of work and its impact on our daily lives.

CRITICAL-THINKING QUESTIONS

1. Do you think it is important to like the job you do?

2. How do you think Mr. Griggs would feel if he ever got fired from his job?

3. What do you think would happen if there were no postal service?

4. What do you think is the most important job in your neighborhood?

5. Why do you feel Mr. Griggs loved his job as much as he did?

6. Besides the fact that Mr. Griggs loved his work, why did people like him so much?

7. Do you think Mr. Griggs would make a good neighbor?

8. Would you enjoy working in the post office?

RELATED BOOKS AND REFERENCES

Adams, Samuel. *The Pony Express*. New York: Random House, 1950.

Arnold, Oren. *Marvels of the United States Mail*. New York: Abelard-Schuman, 1969.

Colunius, Lillian. *At the Post Office*. Los Angeles, Calif.: Melmont, 1983.

Gibbons, Gail. *The Post Office Book: Mail and How It Moves*. New York: Crowell, 1982.

Jensen, Lee. *The Pony Express*. New York: Grosset & Dunlap, 1955.

Jupo, Frank J. *Any Mail for Me? 5,000 Years of Service*. New York: Dodd, 1964.

Kelen, Imri. *Stamps Tell Us the Story of the United Nations*. New York: Meredith, 1968.

ACTIVITIES

1. Encourage students to interview several mail carriers in your town or community. Have students prepare a standard list of questions to ask each individual. After all the interviews are completed, ask students to compare the answers to each of the questions. Do all the carriers enjoy their job as much as Mr. Griggs did?

2. Have students write a story from the perspective of a letter going through the mail system. What adventures does the letter have? What places does it visit? How long does its journey take? After stories are completed, invite a mail carrier into your classroom to discuss the actual travels of a real letter.

3. Have students begin collecting postmarks from throughout the country. Encourage pupils to have their parents, friends, and relatives save letters from different places. These letters can be brought into the classroom, the postmarks cut from each letter, and an interesting collage or display set up on a bulletin board. Place a map of the United States next to the display and fasten pieces of yarn from each postmark to the location of that town on the U.S. map.

4. Invite a philatelist (stamp collector) into your classroom to discuss his or her hobby. What are some of the most unusual stamps in his or her collection? What makes a stamp valuable? What are some different sizes and shapes of stamps? What are some of the rarest stamps in the United States? In the world?

5. Take a field trip to the local post office. What are some of the jobs of the people there? What responsibilities does the postmaster have? How many stamps are sold each day? What are some of the most unusual things postal workers have done on their jobs? Students may wish to collect answers to these and other questions and create a poster of the postal service in their town. If appropriate, the poster can be hung in the post office for all to enjoy.

6. Divide the class into several groups. Direct each group to interview a class of community workers (health workers: doctors, nurses, paramedics; construction workers: plumbers, carpenters, electricians; educators: teachers, professors, counselors, etc.). Have each group construct a collage or scrapbook of their findings for display in the classroom.

7. Students may wish to write thank-you letters to their local postal carriers for the job they do. Students may also wish to write to the postmaster in their town in appreciation of the job he or she does every day.

8. Provide students with copies of the daily newspaper's want ads. Explain the different kinds of abbreviations used in want ads and prepare a sample want ad for classroom display. Ask students to work in groups to design want ads for various classroom jobs. What special qualifications should applicants for each job have? The student-designed ads can be posted periodically when it is time to assign students to classroom chores.

9. Obtain a postal scale from the school district's business office. Bring in several packages of different weights and have students weigh them on the scale. Students may wish to set up a make-believe post office, weighing several different packages, charting the weights on a graph, and determining appropriate postage according to current postal rates. These activities are a wonderful supplement to the math program.

10. Create a contest in which students design their own original stamps. You may wish to have several different categories for the contest: funniest stamp, most original, most unusual, etc. Have the stamps judged by someone from the local post office.

11. Bring in several street maps of your local community. Talk with a mail carrier and ask that individual to trace his or her daily route on the map. Discuss with students the various places that individual visits each day, the sights seen, and the different streets traveled. Students may want to trace their own daily routes on individual maps and compare their routes with that of a mail carrier.

12. Students may wish to create a time line of U.S. stamps. Ask students to bring in examples of U.S. stamps from forty, thirty, twenty, ten, and five years ago. Place each stamp on an index card and post it above a time line constructed over the chalkboard. Have students record significant historical events that took place when those stamps were in effect. Be sure to discuss reasons why stamp prices escalate.

13. Students may wish to set up a classroom post office for all the class correspondence. Choose one student to be the postmaster and several to be postal carriers. All mail (papers turned in to the teacher) must be addressed (to the teacher) and have a return address (the student's name and desk location). The "mail" can then be placed in facsimiles of post office boxes and inspected regularly by the classroom postmaster.

14. Divide the class into three groups. Have each group research one of the three countries mentioned in the story. After conducting their research, each group should make a presentation to the rest of the class on its discoveries.

15. Have students discuss all the elements that are necessary for being happy in one's job. What conditions must be present? What type of people should one work with? What kind of boss should one have? How long should one work each day? Have students record their responses and then compare them to the responses of their parents. What similarities or differences do they note?

16. Have students write a journal of an imagined day in the life of a mail carrier. What things are seen, people met, places visited?

17. Students may enjoy writing to a pen pal in a foreign country (many foreign students can speak and write in English). Have students send their inquiries to: Student Letter Exchange, 215 5th Avenue S.E., Wasecu, MN 56093.

Shaker Lane

Alice Provensen and Martin Provensen
(New York: Viking/Penguin, 1987)

SUMMARY

Shaker Lane is peopled by an odd assortment of bucolic characters. They live simply, are always friendly, and require only the basic necessities of life. But a reservoir changes their life—covering it up, in fact—and another piece of rural America becomes a memory.

SOCIAL STUDIES TOPIC AREAS

History, economics, political science, sociology

CONTENT-RELATED WORDS

crossroads, bales, nuisance, enormous, reservoir, excavation

CURRICULAR PERSPECTIVES

Development. For many people, that word has an evil connotation. Large expanses of tract homes, vast shopping malls spilling over the edges of suburbia, or the polluting giants of industry stinking up the skies and creating eyesores and traffic snarls for the local residents are usually associated with the term. For some, the term means money and power; for others, it means losing a way of life that they and generations before them have tried to preserve and maintain.

Shaker Lane is not unlike any country lane in any rural area of this country. It is peopled by simple folk, families who life close to the land and close to each other. Their dwellings are not fancy: just enough to keep the rain off their heads and keep them warm in winter—in essence, a place that is more home than house. Distinctive personalities and eccentricities are the hallmark of the Shaker Lane people. They are not cast from the same mold but are as varied as the landscape that surrounds them. Indeed, they are as much a part of the land as the trees and rocks.

But Shaker Lane is out of context. Its simple lifestyle and easygoing folk are doomed. A reservoir is to be built and the water will swallow their beloved land. Knowing that there is probably nothing they can do, everyone, save Old Man Van Sloop, leaves. The water rises and soon a housing development is built along the shore of the lake, a development as different from Shaker Lane as night is from day. It is either a new beginning or a sad ending.

Teachers will find this delightfully illustrated book a wonderful introduction to rural living and rural people. It is a well-told tale full of interesting characters and a powerful message. It does not press for eliminating development of land, but it provides students with a forum in which this issue can be rationally discussed. The authors/illustrators have done a marvelous job of recording a semiagrarian lifestyle through drawings and text that are both simple and complex at the same time. This is a book that can be read from many different perspectives and will certainly be read many times. It is a valuable addition to city-versus-country comparisons.

CRITICAL-THINKING QUESTIONS

1. How would you feel if you were evicted from your home?

2. Who was your favorite character in the book? Why? How is that individual like you?

3. Would the people in your neighborhood fight to save their land? What do you think they would do?

4. If the land had never been sold, what do you think Shaker Lane would look like today?

5. Why do you think a reservoir was constructed?

6. Why do you suppose Old Man Van Sloop and the Herkimer sisters stayed on Shaker Lane?

7. Would you enjoy living on Shaker Lane? What would you find most enjoyable? Least enjoyable?

RELATED BOOKS AND REFERENCES

Baroni, Gino. *Saving Urban Neighborhoods* (sound recording). New York: Encyclopedia Americana/CBS News Audio Resource Library—Grolier Educational Corp., 1977.

Baylor, Byrd. *The Best Town in the World*. New York: Scribner's, 1983.

Goodall, John S. *The Story of Main Street*. New York: Macmillan, 1987.

Henkes, Kevin. *Once around the Block*. New York: Greenwillow, 1987.

Neighborhood Safety (video). Rockville, Md.: National Institute of Justice, 1985.

Yeoman, John. *Our Village*. New York: Atheneum, 1988.

ACTIVITIES

1. Direct students to create a questionnaire to interview several of their neighbors. What if a county land agent evicted you from your house to build a reservoir? Would you oppose the eviction or just move to a different area? Have students graph the positive and negative remarks from their neighbors.

2. Invite a local county agent to visit your class. Have the agent discuss the process by which the county acquires land for resource purposes. Who determines who gets moved, which properties are purchased, and how much money is paid for the properties? What recourses do residents have?

3. Have students write a different version of the book. Instead of the residents moving away and not fighting, have the students write a version in which the residents appeal the eviction notice. Display these writings on a bulletin board entitled "Shaker Lane Fights Back."

4. Invite students to prepare a short script about the incident in which the county agent tells the residents they must move. Have several students take on the roles of selected characters (such as Old Man Van Sloop, the Whipple boys, Virgil Dates, etc.), each of whom is interviewed by a news reporter. Videotape the interviews for later viewing.

5. Divide the class into several groups and ask each group to create a song to the tune of "Over the River and through the Woods," using characters or events from "Shaker Lane." Here is an example:

   Over the river and through the woods
   To Shaker Lane we go
   The Herkimer sisters and Old Van Sloop
   Must now learn how to row.

   Students may also wish to create versions of the song using people and events in their own neighborhoods.

6. Invite a representative of the local Welcome Wagon committee to visit the class and discuss the information they share with new residents of the community. Afterwards, direct students to organize a "Welcome Neighbor Gang" for any new students who enroll in school. Have students put together "Welcome Boxes" for new students, including items such as pencils, a school sports schedule, a listing of P.T.O. meetings, notebook paper, and the like.

7. Ask students to create a community newspaper. Students can create current-event articles on the local neighborhood, a series of community cartoons, a sports page, movie and play reviews and schedules, P.T.O. meetings, etc. Try to group students who live in the same neighborhood together and rotate the assignments (sports reporter, fashion editor, etc.) among different students.

8. Have students work with their parents to measure the distances from individual student houses to the school. The distances can be measured by car odometer and converted to feet, yards, and miles. Students can create graphs and charts illustrating the different distances each of them lives from school.

9. Old Man Van Sloop, who lived by himself, had many animals, such as dogs, cats, and goats, to keep him company. Invite a local animal shelter representative to your class to discuss the advantages of pet ownership, including companionship, protection, and safety. Students may wish to make journal entries on the various advantages of different types of household pets.

10. Invite a soil conservationist and/or a landscape architect to the class to discuss the procedures used to build a reservoir. What types of soil and other materials are needed to build an effective reservoir? What safety precautions must be followed? How long does it take? Direct students to construct a visual chart of the steps necessary in planning for, developing, and eventually constructing a reservoir.

11. You may wish to initiate a simulation of the creation of a new neighborhood. Divide the class into small groups and invite them to respond to the following questions:

    Where will the new neighborhood be located?

    What kinds of buildings will be in the new neighborhood?

    What kinds of resources or supplies must be taken to the new neighborhood?

    How many people will live in the new neighborhood?

    What kinds of people do you want in your neighborhood?

    What rules or laws must be set up in your new neighborhood?

After each group has generated some responses to those questions, ask them to decide how they will handle one of the following challenges to the new neighborhood:

A group of land developers wants to construct a new shopping mall

The town council decides to tear down five of the buildings

One hundred new residents move to the area and demand new housing

A reservoir will be built on the edge of town.

12. Have a "Neighborhood Day" in your classroom. Invite various people from your community to visit and share information about their occupations. You may want to invite the mayor, fire chief, postmaster, a doctor, a nurse, the owner of a lumber store, a sanitation worker, a seamstress, an insurance salesperson, or representatives of other occupational groups. Provide a forum in which students can interview each of the visitors and collect the data in the form of a scrapbook or series of brochures.

13. Schedule a "Neighborhood of the Week." Each week, direct one or more students to bring in photographs of their neighborhood, a listing of events that take place in the neighborhood, special attractions, or unusual buildings. Descriptions and captions for each of these can be prepared and posted on the bulletin board.

14. Direct students to write journal entries about one thing in their own neighborhood they would like to change. Why did they select that particular item? How would they change it? How would that change benefit other neighborhood residents?

15. Have students conduct tape-recorded interviews with several of their neighbors. What does each individual like or dislike about the neighborhood? Why do they live there? What changes would they like to see?

16. Direct students to create a telephone directory for the residents of Shaker Lane. Students can invent street addresses and telephone numbers for each of the people mentioned in the book. A set of Yellow Pages can also be included, with listings for the county agent, the water reservoir office, recreational supplies, hardware stores, and the like.

17. Call several real estate agents to get prices on an acre of land. Select areas in the immediate community, other parts of the county, and in other parts of the state. Share that information with students and have them create bar graphs listing the locations and land prices.

18. Rural folks are used to "making do." Simple lifestyles and simple foods are the norm. Here is a recipe for a simple and inexpensive treat children can make and enjoy called Honey Balls:

1 cup peanut butter
1 cup honey
1 cup nonfat dry milk
wheat germ

Mix honey and peanut butter. Gradually add nonfat milk and mix well. Form into balls with greased hands and roll in wheat germ. Chill.

8—City and Country

Grandpa Had a Windmill, Grandma Had a Churn
Louise A. Jackson
(New York: Parent's Magazine Press, 1977)

SUMMARY

This is an intriguing story of life on the farm told through the eyes of a young girl. The girl demonstrates her fascination with farm objects such as a windmill, churn, whetstone, and corn sheller. Through her eyes, readers have opportunities to compare urban/suburban lifestyles with those of farm residents.

SOCIAL STUDIES TOPIC AREAS

History, anthropology, sociology

CONTENT-RELATED WORDS

whetstone, churn, shucked, cellar, quilting frame, corn sheller

CURRICULAR PERSPECTIVES

Farm life has never been easy. Animals must be fed, vegetables canned, machines repaired, and a host of other chores completed every day. Life on the farm is both simple and complex and seemingly without end. Nevertheless, it is a life full of activity and adventure, with never a dull moment.

However, farm life is slowly being taken over by mechanization and modernization. Some reports indicate that less than 3 percent of the available land in this country is used as farmland. That is certainly a sharp decline from the turn of the century, when farmers and farms proliferated. What may have been the norm years ago is, in some parts of this country, fast becoming a memory. The farmer and the family farm are quickly going the way of the Model T and the washboard. Farms and farmers today are struggling for their very existence. That which was so much a part of our past has an uncertain future.

This book provides youngsters with a brief yet realistic peek into the activities of a family farm. Told through the eyes of a young girl, readers get a sense of the magnitude of a farm, the chores that must be done to keep it functioning, and the labor of love that makes farming the special occupation it is. For children raised in urban settings, this book provides a delightful glimpse into selected features of a typical farm. Days begin early and end late and are filled with plenty of jobs, both large and small.

This book should be an important addition to any social studies program. It describes the workings of a farm with an emphasis on the individuals who make it run. Children get an idea of a part of Americana they may seldom see, yet which is intrinsically part of their cultural history. Although many children may never visit a farm, they can experience one through the pages of this book.

CRITICAL-THINKING QUESTIONS

1. Would you like to live on a farm? All year long? For just the summer?

2. How are the grandparents in this story different from or similar to your own grandparents?

3. What are some stories your grandparents may have told you about life when they were young?

4. What kinds of activities have your grandparents done with you that are similar to activities mentioned in the book?

5. What would be some of your favorite farm activities? Your least favorite farm activities?

6. How would you enjoy spending part of your day churning butter, sharpening axes, or sawing wood by hand? What are some advantages or disadvantages of that kind of daily life?

7. How do you think the girl feels about her grandparents?

8. What chore would you enjoy doing the most?

RELATED BOOKS AND REFERENCES

Bolwell, Laurie, and Clifford Lines. *Farms and Farmlife*. London, England: Wayland, 1984.

Humphrey, Henry. *The Farm*. New York: Doubleday, 1978.

Nakatani, Chiyoke. *My Day on the Farm*. New York: Crowell, 1975.

Olney, Ross R. *Farm Giants*. Canada: McClelland and Stewart, 1982.

Oxenbury, Helen. *Grandma and Grandpa*. New York: Dial, 1984.

ACTIVITIES

1. Ask each student to bring in a scrap of material from home. Have the students trim each scrap into a designated size (12" x 12", for example). Instruct students in some rudimentary sewing techniques (threading a needle, stitching, etc.). Have students work in teams to assemble a quilt made from all the fabric samples.

2. Most students probably have not tasted homemade bread. Here is a recipe to share with your class:

>   3 to 3½ cups all-purpose flour
>   1 package active dry yeast
>   ⅓ cup packed brown sugar
>   1¾ cups water
>   1 teaspoon salt
>   3 tablespoons shortening, margarine, or butter
>   2 cups whole wheat flour

Combine 2 cups all-purpose flour and yeast. Heat and stir brown sugar, shortening, water, and salt until warm. Add to flour mixture and beat for 3 minutes with a mixer on high speed. Stir in whole wheat flour and as much of the remaining all-purpose flour as you can. Knead until moderately stiff. Shape into a ball, place in a lightly greased bowl and let rise in a warm place for 1 to 2 hours. Punch dough down and let rest for 10 minutes. Separate into 2 equal parts and place each into a lightly greased loaf pan. Bake in a 375-degree oven for 40 to 45 minutes. Remove from pans, slice, spread with butter or homemade jam, and enjoy!

3. Establish a special place in the classroom as a "Grandparent's Gallery." Direct students to bring in as many photographs of their grandparents as they can. Post these over the display. Students may also be able to bring in some artifacts or memorabilia from their grandparents to display (be sure each piece is labeled with the student's name so it can be properly returned). Encourage students to think of other items which could be displayed in the exhibit.

4. Students may enjoy making their own homemade ice cream. The following recipe, although simple, will give students a sample of real ice cream without the usual additives found in store-bought ice cream.

2 cups heavy cream	a large Styrofoam™ cup (10 oz.)
½ cup granulated sugar	crushed ice
½ teaspoon vanilla	salt
bowl	wooden stirring sticks
a small paper cup (4 oz.)	

Mix the cream, vanilla, and sugar together in the bowl. Fill the paper cup about ¾ full with the cream mixture. Fill the Styrofoam cup about ⅓ full with ice and add about 3 to 4 tablespoons of salt. Stir with a stick until the ice begins to melt. Push the paper cup into the middle of the slushy ice until it is just barely above the level of the ice. Slowly stir the ice cream mixture with another stick. Stop every so often to allow the mixture to solidify and crystallize (you may need to add more ice and salt to the Styrofoam cup from time to time). This process may take up to ½ hour (until the ice cream is slightly soft). Spoon into cups, eat, and enjoy!

Teams of students can each prepare their own flavors of ice cream by adding chocolate syrup, cinnamon, mint flavoring, strawberry topping, or other flavorings to the ice cream just before serving.

5. Set up a field trip during which students visit a local retirement home or senior citizen center. Work with the staff beforehand to plan for some appropriate activities for both students and the senior citizens. These may include, but are not limited to, some of the following:

A planned lunch together

A skit prepared and presented by students

A games festival (checkers, chess, Ping-Pong™)

A read-aloud session

A movie night

A letter exchange

6. Students may enjoy eating corn on the cob for lunch one day. Depending on the season, obtain several ears of corn from a local vegetable stand or your local supermarket (one for each student). Bring these into school along with a large pot. Have students shuck the ears and place them in a pot full of water. Boil the corn and serve hot with lots of butter.

7. Students may also enjoy growing their own corn. Depending on your location or the season of the year (early spring is best), set out a plot of land somewhere on the school grounds (be sure to obtain permission first). Obtain several packets of corn seed from your local nursery or garden center. Follow the instructions and have each student plant part of a row of corn. Weed and water carefully and in about ninety days you and your students may be able to harvest your own crop of homegrown corn. Be sure to enjoy as in activity 6!

8. Students may enjoy interviewing someone who lives on a farm. Ask a local farmer to come to your class for the interview. If someone is not available locally, you can call your county extension agent and obtain the name of someone who might be able to give your students a telephone interview. Be sure your students have prepared a stock of questions beforehand to pose to the farmer.

9. Someone from the local hardware store (or perhaps a parent) might visit your classroom to demonstrate the use of a whetstone (be sure students understand that knife and ax sharpening can be dangerous and should only be done by adults). Have students list all the steps the presenter uses. Later, they can construct brochures on the proper use of a whetstone.

10. Have students each write a series of journal entries on what life was like in "the good old days." Ask them to speculate on the activities or pastimes that made those days "good old ones." Invite one or more elderly people into your classroom to discuss their recollections of the good old days and whether they were appropriately named.

11. Students may enjoy playing a game of charades using the actions and activities (churning butter, sharpening axes, feeding fish) mentioned in the book.

12. Set up a fishbowl (with goldfish) in your classroom. Assign students various tasks related to the care of the fish (feeding, cleaning, changing the water, etc.). Rotate the jobs among the students so that everyone has a chance to care for the fish.

13. Divide the class into several groups. Tell each group that it will be creating its own farm. Ask each group to make the following decisions:

    What animals will you have?

    What tools will you need?

    What crops will you grow?

    Where will you locate your farm?

    After each group has decided on how it will initiate its farm, have the groups come together to discuss the differences or similarities of their respective farms.

14. Obtain and show a copy of *The Heartland* (No. 51090), a twenty-five minute color video available from the National Geographic Society (Washington, D.C., 1983). This film describes the Farm Belt region of the United States in colorful detail.

15. Generations of children and their grandparents have enjoyed making homemade fudge. Here is a quick and easy no-bake recipe for "Fabulous Farm Fudge" your students will enjoy:

1 pound confectioner's sugar	⅓ cup margarine
1 package instant chocolate pudding	2 tablespoons milk
½ cup peanut butter	1 egg white

    Combine all ingredients in a large bowl. (Dough will be very stiff.) Roll to ½" thickness and cut into pieces or mold with hands.

Night in the Country

Cynthia Rylant
(New York: Bradbury, 1986)

SUMMARY

Listen to the mysterious sounds of nighttime in the country. Take a journey through the darkness, inside the farmhouse, out in the barn, over the fields, and through the woods. The sights and sounds of night in the country come alive through the pictures and words in this book.

SOCIAL STUDIES TOPIC AREAS

Geography, anthropology

CONTENT-RELATED WORDS

country, patter, nuzzles, clink

CURRICULAR PERSPECTIVES

We are constantly bombarded with sounds. Traffic noises. Work sounds. Sounds of children talking. Airplane noises. Our days are so often filled with a cacophony of sounds that moments of silence seem almost deafening by comparison.

This book takes a gentle and perceptive look at the nighttime sounds of the country, which we may seldom hear but are indigenous to open fields, large barns, and back yards in rural areas everywhere. The sound of an owl, the rattling of a dog's chain, and the nearly silent nibbling of a rabbit are all part of the sounds of the country when people are asleep and the animals are carrying out their nocturnal activities.

For many children raised in urban or suburban environments, Cynthia Rylant's book will be a welcome introduction to life in the country. Its colorful and descriptive illustrations and sparse text provide gentle relief from the harshness of city living. This is a book about the sounds we seldom hear and a lifestyle too few of us experience. Nevertheless, it is an important part of the tapestry of America. Students will learn that there are many things that happen around them all the time; by taking a few moments, we may experience scenes and sounds previously undiscovered.

Teachers will find this book a perfect platform for discussions on country life, comparisons between urban and suburban living, explorations into animal habits, journeys through colorful landscapes, and decision-making on environmental concerns. In short, this book offers teachers and students a vast array of possibilities for learning more about their world, whether that world is their own neighborhood or some distant place across the country.

CRITICAL-THINKING QUESTIONS

1. What kinds of sounds do you hear at night when you lie in bed? Are the sounds of summer different from the sounds of winter?

2. What kinds of city sounds are similar to country sounds?

3. Why do people who live in the city like to visit the country?

4. What if there were no animals in the country?

5. If you were to visit the country, what would you like to see or hear?

6. What did you enjoy most about the story?

7. Should we be afraid of unknown sounds at night? What about sounds we know?

8. Would you like to be one of the creatures who stays awake all night? If so, which one?

9. What kinds of sounds do you hear at night but do not hear during the day?

RELATED BOOKS AND REFERENCES

Allen, T. B. *On Granddaddy's Farm*. New York: Knopf, 1989.

Asch, Frank. *Country Pie*. New York: Greenwillow, 1979.

Bozzo, Maxine Zohn. *Toby in the Country, Toby in the City*. New York: Greenwillow, 1982.

Buxbaum, Susan Kovacs. *Body Noises*. New York: Knopf, 1983.

Chwast, Seymour. *Tall City, Wide Country: A Book to Read Forward and Backward*. New York: Viking, 1983.

Cohen, Daniel. *Animals of the City*. New York: McGraw-Hill, 1969.

Enright, Elizabeth. *Thimble Summer*. New York: Holt, Rinehart and Winston, 1966.

Good, Elaine. *That's What Happens When It's Spring*. Intercourse, Pa.: Good Books, 1987.

Hall, Donald. *The Man Who Lived Alone*. Boston: D. R. Godine, 1984.

Little Schoolhouse: All about Sounds (video). Santa Monica, Calif.: Hi-Tops (A Division of Heron Communication, Inc.), 1987.

Moncure, Jane. *Sounds All Around*. Chicago: Children's Press, 1982.

Provensen, Alice, and Martin Provensen. *Town and Country*. New York: Crown, 1985.

Robbins, Kim. *City/Country: A Car Trip in Photographs*. New York: Viking, 1985.

Ruff, Bob, and Jack Murtha. *The Fundamentals of Square Dancing: Party Series, Level One* (sound recording). Los Angeles, Calif.: American Square Dance Society, 1975.

Stanley, Diane. *A Country Tale*. New York: Four Winds, 1985.

ACTIVITIES

1. Share some night poetry with your students. Included could be "At Night" by Aileen Fisher and "The Night Is a Big Black Cat" by G. Orr Clark.

2. Have students rewrite the book from the point of view of one of the animals. For example, what sounds would a frog hear? What human sounds (if any) would animals hear at night?

3. Students may enjoy having a campout at school. Send a letter to parents explaining the nature of your project. Invite students to bring sleeping bags, tents, and other camping equipment to

school on a Friday or Saturday afternoon. If possible, have a campfire and tell stories. Schedule some time when you and the students can listen for night sounds in and around the school. Discuss the sounds and their sources on the following school day.

4. Obtain *What You Can See and Hear* (No. 30081) (Washington, D.C.: National Geographic Society, 1985). This two-filmstrip series (with sound) covers the sights and sounds of animals in the forest and animals in the city. Have students compare the sounds on these filmstrips with sounds in their own neighborhoods.

5. Have students imagine what their lives would be like if they were awake during the night and slept during the day. What changes would occur in their lives? What adjustments would they have to make?

6. Direct students to create a bulletin-board display of sounds in the country and sounds in the city. Magazine pictures and photographs brought from home can be posted in each of the two categories. Have students discuss whether some pictures could go in both groupings or are specific to only one.

7. Trees play an important role in the ecological balance of the country as well as the city. They also play an important role in human terms, too—Americans consume more than one-and-a-half billion trees a year in paper, wood, and other products, an average of seven trees per person per year. Get your students involved in one or more tree-planting projects. Information can be obtained from the National Arbor Day Foundation (Arbor Lodge 100, Nebraska City, NE 68410) or Tree People (12601 Mulholland Drive, Beverly Hills, CA 90210).

8. Have students write a letter to their local state representative on why country areas should be preserved in the form of parks, wildlife areas, or preserves. Students may be surprised if they receive a reply. Be sure to discuss their reactions to any reply.

9. Have students prepare a tape recording of various sounds heard in the classroom, in the hallway, or in the library. What similarities do those sounds have? What differences? How do those sounds compare with sounds in the country?

10. Students may wish to write a "Country Newspaper" that includes all the happenings and events of the country in newspaper format. Students can take on the role of reporters and describe animal attractions, goings and comings of various species, fashion, sports events, and the like.

11. Bring in a copy or two of *The Farmer's Almanac*. Have students look up weather predictions, crop forecasts, phases of the moon, and other tidbits of information. What data can they gather for the local area? Can that information be combined into a mini-almanac for your region of the country?

12. Have students bring in cameras from home or provide individual groups of students with a school camera. Direct students to take photographs of the various animals that live around the school and create a collage of the photographs.

13. Direct each student to select one farm or country animal and pretend to interview the animal about its life in the country. Have students write their interviews on animal-shaped papers.

14. Give students several farm headlines such as "Cow's Milk Supply Dries Up!" or "Farmer Grows Corn the Size of Watermelon!" Tell students they are journalists for the magazine *Fantastic Farm Facts and Frolics* and must write articles about their headlines. Organize the articles into a magazine and make copies for each student.

15. To tie this book to a study of farm products, students may enjoy making their own homemade butter:

> Whipping cream or heavy cream (3 or 4 pints)
> Salt
> Baby food jars with tight-fitting lids (one for each student)

Allow the cream to come to room temperature. Fill each of the jars half full with cream. Screw the lids on tightly and allow the students to shake the jars for approximately 15 to 20 minutes, or until butter forms. Carefully rinse off the excess liquid and add a pinch of salt. Have students spread their butter on crackers and enjoy!

Students may wish to suggest a brand name for their butter and write a jingle to advertise its "fresh country taste."

As students shake their butter, teach them the following rhyme:

> Come butter come
> Come butter come
> Peter standing at the gate
> Waiting for a butter cake
> Come butter come.

Explain to students that because the job of making butter is not difficult but can get boring, parents used to give this task to the children. To pass the time, children chanted rhymes. Your students may enjoy creating their own butter rhymes.

16. Turn the class into a country jug band. Let students create their own band instruments, using jugs, combs, spoons, washboards, pots, bells, or anything else that makes an interesting sound. Provide time for students to practice creating rhythms. It might work better to have students work in small groups before attempting to play as an entire class.

17. Teach students some square dances (use *Square Dances of Today and How to Teach and Call Them* by Richard Kraus (New York: Ronald Press, 1950). Arrange for a country hoedown. Ask parents to donate baked goods, bring in gingham tablecloths, and some straw if available. Students and their parents can come dressed in country clothes and participate together in a family square dance. For a recording with square dances and instructions, use *Learn Square Dancing with Ed Gilmore* (Universal City, Calif.: MCA Records, 1980).

18. Students may also enjoy making their own applesauce. Here is an easy recipe:

> 20 medium apples
> water
> cinnamon

Have students wash the apples in a tub of water. Cut the apples in quarters and remove the cores. Place apples in a large cooking pot with one cup of water. Bring to a boil, cover, and simmer over low heat until apples are mushy. Let each student have a turn grinding apples into sauce using a food mill. There is no need to add sugar, but students may enjoy adding some cinnamon and eating warm applesauce.

19. Read students the poem "Rudolph Is Tired of the City" by Gwendolyn Brooks and then read "City, Oh City" by Jack Prelutsky (both poems can be found in *The Random House Book of Poetry for Children*, edited by Jack Prelutsky [New York: Random House, 1983]). Ask students to compare the two poems. How does the person in the first poem feel about the city? The second poem? Have students write a poem expressing their views of the city.

Sam Johnson and the Blue Ribbon Quilt
Lisa Campbell Ernst
(New York: Lothrop, Lee and Shepard, 1983)

SUMMARY

By accident, Sam Johnson discovers that he enjoys sewing. Attempting to pursue his newfound hobby, he decides to join the women's quilting club. When met with resistance, he forms a men's quilting club. Fate steps in at the county fair as the two groups join forces to create a single blue ribbon quilt.

SOCIAL STUDIES TOPIC AREAS

Sociology, economics

CONTENT-RELATED WORDS

awning, masterpiece, handiwork, lingering, chorus, awkwardly, stalked, rousing, smug

CURRICULAR PERSPECTIVES

Life is full of sexual stereotypes. Men tend the fields; women cook the food. Men become doctors; women become nurses. Boys play with trucks; girls play with dolls. Men are strong and tough; women are quiet and docile. What is unfortunate is that many of these stereotypes are so ingrained in our culture that they are often difficult to eradicate and are passed down from one generation to the next. What is fortunate is that we are beginning to realize the effects of those stereotypes on the occupational and social choices we provide children and that we can do something about those effects.

This book presents a gentle lesson to the reader: namely, there is no such thing as "men-only" pursuits or "women-only" pursuits. No matter what our gender, we can all participate in activities simply because we enjoy them, not because of our gender. The book, however, is not dogmatic—children are not beaten over the head with a message. Rather, they are introduced to alternatives in an engaging and pleasant story that carefully erases lines of distinction and demonstrates true sexual equality.

Through the pages of this book, children begin to realize that if something interests them, they should pursue it. Quite naturally, children will wonder what their friends think of their choices, but more important is the fact that there are opportunities waiting to be taken that should not be eliminated simply because of artificially created barriers. The decisions Sam Johnson makes can be made by any individual willing to take a risk and pursue whatever interests him or her.

This is a wonderful book that can be made part of any social studies program. Delightful and purposeful illustrations highlight the text and provide a valuable backdrop to the story line. As you might expect, this book will engender a great deal of classroom discussion about the roles of men and women. That discussion can be a healthy introduction to a variety of nongender-specific activities, hobbies, vocations, avocations, and pastimes.

CRITICAL-THINKING QUESTIONS

1. How do you think Sam felt when he was not allowed to join the women's club?

2. How would you feel if you were not allowed to do something you really enjoyed?

3. Which quilt do you think would have won the blue ribbon if they had not both fallen into the mud puddle? Why?

4. Do you know any women who do jobs that are typically "man's work"? Do you know any men who do jobs that are typically "woman's work"?

5. In some occupations, women get paid less for doing the same job as a man. How do you feel about that?

6. If you are a boy, how do you think your parents would feel if you decided to become a nurse? If you are a girl, how do you think your parents would feel if you decided to become a construction worker?

7. What are some jobs in which men and women work together equally?

RELATED BOOKS AND REFERENCES

Burt, Stephanie. *A Visit to the Farm* (thirty-minute videotape). New York: New World Video, 1985.

Fair, Sylvia. *The Bedspread*. New York: Morrow, 1982.

Fleisher, Robbin. *Quilts in the Attic*. New York: Macmillan, 1978.

Flournoy, Valerie. *The Patchwork Quilt*. New York: Dial, 1985.

Johnson, Tony, and Tomie dePaola. *The Quilt Story*. New York: G. P. Putnam's Sons, 1985.

Techniques of Quilt Making (series of eight filmstrips). Huntsville, Tex.: Visual Aids Studio, 1975.

Wiseman, Ann. *Making Things: The Handbook of Creative Discovery*. Boston: Little, Brown, 1973.

ACTIVITIES

1. Have each student bring in a piece of fabric from an outgrown item of clothing. Create a classroom quilt by using tacky glue and attaching the fabric squares to cardboard. Students may also wish to work in small groups and stitch the squares into strips, which can then be combined to form a large quilt top. This top can be sewn to a plain blanket and hung on one wall of the classroom. Refer to *Quilting and Patchwork* (San Francisco, Calif.: Lane, 1973).

2. Bring in a handmade quilt and a machine-made quilt. Have the students examine the two quilts for similarities and differences. Ask students to take on the role of quality inspectors to decide which quilt has the better construction.

3. Invite a male nurse and a female construction worker into your class to discuss their choices of occupation. Have they experienced any job discrimination? What do their friends think about their occupations? Why did they choose those jobs?

4. Divide the class into two groups, boys and girls. Ask each group to prepare a "Declaration of Independence" outlining roles and responsibilities of boys and roles and responsibilities of girls. Afterwards, divide the class into four groups, each with both boys and girls. Direct each group to design alternate "Declarations of Independence" with an emphasis on equal roles and responsibilities. Have students discuss any differences between the declarations.

5. Schedule a "club time" each week. Form various clubs within the classroom such as a cooking club, model airplane club, sewing club, or baseball club (clubs which are often associated with either boys or girls). Encourage all students to participate in selected clubs throughout the year. Have club members keep journals and write down their individual thoughts about membership in the clubs. Use the journals as a basis for classroom discussions.

6. Have students construct a model of Sam Johnson's home. They can use different materials such as clay, construction paper, shoe boxes, or pipe cleaners. Different groups may enjoy constructing a house, barn, a field, farm animals, or Sam and his wife, Sarah.

7. Check with a local women's club or in the telephone book for a sewing or quilting organization. Invite several members of the group to demonstrate their craft to students. Provide an opportunity for students to interview club members on the intricacies of quilt-making.

8. Have the students rewrite the story from the perspective of Sam's dog. What kinds of things does he observe? How does he feel about Sam's new venture?

9. Encourage students to engage in a debate on equal rights. Should boys and girls have equal rights and responsibilities? Should men and women have equal rights and responsibilities? What does *equal rights* mean? How can it be promoted in the classroom? In the school? In the local community?

10. Students may enjoy making simple looms. Provide each student with a 6" x 8" piece of scrapwood. Along each 6-inch end hammer 6 nails, evenly spaced. Have students use string or twine and wrap tightly between the nails (these vertical threads are called the *warp*). Then have students use colorful yarn, ribbon, or fabric strips and weave over and under the warp threads (the horizontal threads are called the *woof*). Have them tighten each row with a comb or fork. The loose ends can be tied off or tucked into the fabric. The finished products can be displayed throughout the room.

11. Have students interview their grandparents or other older people about their recollections of country fairs or similar community celebrations. Students can compare and share the results of their interviews with each other.

12. Have students create a large collage on quilting or sewing. Direct them to cut out pictures and illustrations from old magazines and paste them to a large sheet of paper. Examples of clothing, sewing materials, dyes, sewing machines, etc., can all be included on the collage. Ask students to prepare an explanatory sheet of the finished product.

13. Country fairs mean lots of good food. Here is a recipe for some blue ribbon oatmeal muffins your students may enjoy preparing:

1 egg
1 cup buttermilk
½ cup brown sugar
⅓ cup shortening
1 cup quick-cooking oats
1 cup flour
1 teaspoon baking powder
1 teaspoon salt
½ teaspoon baking soda

Heat oven to 400 degrees. Grease bottoms of 12 medium muffin cups. Beat egg; stir in buttermilk, brown sugar, and shortening. Mix in remaining ingredients until flour is moistened. Batter should be lumpy. Fill cups and bake for 20 to 25 minutes. Remove from cups immediately.

14. Assign the role of Sam Johnson to a girl and the role of Sarah Johnson to a boy. Ask the two students to simulate a conversation between Sam and his wife. What difficulties do the students have in recreating those two roles? Would it be easier if the role of Sam were played by a boy and the role of Sarah by a girl? Why?

15. Ask children to list all the occupations of their parents. Post the list and ask students which of the jobs could be held by either a man or a woman. Are there jobs on the list that can only be done by a man or by a woman? Why? This activity can be repeated with a listing of all the avocations of parents.

Town and Country
Alice Provensen and Martin Provensen
(New York: Crown, 1985)

SUMMARY

This book weaves a rich tapestry of life in rural and urban America. The text describes a bustling town with restaurants, stores, museums, ports, and parks. It concludes with scenes of the farmhouses, general stores, big fields, and winding roads of the country.

SOCIAL STUDIES TOPIC AREAS

Sociology, geography, economics

CONTENT-RELATED WORDS

city, farms, homes, people, jobs, stores

CURRICULAR PERSPECTIVES

Often children take their places of residence for granted. They may give little thought to where they live, the dynamics of neighborhoods and local communities, the ebb and flow of people on their way to work or play, or even the sights and sounds that surround them during the day. While each of us may live in a different region of the country or different type of dwelling, it is important for us to understand the comparisons and contrasts between our individual spaces and what makes them unique.

This book provides a panorama of words and pictures to illustrate the variety of places and people that compose the city and the country. The text is as rich in description of the sights, sounds, smells, and tastes of city life as it is of country life. Readers get perceptive and varied insights into the dimensions of urban and country living. In so doing, the authors/illustrators give students an opportunity to appreciate their own styles of living as well as the styles of those in other venues.

The book describes, in wonderful detail, elements of life in the city and country, what children do in school, how they play, and the variety of activities they have to participate in during the day. The emphasis is not to illustrate the differences but rather to celebrate the similarity of lifestyles all children have, no matter where they live. This book is thus a wonderfully varied description of daily living, wherever it may occur.

Teachers will want to use this book to supplement any discussions about country or city living. Indeed, the book can serve as a focal point for explorations into the towns, hamlets, villages, cities, metropolises, and rural areas found throughout this country. Children will develop an appreciation for different living conditions and the similarities of daily existence.

CRITICAL-THINKING QUESTIONS

1. When you grow up, where would you like to live, in the city or in the country? Why?

2. What types of responsibilities do children living in the city have? What about children in the country? How are they similar? How are they different?

3. Why do you think there is such a wide variety of people living in the city?

4. If you lived in the city, what would be your chief reason for visiting the country? If you lived in the country, what would be your main reason for visiting the city?

5. How is the city or country portrayed in the book different from the area in which you live?

6. Are any of the people described in the book similar to people in your neighborhood? Who are they and why are they similar?

7. What are some noises that would be the same in the city as in the country?

8. What might be some dangers for children living in the city? What would be some dangers for children living in the country? How could those dangers be reduced?

RELATED BOOKS AND REFERENCES

Bates, Betty. *Ask Me Tomorrow*. New York: Holiday House, 1987.

Baylor, Byrd. *The Best Town in the World*. New York: Aladdin, 1986.

Bozzo, Maxine Zohn. *Toby in the Country, Toby in the City*. New York: Greenwillow, 1982.

Chwast, Seymour. *Tall City, Wide Country*. New York: Viking, 1983.

Davis, Penelope. *Town Life in the Middle Ages*. Hove, England: Wayland, 1980.

Higgins, Alfred. *Cities, What Are They* (seventeen-minute video). Los Angeles, Calif.: Alfred Higgins Productions, 1984.

Martin, Ann M. *Ten Kids, No Pets*. New York: Holiday House, 1988.

Saullnier, Karen L. *Oliver in the City*. Washington, D.C.: Gallaudet College Press, 1975.

ACTIVITIES

1. Direct students to generate a master list of some of the major cities of the United States. Invite each student to select one city from the list and create a travel guide to that city. Have the class discuss the types of information, such as tourist attractions, museums, parks, selected hotels, etc., to be included in each guide. An extended period of library research may be necessary to complete the guides.

2. Have students create several posters, each highlighting a major city from anywhere in the world.

3. Using an overhead projector, create an oversize outline of your state. Trace that outline on a sheet of newsprint. Direct students to identify major urban areas within your state as well as large rural areas. Students can color in the appropriate areas with colored pencils.

4. Have students imagine they are living in the country and are writing to a friend to convince him or her to visit for several days. What features or attractions should be pointed out in the letter? Afterwards, have students imagine they are in the city and writing to a friend inviting that person for a visit.

5. Obtain one or more topological maps of a portion of your state from the public library or geography department of a nearby college. Divide the class into several groups and direct each group to plot the location of one or more imaginary cities on its map. Ask students to consider geographical features, natural resources, and climate as determining factors in the location of urban areas. Have students defend their placement of the cities.

6. Have the class brainstorm for the advantages and disadvantages of living in the city as well as the advantages and disadvantages of living in the country. Which list has the most items? Does that influence students' choices of where they want to live when they grow up? Why?

7. Have students draw an illustration of their local area as though they were hawks flying overhead. What distinctive or unusual features should be highlighted in the illustration?

8. Have students prepare a description of their local area from the perspective of an inanimate object. For example, if they live in an urban area, how would that area look from the viewpoint of a factory? If they live in a suburban area, how would the area look from the viewpoint of a stop sign? If living in a rural area, how would the area look from the viewpoint of a barn?

9. Students may enjoy creating a collage of how food moves from farms into the city. Students can cut out pictures from several old magazines depicting growing crops, rainstorms, harvesting, loading trucks, trucks rolling down the road, trucks being unloaded, markets being stocked, and people buying groceries, for example.

10. Have students produce a videotaped walking or automobile tour of your town or area. Students can design a route that includes major highlights of the area and write appropriate narration for inclusion on the videotape. These productions can be shared with students in other classes.

11. Have students create a classroom museum of artifacts and information about your town. Local newspaper clippings, documents, photographs, and other memorabilia can be arranged in an attractive display set up in one corner of the room. Encourage students to contribute as many items as possible so that visitors can get the real flavor of your locality.

12. Using milk cartons, small boxes, shoe boxes, and other similar materials, have students create a miniature city. Boxes can be painted and set up in a variety of ways.

13. Try to locate someone in the local area who has a model railroad setup. Invite that individual to bring slides or photographs of his or her setup to your classroom and discuss reasons why certain buildings and models were put in specific locations. You may be able to make arrangements for students to visit a model railroad layout.

14. Show *Portrait of a Wheat Farmer* (No. 51179) (Washington, D.C.: National Geographic Society, 1980) to your class. This fifteen-minute color video shows some of the processes farmers must go through to ensure that their crops get to market. Ask students how the farmer's job is similar to or different from the jobs students' parents have.

15. Divide the class into two groups. Direct each group to create a special dictionary: one group will create a dictionary of country words, while the other group will create a dictionary of city words. You may wish to show them several examples of children's dictionaries for ideas on format and design. After the dictionaries are complete, have the groups compare their lists. Are there words that appear on both lists? If so, why?

16. Have students follow the weather reports for certain selected urban areas around the state as well as some rural areas. Groups of students may wish to follow these weather patterns for an extended period of time (several months, for example) to note any trends. Have students speculate on the effects of weather on the lifestyles of the people who live in that particular region.

17. Students may enjoy setting up their own garden or farm on a plot of land on the school grounds. (Be sure to get permission from your administrator first!) Two excellent sources of information include *The Victory Garden Kids' Book* by Marjorie Waters (Boston: Houghton Mifflin, 1988) and *Your First Garden Book* by Marc Brown (Boston: Little, Brown, 1981).

18. Share some gardening poetry with your students. These poems could include "Little Seeds" by Else Holmelund Minarek, "Maytime Magic" by Mabel Watts, and "A Spike of Green" by Barbara Baker.

9—States and Regions

Aurora Means Dawn
Scott Russell Sanders
(New York: Bradbury, 1989)

SUMMARY

A family of nine makes the long, arduous journey from Connecticut to the wilderness of Ohio in the year 1800. When they arrive, what they thought would be a bustling town is nothing more than a surveyor's stake. Thus, they become the first settlers of the new town of Aurora, Ohio.

SOCIAL STUDIES TOPIC AREAS

History, geography, sociology

CONTENT-RELATED WORDS

precisely, deluge, glinted

CURRICULAR PERSPECTIVES

In 1800, "wilderness" was considered to be anything beyond the Atlantic seaboard. Ohio seemed like a continent away. Unsettled, wild, and unknown, it meant untold dangers for anyone brave enough or foolish enough to travel there. However, it was also a land of opportunity, representing a chance to establish a new life or create a better life for one's family, although it meant hardships during the journey and certainly hardships at the ultimate destination.

It took a special breed of rugged individualists to strike out from the comfort of the East into the unknowns of the West, though it held promise and unrealized potential for the future. For many families, it meant leaving behind the comfort of an established lifestyle and risking everything for a lot of uncertainties, but many families were willing to take that risk. Their determination became the backbone of the westward movement—a movement unlike any in history.

This book provides young readers with an accurate look into the toils and troubles of those westward pioneers. This is nothing like the pictures children see on Saturday morning cartoons or grade B Hollywood movies. This is life as it was really lived. All work and very little play; long, dusty days and lonely, dark nights; many promises and few rewards—but it was a life that many sought and many cherished. Through the pages of this book, readers will get a keen sense of the promises and disappointments of that westward movement.

An important message here is that the American West was much more than cattle drives through Texas or cowboys and Indians in Arizona. It was the story of little-known families who looked beyond the next mountain or were willing to ford the next stream, not for glory or gold but to create a better life for themselves and their families. In many ways, that may be the true and original story of the American West.

CRITICAL-THINKING QUESTIONS

1. Why do you think the family wanted to move from Connecticut?

2. What did the family expect to find in their new home?

3. Aside from the storm, what were some other hardships the family might have faced during their journey?

4. Would you want to make a trip of this length by wagon train? What would appeal to you most about the journey?

5. If you had an opportunity to settle anywhere in the country, where would it be? Why?

6. Why do you think the townspeople helped the family?

7. Why did it take so long for another family to settle in Aurora?

8. What were some of the jobs the family had to do to begin their new life?

RELATED BOOKS AND REFERENCES

Freedman, Russell. *Children of the Wild West*. Boston: Houghton Mifflin, 1983.

Gorsline, Marie, and D. W. Gorsline. *The Pioneers*. New York: Random House, 1982.

Tunis, Edwin. *Frontier Living*. New York: Harper, 1976.

Walker, Barbara M. *The Little House Cookbook: Frontier Foods from Laura Ingalls Wilder's Classic Stories*. New York: Harper, 1979.

ACTIVITIES

1. Invite students to write letters to students in another class as though your students were members of the Sheldon family. Have students describe the adventures encountered on the journey from Connecticut to Ohio, the activities and chores that had to be done, and how they felt when they arrived at their new homesite. Encourage students from the other class to respond to those letters as though they were friends of the family still living in 1800s Connecticut.

2. Students may wish to consult books such as *The Old Farmer's Almanac Book of Weather Lore* by Edward F. Dolan (Dublin, N.H.: Yankee, 1988), *Questions and Answers about Weather* by M. Jean Craig (New York: Four Winds, 1969), or *Weather* by Paul E. Lehr (New York: Golden, 1965). Encourage students to create a series of weather maps for the state of Ohio during different seasons of the year. Based on the information available, ask them to determine the best part of the year for traveling to Ohio by wagon in the 1800s.

3. Direct students to create a travel guide for the Sheldon family. Obtain a collection of maps and travel guides for the states between Connecticut and Ohio by writing to the various state departments of tourism. Addresses can be found in any U.S. road atlas or obtained through your local automobile club. Have students put together an itinerary the Sheldon family could have used for the trip.

4. Share some books on nature and weather folklore with your students. Books such as *The Earth Is on a Fish's Back: Tales of Beginnings* by Natalia Belting (New York: Holt, Rinehart and Winston, 1965); *Star Tales: North American Indian Stories about the Stars* by Gretchen Will Mayo (New York: Walker, 1987); and *A January Fog Will Freeze a Hog and Other Weather Folklore* by Hubert Davis (New York: Crown, 1977) are all appropriate. Students may wish to create their folklore book about events or conditions in their own community or neighborhood. Encourage students to use a large dose of imagination in their explanations of traditions or beliefs in their area of the country.

5. Divide the class into several groups and direct each to plan a trip from Connecticut to Ohio in the 1800s. Have each group put together a list of supplies and equipment they would need on their journey. What would be some essential items? What would be some desirable but nonessential items? Have students compare their lists and post them on the bulletin board for whole-class discussion.

6. Building houses on the frontier was not easy. The time and labor involved were enormous. To demonstrate to students some of the difficulties frontier families had in constructing their homes, provide small groups of students each with a large quantity of popsicle sticks (available at any hobby or variety store) and some white glue. Direct each group to construct a complete house (walls, roof, windows, door, etc.) without using any drawings or plans. When completed, encourage students to discuss the difficulties they had and to compare their difficulties with those the pioneers may have had in constructing their homes on the frontier.

7. Have students each write a series of observations as though they were visitors to the Hudson post office. What types of people visit the post office? What do they discuss? Where do they come from? Where do they go when they leave the post office? What are their families like? You may want to show the video *The Post Office* (No. 51472) (Washington, D.C.: National Geographic Society, 1991) and ask students to compare the post office of today with the post office of the 1800s.

8. Students will enjoy seeing the filmstrip series entitled The Westward Movement (No. 04102) (Washington, D.C.: National Geographic Society, 1979). This two-part series describes the forces that influenced westward expansion and the men and women who made it happen. Although this series is geared for an older audience (grades 5-12), younger students will also find it to be an appropriate introduction to pioneer life, particularly if followed by lots of classroom discussion.

9. Have students create a skit based on a friendly meeting between the Sheldon family and a group of Native Americans. What kinds of things would be discussed? What kinds of communication difficulties would have to be overcome? Would any trading occur?

10. To make a covered wagon, obtain a refrigerator box or other large box. Cut off one side of the box. Place the box on the floor with the open section on top. Open up several wire coat hangers and bend them into semicircles. Fix the ends of each hanger into opposite sides of the box. Cut an old bedsheet to an appropriate size and lay it over the hangers. Have students cut out wheels from the discarded section of the box, color them, and affix them to the sides of the box. Turn your covered wagon into a reading area for students to peruse books on pioneers or frontier life.

11. Invite a parent or local person to your class to demonstrate (outside) the chopping of wood. Be sure the visitor emphasizes all the safety procedures necessary for safe use of an ax. Videotape the presentation and have students write an accompanying guidebook.

12. Divide the class into several groups, with each group being responsible for writing and creating a story or tale for sharing around a campfire. To set up an imaginary campfire, place some logs in the middle of the classroom, create some flames out of orange and red construction paper, and arrange some flashlights in between the logs to give the illusion of light. Have students gather around the campfire to share their tales and stories with each other. Afterwards, discuss with students the fact that this type of activity was one of the few recreational opportunities families had on the frontier. Ask students to compare that activity with some of the things they do in the evenings.

13. Songs and singing were an important part of frontier life. There are many collections you can obtain to introduce your students to the ballads and folk songs that were and still are a part of our heritage. Here are some song books to get you started: *The Woody Guthrie Songbook*, edited by Harold Levanthal (New York: Grosset & Dunlap, 1976); *Sail Away: 155 American Folk Songs*, edited by Eleanor Locke (New York: Boosey & Hawkes, 1988); and *American Folk Music: Songs of the Frontier and Prairie* (North Hollywood, Calif.: Center for Cassette Studies, 1972).

14. Of necessity, food recipes on the frontier were quite simple, requiring a minimum of ingredients. Here is one for apple fritters you may enjoy making with the help of your students:

> 1½ cups flour
> 2 level teaspoons baking powder
> ⅔ cup milk
> 1 egg, well beaten
> 2 apples, cut in thin slices
> powdered sugar (optional)
> pinch of salt

Sift together the flour, baking powder, and salt. Add the egg and milk, then the sliced apples. Drop by teaspoonfuls into a deep pan of ½" hot cooking oil (the oil should be hot enough to brown a piece of white bread). Drain the fritters on paper towels and sprinkle with powdered sugar.

Note: The use of hot oil requires extreme caution.

15. Have students draft a "constitution" for a new settlement on the American frontier. What laws should be established early on to ensure the survival of the new settlement? How should the settlement be governed? Who should run it and how should they be chosen? Have students debate these concerns as they draft their constitution.

Just Us Women

Jeannette Caines

(New York: Harper & Row, 1982)

SUMMARY

A young girl and her favorite aunt, Martha, share the excitement of planning a very special car trip to North Carolina for just the two of them.

SOCIAL STUDIES TOPIC AREAS

Geography, sociology, history

CONTENT-RELATED WORDS

double-checked, poisonous, omelette

CURRICULAR PERSPECTIVES

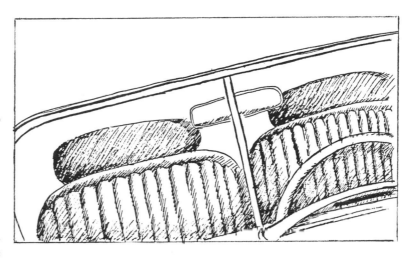

Familial friendships and distant destinations are the theme of this book. Two travelers, one aunt and one niece, plan a car trip through several states. Although they see many sites and experience a variety of scenery along the way, the story is more about the time and talk they share, getting to know each other and themselves a little better.

Although we do not know the length of time involved in this story, we know that the travelers' trip through New Jersey, Pennsylvania, Maryland, West Virginia, Virginia, and North Carolina exposes them to a host of people and places, country and city life, and interests and exhibits which help them appreciate the diversity of people in this country. The sites, however, are not the focal point of this story about their travels; it is the fact that two people can take time from busy schedules and responsibilities to learn more about each other. This book is much more than a brief travelogue through some eastern states. It chronicles a journey of discovery that cements a friendship and provides a vehicle for discussion and conversation.

Children will enjoy this book not just because of the simplicity of language but because it painlessly weaves geography into a tale of a developing friendship between two relatives. When reading this, students get a sense that geography is much more than places on a map (physical geography), because the book also focuses on people (cultural geography). Children learn that although many geography lessons focus on places and positions, relations and cultures are also an integral element of geographical literacy.

CRITICAL-THINKING QUESTIONS

1. Would you want to have Aunt Martha as a relative?
2. How would the story be similar or different if Aunt Martha and her niece had taken a bus? A train? A plane?

3. What kinds of places would you like to travel to? Why?

4. Why do you think Aunt Martha and her niece did not want men or boys to go along on the trip?

5. Would your friends enjoy this story? Why or why not?

6. Did you ever take a trip like this one? How was it the same or different from this trip?

7. What types of adventures would you like to take without your parents?

8. Why do you think the narrator wanted to turn breakfast and supper times around?

RELATED BOOKS AND REFERENCES

Atlas of the World. 6th ed. Washington, D.C.: National Geographic Society, 1990.

Geography of the United States Series, *Part V—New England & The Mid-Atlantic States* (two sixteen-minute sound filmstrips). Washington, D.C.: National Geographic Society, 1979 (No. 04095).

Hoff, Syd. *My Aunt Rosie*. New York: Harper & Row, 1972.

Khalsa, Dayal Kaur. *My Family Vacation*. New York: Crown, 1988.

Lazard, Naomi. *What Amanda Saw*. New York: Lothrop, 1971.

The Mid-Atlantic States (twenty-seven-minute color video). Washington, D.C.: National Geographic Society, 1983 (No. 51144).

Young, Miriam Burt. *If I Drove a Car*. New York: Lothrop, 1971.

ACTIVITIES

1. Have students keep a journal or diary about Aunt Martha and her niece's journey to North Carolina.

2. Students may wish to make a tape recording of an oral reading of the book. Students may select and include appropriate musical selections for background music. Sound effects (alarm clock ringing, teapot whistling, car engine starting, eggs frying, rain falling) could be added to the recording.

3. Using a map of the United States, have students put push pins into all the places Aunt Martha and her niece visited or drove through during their trip.

4. Have students write a prequel or sequel to the story. What other events could have taken place after the story or before the story began? What might have prompted Aunt Martha and her niece to take the trip? What will happen after they arrive in North Carolina?

5. Write for and bring in some brochures about the states mentioned in the book. Have students prepare a travel itinerary for visiting those states. Students may wish to create similar brochures for their own state or a state where a favorite relative lives. (Note: Tourist information on North Carolina can be obtained from Travel and Tourism Division, 430 N. Salisbury Street, Raleigh, NC 27611; (800) 847-4862 or (919) 733-4171.)

6. Have students pretend they are visiting North Carolina or another state mentioned in the book. Have them create some make-believe postcards to send back to their families at home. These postcards can be posted on a bulletin board.

7. Ask students to collect several copies of travel magazines and brochures and prepare a collage of pictures clipped from those periodicals. Students may want to create collages comparing their state and North Carolina (North Carolina students can compare their state with any other of their choosing).

8. Have students create a poster or advertisement for visiting a particular state mentioned in the book. What kind of data or illustrations need to be included to interest people in visiting that state?

9. What kinds of services will Aunt Martha and her niece need prior to their trip? Have students look in the telephone book Yellow Pages and create a list of those services. For example, a service station, a grocery store or delicatessen, a clothing store, a travel agent, and a bank are all possibilities. Have students create their own special Yellow Pages specifically for this trip.

10. Ask students to create a budget for travel to North Carolina. How much money should be allocated for food, gas, hotels, entertainment, etc.?

11. Have students bring in different examples of omelette recipes. Prepare several of these omelettes and share them with all class members. Students may wish to create an omelette recipe book of their favorites. Here is a simple recipe to get you started (serves four):

    > 6 eggs
    > ⅓ cup milk
    > ¾ teaspoon salt
    > 1/8 teaspoon pepper
    > 2 tablespoons butter

    Beat the eggs until the whites and yolks are thoroughly mixed. Add the milk, salt, and pepper. Melt the butter in a skillet. Pour in the egg mixture and place over moderate heat. While the eggs are cooking, lift the edges and tip the skillet so the uncooked mixture flows underneath the cooked portion. When the bottom is browned, fold over, remove from skillet, and serve.

12. Have students write a logbook or chart on the weather patterns and climate of North Carolina. Have them decide the best time of year to take a trip to North Carolina. They should also decide on the type of clothing to be taken.

13. Have students pantomime selected events from the story. Turn the activity into a game of charades and make up event situation cards for the students to select and act out.

14. Students may wish to make a cool, nutritious drink that is great for traveling. Portions for four can be made using the following recipe:

    > 2½ cups pineapple juice
    > 1½ cups grape juice
    > 2½ cups yogurt
    > one ripe banana

    Have students measure the ingredients. Mix them in a blender, pour into cups, add ice, and serve as a snack. While they sip their drinks, students may want to describe their ideal vacations.

15. Each week students can pretend to be living in a different city in the states where the story took place. One student can check the daily weather reports (using the local newspaper or television news broadcast) for his or her adopted city. Another can give capsule summaries of important events in that particular city. Another can report the sports scores of the major-league teams from that city. Mini-bulletin boards can be set up for each city to allow students to record their data collection throughout the week.

16. A fun-to-make and fun-to-eat treat that travelers have been using for many years is granola. Provide your students with an opportunity to create this wholesome snack.

> 4 cups oatmeal
> ½ cup wheat germ
> ½ cup coconut
> 1 teaspoon salt
> ½ cup honey
> 4 teaspoons butter
> ½ cup raisins
> 2 tablespoons sunflower seeds
> ½ cup nuts
> ½ teaspoon vanilla

Mix all the dry ingredients (except the oatmeal) in a bowl. Melt the butter in a pan and brown the oatmeal. Add oatmeal, vanilla, and honey to the dry food mix and mix thoroughly. Place the granola on a cookie sheet in the oven at 250 degrees until toasted.

Your Best Friend Kate

Pat Brisson

(New York: Bradbury, 1989)

SUMMARY

Kate and her family take a trip and visit several sites along the East Coast. While she is gone, Kate sends several postcards to her friend Lucy, who is caring for Kate's pet fish.

SOCIAL STUDIES TOPIC AREAS

Geography, history, anthropology, sociology

CONTENT-RELATED WORDS

Eastern Standard Time, stalactites, stalagmites, souvenir, Beluga whales, Anhinga bird

CURRICULAR PERSPECTIVES

Children love to travel! Seeing new sites, new people, and new areas for exploration and discovery are all part of the fascination of travel. Travel not only gives children an opportunity to see what is beyond their immediate world but also provides them new perspectives on how people live and work. When children move out into other areas of their environment, their background knowledge increases and provides a wonderful foundation for all sorts of learning.

This story concerns the travels of a young girl and her family as they set out by car to observe some distant locations and interesting people. This is more than just a geography lesson, though; it is a vehicle by which readers are transported to all manner of vistas, environments, and venues, each different and each distinctive. Children soon learn that this country is made up of many colors and many hues, each adding a richness to the American landscape—a landscape that grows larger with each journey.

The story, told as one youngster writes postcards to another youngster, is an insight into how children view the world around them and what they consider to be important in their lives. This story also paints a picture of sights and sounds that are different and uniquely American. The reader is led to believe that there is always a new discovery around the corner or a new adventure just down the road.

Although this is geography in a fictionalized rendering, it is also an accounting of the diversity of America and of the many sites that await the traveler willing to step off his or her front porch into a world full of people and scenery. A car, a map, and a destination are all that are needed for geography to come alive.

CRITICAL-THINKING QUESTIONS

1. Do you enjoy traveling with your family? Why?

2. After reading the book, are you tempted to travel to any of the spots mentioned?

3. Do you think the story would change if Kate had a sister instead of a brother?

4. On Kate's trip, she passed through time zones. Why do you think the country is divided into time zones?

5. Do you think Kate's parents had a good time on the trip? In what ways can you show that from the book?

6. Why do you think Kate's family decided to travel by car? Do you agree with their decision?

7. In what ways is Kate like you?

8. Do you suppose Kate got homesick while she was on vacation?

RELATED BOOKS AND REFERENCES

Aylesworth, Thomas G., and Virginia L. Aylesworth. *Mid-Atlantic States*. New York: Chelsea, 1988.

Bate, Lucy. *How Georgina Drove the Car Very Carefully from Boston to New York*. New York: Crown, 1989.

Blume, Judy. *The Pain and the Great One*. New York: Bradbury, 1974.

Bridgeman, Elizabeth. *How to Travel with Grown Ups*. New York: Ticknor, 1989.

Family Adventure Road Atlas. Chicago: Rand McNally, 1967.

Galster, Robert. *North, South, East, West*. New York: Crowell, 1990.

Grahame, Kenneth. *The Open Road*. New York: Scribner's, 1980.

Khalsa, Dayal. *My Family Vacation*. New York: Crown, 1988.

ACTIVITIES

1. Have each student bring in a picture of a place he or she has visited or been to on a vacation. Have students write a description of those locations, or a reason why other children should visit that spot, on a 3" x 5" index card. Post a map of the United States on a bulletin board and have students tack their index cards to the corresponding locations on the map.

2. Encourage children to visit a local travel agency and select one travel brochure on a U.S. vacation spot. When several have been collected, have students create an attractive collage using all the brochures.

3. As an adjunct to activity 2, have students create a travel brochure for their home town. Have them follow the design of other travel brochures in designing one for their locale. These can be displayed, too.

4. Have students write to several state departments of tourism. Most public libraries will have addresses, as will current issues of the *Mobil Travel Guide* or the *Mobil Road Atlas and Trip Planning Guide*. Also, the local American Automobile Association office will have addresses. Students can ask for tourist information, maps, and other free information, all of which can be collected and displayed around the classroom.

5. Students may wish to write to one or more map publishers to obtain a list of the different kinds of city, county, and state maps they produce. Here are four sources: Arrow Publishing Company, Tauton, MA 02780; Unique Media Incorporated, Box 4400, Don Mills, Ontario, Canada, M3C 2T9; Marshall Penn-York Co., 538 Erie Boulevard West, Syracuse, NY 13204; and Gousha Travel Publications, P.O. Box 49006, San Jose, CA 95161. Other sources can be obtained by looking on the back of any road map for the name and address of the publisher. After obtaining lists and catalogs, have students plan a trip to a vacation spot 500 to 750 miles from your town.

6. Have students create mobiles. On the first level of the mobile, write a specific vacation location in the United States. On the second level, hang names of tourist spots students would like to visit. On the third level, hang the names of historical sites they would like to see.

7. Have each student identify a popular tourist spot somewhere in the United States. Direct each student to develop a geographical guide to that particular place. For example, students can list any nearby rivers, mountains, lakes, and streams. What airports, large cities, or other attractions are located in the vicinity? Can students describe the topography of the land? They may wish to combine this information into a scrapbook display.

8. Have students create several collages of all the different forms of transportation that could be used to get to, or while staying at, a vacation spot. Besides the usual (car, airplane, boat, motorcycle), have students brainstorm for some unusual modes of vacation transportation (dogsled, parachute, skates). Pictures illustrating these modes of transportation can be cut from old magazines and glued to a large sheet of construction paper. Students may wish to organize the finished collages into several categories (water transportation, air transportation, mechanical-powered, human-powered, etc.).

9. Have each student write a detailed itinerary from his or her house to the school. Have students outline the travel route, the landscape, interesting sites, and perhaps some historical comments. Post these on the bulletin board.

10. Have students write postcards to all their friends and relatives who live out of state. Students can request a sampling of postcards from each person they write to. Assemble all the postcards sent in and direct students to construct travel routes and itineraries that would allow them to visit all the designated locations.

11. Check with the reference librarian at your public library and obtain an address list of several out-of-state, medium-sized newspapers. Have your students compose a letter (a form letter will do) to be sent to the "Letters to the Editor" section of each newspaper requesting data, information, maps, and postcards from some of the people living in that area. When material arrives, be sure students send appropriate thank-you letters in return. Have the class put together a scrapbook of all the items sent.

12. Have students write a story from the perspective of the parents in the book. Have students focus on how the parents feel about how the children behaved during the trip.

13. Ask students to brainstorm for a list of travel games that could be taken along on a car vacation. What would be some good games? What criteria should be used in selecting appropriate games? What games should definitely not be taken along?

14. Have students make clock faces from paper plates, construction paper hands, and a paper fastener. Divide the class into four time zone groups. Those students in the Eastern time zone group should arrange their clock hands at 1:00; those in the Central time zone at 12:00; those in the Mountain time zone at 11:00; and those in the Pacific time zone at 10:00. Ask students in one time zone to change the position of the hands on their clock. Direct the students in the other time zones to change their clock hands to the appropriate time. For example, tell students in the Mountain time zone to put their clock hands at 5:30. At what times should the students in the other three time zones set their clocks?

15. Have students collect pictures of the state birds for all the states Kate and her family visited. Students may wish to construct a mobile or diorama of the birds. The same can be done for state flowers.

16. Have students collect postmarks from the letters their parents receive at home. Have students organize the postmarks into several categories (by time zone, by region of the country, or by state). A scrapbook of postmarks for each of the designated categories can be organized and maintained by separate groups of students.

17. Bring in a suitcase and ask students to decide what they should pack in the suitcase if they are taking a vacation the same length as the one Kate and her family took. Have students make up individual lists of items to be packed. Encourage group discussion on the items needed for a short trip (a few days) and those needed for a long trip (several weeks).

18. Have students write an ending for the story. What do they think Kate did after she returned home?

10—Nation and Country

Anno's U.S.A.
Mitsumasa Anno
(New York: Philomel, 1983)

SUMMARY

A traveler arrives on the West Coast of the United States and journeys toward the east, stopping along the way in different cities. As he travels, the pages of time are turned back as he visits key historic sites.

SOCIAL STUDIES TOPIC AREAS

Geography, history, sociology, economics

CONTENT-RELATED WORDS

(none)

CURRICULAR PERSPECTIVES

Rich in history and tradition, the United States is filled with intriguing stories and exciting tales. Understanding the historical antecedents of modern society is an important part of the elementary curriculum and a basis on which children can learn to appreciate the country in which they live.

It is unfortunate that the subject of history is anathema to many students. Often bombarded with a host of facts, dates, figures, and names, students frequently get the idea that history is composed primarily of rote memorization and verbal regurgitation. As a result, too many youngsters have a negative view of what history is or its relationship to their own lives.

What makes history exciting for young people is when the emphasis is placed on the last two syllables: "*story*." When children understand that history is a sequence of stories, tales, and adventures, they begin to comprehend the inherent excitement of the past. Thus, we can use this book, which takes an intriguing look at the past and weaves it into a story line but does so without words!

A cursory reading of this book will not do justice to all the adventures of the mysterious traveler. By spending time on each page, students and teachers will discover a wealth of interesting and fascinating details that add immensely to the telling of the tale. It is important to note that students enjoy this book not only because it is a story but also because they can embellish it with narration and their own personal sense of the natural order of familiar (and unfamiliar) events. This book will be used time and time again.

CRITICAL-THINKING QUESTIONS

1. Which place from the book would you most like to visit? Why?

2. Name all the different forms of transportation you see in the book. Give examples of each. Which would you like to travel in most?

3. Which area was the most exciting to visit? What makes you choose that area?

4. Would you like to travel the United States alone, like the traveler in the book? With a friend? Explain your answer.

5. Would you recommend this book to a friend? Why or why not?

6. Do you think the traveler got lonely? Explain.

7. Why do you think there are so many pictures of animals in the book?

8. What might have changed if the traveler had been a woman?

9. What other U.S. locations do you think should be added to the book?

10. Would you like to go back in time? Where and when would you like to visit?

11. If you could live on any page in the book, which page would it be? Why?

12. If you could meet the author, what would you like to tell him about his book?

RELATED BOOKS AND REFERENCES

Barchers, Suzanne, and Patricia Marden. *Cooking Up U.S. History*. Englewood, Colo.: Libraries Unlimited, 1991.

Dalgliesh, Alice. *The Columbus Story*. New York: Scribner's, 1955.

_____. *The Courage of Sarah Noble*. New York: Charles Scribner's Sons, 1954.

d'Aulaire, Ingrid, and Edgar Parin d'Aulaire. *Ben Franklin*. New York: Doubleday, 1950.

Fisher, Leonard Everett. *The Statue of Liberty*. New York: Holiday House, 1985.

George Washington (filmstrip with record). Society for Visual Education, 1970.

Martin, Patricia Miles. *Pocahontas*. New York: Putnam, 1964.

McGinley, Phyllis. *All around the Town* (poetry). New York: Lippincott, 1948.

Stolz, Mary. *Noonday Friends* (record). New York: Newbery Award Records, 1975.

Twain, Mark. *The Adventures of Tom Sawyer*. New York: Harper & Row, 1938.

ACTIVITIES

1. Invite a travel agent to the class to discuss the arrangements and procedures used in planning a trip. Ask the agent to arrange an imaginary trip for the class to travel across the United States.

2. Have students research pineapple production in Hawaii. Students may wish to make a collage of pictures, clipped from old magazines, that display the pineapple industry. Bring in several fresh pineapples to class, cut them up, and let students enjoy this natural treat.

3. Have students make an Anno-type mural of their town or city. What elements or features would they like to include in their mural? Which ones should be left out?

4. Have a class "Rodeo Day." Wear western clothes and hold several rodeo-type events, such as "Lasso the Post" (string lariats and pencils set in clay), pogo stick ride (timed), barrel foot races on the playground, etc. Encourage your students to create other events similar to those in the book.

5. Ask the school's music teacher to suggest some western or cowboy songs for students to sing. Songs such as "Streets of Laredo," or "She'll Be Comin' round the Mountain" would be appropriate to share in class.

6. Have students trace the Mississippi River on a map of the United States. Ask them to create a scale model of the river on the playground with chalk. Have them label the mouth, delta, plain, bed, and other features of the river.

7. Encourage students to make several different types of kites. Create one similar to Ben Franklin's. Schedule a day on which students can fly their kites. You may wish to make it competitive by awarding prizes for the largest kite, the smallest kite, the kite that flies the highest, etc.

8. Direct students to write an imaginary letter to Ben Franklin. What questions would they like to ask him? How would he feel if he were to walk into the classroom?

9. Students may wish to create some word poems about selected cities in the book. Write the name of a city vertically down the left side of the chalkboard or a piece of posterboard. Have students select words or phrases that are indicative of the city for each of the letters in the city's name. Following is an example for Washington, D.C.:

   Where the Potomac flows by
   Among the cherry trees
   South of New York
   Historical
   Interesting
   Near Baltimore, Maryland
   Great National Zoo
   Thomas Jefferson Memorial
   Our president lives there
   National capital

   Dulles Airport
   Congress

10. Have students calculate the approximate number of miles from one stop to another. These figures can be obtained from an almanac or road map. Students can develop and work on problems such as the following: New York is 200 miles from Washington, D.C. Philadelphia is 75 miles from Washington, D.C. How far is it from Philadelphia to New York?

11. Discuss the directional relationship between any two places that the traveler visited. Students may wish to create problems for each other (using the "Twenty Questions" game format), such as "I'm thinking of a city that is northwest of Arizona" (San Francisco).

12. Bring in several paper cups, some soil, and some pumpkin seeds. Have students plant their pumpkin seeds and chart the growth pattern over the course of several weeks. Students may wish to calculate the average germination time and growth rates for all the plants started.

13. A traditional American treat is homemade apple butter. Your students may enjoy making their own apple butter. Here is a recipe:

> 12 to 14 apples (Jonathan or Winesap)
> 2 cups apple juice
> sugar
> cinnamon
> allspice
> cloves

Wash, core, and quarter apples (do not peel). Combine apples and juice in lightly oiled crock pot. Cover and cook on high for 2 to 4 hours. Put cooked fruit through a food mill to remove peel. For each pint of cooked fruit, add 1 cup of sugar, 1 teaspoon cinnamon, ½ teaspoon allspice, and ½ teaspoon cloves. Stir well. Cover and cook on high for 6 to 8 hours, stirring about every 2 hours. Remove cover after 3 hours to allow fruit and juice to cook down. Allow to cool and spread on bread or toast.

14. Students may wish to compare and contrast the various types of housing found in this book. They may want to set up a "Housing through the Years" bulletin board using pictures cut from old magazines.

15. Obtain the sixteen-minute filmstrip *North America: Land of Many Peoples* (No. 04659) (Washington, D.C.: National Geographic Society, 1983) and show it to your students. Discuss the relationship between the places and sights shown in the filmstrip and those depicted in the book. What similarities and/or differences do students note?

16. The most important contribution of the Native American tribes to our modern diet is corn. Here's a recipe for "Blue Corn Bread"* students will enjoy preparing:

> 1 cup flour
> 1 cup blue or yellow cornmeal
> ¼ cup sugar
> 4 teaspoons baking powder
> ¾ teaspoon salt
> 2 beaten eggs
> 1 cup milk
> ¼ cup cooking oil

Grease a baking pan. In a mixing bowl, stir together flour, cornmeal, sugar, baking powder, and salt. Add the beaten eggs, milk, and cooking oil to the dry ingredients and beat until smooth. Pour into pan and bake at 425 degrees for 20 to 25 minutes or until brown.

*Historical note: The Navajo Indians of the southwestern United States used blue cornmeal and baked their bread in juniper ashes.

John Henry
Ezra Jack Keats
(New York: Pantheon, 1965)

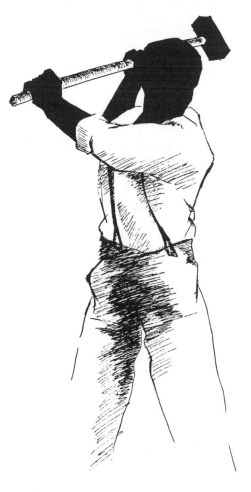

SUMMARY

John Henry is a mighty hero of American folklore. The "man who was born with a hammer in his hand" challenges a new steamdrill to a contest of strength, stamina, and power. The contest, more than a story of man against machine, is a tale of will and determination.

SOCIAL STUDIES TOPIC AREAS

History, geography, anthropology, economics

CONTENT-RELATED WORDS

steamdrill, riverboat, locomotive, legend, tall tale

CURRICULAR PERSPECTIVES

The railroad. Powerful. Sweeping. All-encompassing. It was the railroad that swept across the vast and often unknown frontier of the American West, opening it up for discovery and settlement. It was the railroad that charted new territories, scaled majestic mountains, and crossed vast expanses of prairie. It was the railroad that invaded the lands of Native Americans, creating disturbances, squabbles, and wars, some of which are still being fought today. It was the railroad that united this country and gave it a vision for the future.

The railroad. As we read our history books we are often struck by the impact this single form of transportation had on the creation of this country. In many ways, the railroad achieved heroic proportions, becoming bigger than all its parts—always moving forward, always seeking new conquests. It is not surprising, then, that the railroad created legends and folktales that transcend time and place. The laying of the golden spike, the wholesale massacre of buffaloes, and, of course, John Henry.

No one is quite sure how the legend of John Henry came to be. Perhaps it is not important. What is important, however, is that this story, with all its embellishments, is an integral part of American folklore. It describes the vision and power of territorial conquests, it provides an insight into the people who made the railroad run, and it offers a glimpse into the pride of the men and women who made the railroad possible. Although it is a story of man against machine, it is also a tale of virtue, strength, and fortitude, three qualities that were instrumental in the settlement of this country.

Whether students believe that John Henry was an actual person or not, teachers will find this wonderfully illustrated book to be a perfect addition to the literature about the 1800s and their collections of traditional American folktales, as well as an insight into what made this country grow. Students will delight in the contest and begin to get a sense of personal motivation and energy.

CRITICAL-THINKING QUESTIONS

1. If you were to challenge the steamdrill to a contest, what tools would you have chosen? Why?

2. If you were the author of this story, would you want to change the ending? If so, how would you change it? If not, why?

3. Why was John Henry such a proud man?

4. Why did the author say that John Henry was born with a hammer in his hands?

5. Why does John Henry say "My hands are just itchin' to hold a hammer again"?

6. What other tools do you think John Henry would be able to use with the same skill as the hammer?

7. What makes John Henry an American folk hero?

8. Why do you think the story of John Henry has lasted for so many years?

RELATED BOOKS AND REFERENCES

Broekel, Ray. *Trains*. Chicago: Children's Press, 1981.

Bucknall, Roxon. *Trains*. New York: Grosset & Dunlap, 1971.

Fisher, Leonard Everett. *The Railroads*. New York: Holiday House, 1979.

Harding, Mary. *All Aboard Trains*. New York: Platt and Munk, 1989.

Kanetzke, Howard W. *Trains and Railroad Stations*. Milwaukee, Wis.: Raintree, 1978.

Rines, Glen. *End O' Steel: Men and Rails across the Wilderness*. New York: Macmillan, 1963.

Rosenfield, Bernard. *Let's Go Build the First Transcontinental Railroad*. New York: Putnam, 1963.

Sheffer, H. R. *Trains*. Mankato, Minn.: Crestwood House, 1982.

Waden, Corinne. *John Henry*. Mahwah, N.J.: Troll Associates, 1980.

ACTIVITIES

1. Weston Woods (Weston, Connecticut) produces a number of sound filmstrips about legends and American folktales. Included in their series are filmstrips on "Casey Jones" and "She'll Be Comin' round the Mountain," among others. Check with the school's music teacher and obtain one or more of these filmstrips to share with your students. Encourage students to compare and contrast the various stories about the early days of the railroad in this country. Have them discuss reasons why so many legends sprang up around the railroad.

2. Divide the class into several small groups. Direct each group to create a daily schedule for John Henry. When did he wake up? What chores did he tend to in the morning, in the afternoon, at night? When did he rest? When did he eat? Some groups may wish to plot these daily activities in the form of diary entries. Others may want to chart the activities as a daily time line. Still others may wish to construct a series of illustrations about a typical day in the life of John Henry.

3. Invite a parent or person from the local community to demonstrate his or her model train layout or collection. Many people in this country are model railroad enthusiasts, so there should be little problem in locating a local collector. Have students prepare a series of questions before the visit. You may wish to have students query the visitor on the history of the railroad or the specific time period in which John Henry's story took place.

4. Provide each of several groups with copies of topographical maps of the United States (these can be obtained through your local public library or nearby college). Challenge each group to plot a course for a railroad across the country, taking into account all the geographical features that would be encountered. Ask student groups to defend their various routes. Have students compare their routes with the route taken by the first transcontinental railroad. What differences do they note?

5. Obtain a copy of the video *Love Those Trains* (No. 51382) (Washington, D.C.: National Geographic Society) to show your students. Ask students to compare the different types of trains portrayed. Students may wish to create lists of the advantages of trains over other forms of transportation. Challenge them to create a list of 100 advantages (or 25 or 50).

6. Individual students may wish to create a travel journal for John Henry. Ask each student to imagine he or she is John Henry and to record his or her thoughts and observations about growing up, work, and trains as seen through the eyes of John Henry. Later, journals can be posted on the bulletin board for sharing.

7. Have students develop advertisements or video commercials for the contest between John Henry and the steamdrill. What enticements, slogans, or testimonials can they use to promote the competition? Students may wish to look at promotions used for sports events in the newspaper or magazines for ideas. Be sure these ads are shared with students throughout the school.

8. Have students create a script in which John Henry finds himself in modern-day America. How would he react to the technology present today? What would he think about the evolution of the American railroad? How would he like to be a railroad worker now? Direct students to create responses to these and other questions in the form of a brief play. Assign roles and have students act out the skit for another class. Be sure to solicit reactions from the other class and encourage them to read the "real" story.

9. You may be able to arrange to have a representative from Amtrak or a local railroad depot speak to your class on what the railroad does today. Many youngsters, raised in an era of jet planes and fast cars, may not realize that the railroad is still a fully functioning part of the American transportation system.

10. Obtain a copy of a local railroad schedule. Use it to create several math problems for your students. Have them note departure and arrival times between selected cities. Have them compute the amount of time needed to travel between two designated cities or between several selected cities. Provide opportunities for students to create their own word problems by duplicating train schedules and directing small groups to devise problems for each other.

11. Ask students, in small groups, to create an imaginary machine that could be used to drill through mountains. What would their machines look like? How would the blueprints be designed? What special features would the machines have? How would they be powered? Using a variety of art materials (popsicle sticks, pipe cleaners, glue, construction paper, etc.), students may wish to construct models of their machines.

12. Children may enjoy cutting out pictures from several old magazines and creating a notebook of trains throughout U.S. history. Post a selected picture of a train from a certain time period at the top of a sheet of paper. Write facts about that train and its contributions below. Several of these sheets can be gathered into a notebook for class sharing. This project can take several weeks, with some students collecting pictures, others obtaining data from the library, some contributing illustrations, and other producing the final notebook.

13. Have each student create a postcard John Henry might have sent home to his parents while he was working on the railroad. Have students decide on a colorful illustration for the front of the postcard. Be sure these are appropriately displayed.

14. Visit a local factory or business and obtain copies of its job application (applications for manual labor jobs would be particularly appropriate). Have small groups of students fill out each of these applications as though they were John Henry applying for a railroad job. Invite students to use some imagination in completing some of the application sections (home address, schools attended, work history, etc.).

15. Have students create a newscast about John Henry's contest with the steamdrill. Ask students to watch several television newscasts to get an idea of how they are produced. Afterwards, let students create their own newscast with several reporters, eyewitnesses, and, of course, John Henry. Students may enjoy videotaping the newscast for later viewing.

16. Ask students to make a comparative chart of the tools used by workers in the 1800s and workers today. What similarities are there? What differences do they note? What changes have occurred in tools over the last 200, 150, 100, or 50 years?

17. Have each student take on the role of a hammer manufacturer and write a letter to John Henry trying to convince him to use their company's newest hammer. What characteristics or attributes does the new hammer have that would make it ideal for John Henry's work? What makes the new hammer better than any other? Why should John Henry buy the new hammer?

A Picture Book of Abraham Lincoln
David A. Adler
(New York: Holiday House, 1989)

SUMMARY

The life and times of Abraham Lincoln are chronicled in this story of one of the United States' greatest leaders. From his simple beginnings, his failures and successes, to some of the major decisions he made as president, this book provides an enjoyable insight into a heralded statesman.

SOCIAL STUDIES TOPIC AREAS

Sociology, history, political science

CONTENT-RELATED WORDS

widow, New Orleans, miserable, politics, legislature, representatives, debate, Confederate, Emancipation Proclamation, surrendered

CURRICULAR PERSPECTIVES

The life of Abraham Lincoln is often surrounded with a charismatic or mystical quality. Students almost ritualistically study Abraham Lincoln as one of the great presidents of American history. Most children can cite incidents from Lincoln's life, such as growing up in a log cabin, studying by the light of a fireplace, walking many miles to school, campaigning for and losing many elections, his failing business ventures, his trials and tribulations during the Civil War, and his untimely death. What students may not understand is how those facts combined to create one of the most distinctive personalities in American history.

Aside from the common data about Lincoln, children need to understand that he was a product of his times. The hardships he went through, the decisions he had to make, and the personal tragedies he suffered were not uncommon for that time period. What may well have been uncommon was Lincoln's resolve to rise above those setbacks and disappointments to become the leader the fragile nation so desperately needed.

The author of this book provides readers with some important and valuable insights into the life of our sixteenth president. Told in an engaging and simple format, this book offers a host of delightful facts about Lincoln in a style that children can understand and appreciate. In fact, this book, along with the others in David Adler's series, would make a wonderful addition to the library of any classroom. Clear and expressive illustrations complement the text and provide readers with just the right amount of information and data.

CRITICAL-THINKING QUESTIONS

1. How far would you walk to get to school? To get to a playground or swimming pool? To get to a shopping mall?

2. What are some of the jobs you must do at home? Which ones would you rather not do? Which ones are necessary for the family to run smoothly?

3. What do you think might have happened if Lincoln had not been shot?

4. What kind of problems do you think the slaves had when they were freed?

5. Would you vote for Lincoln if he were running for president today? Why?

6. Why did people refer to him as "Honest Abe"?

7. What are some of the similarities between Abraham Lincoln and our current president? What are some differences?

RELATED BOOKS AND REFERENCES

Adler, David A. *A Picture Book of George Washington*. New York: Holiday House, 1989.

Goldstein, Nathan. *Abe Lincoln: Man of Courage*. Boston: Houghton Mifflin, 1960.

Judson, Clara Ingram. *Abraham Lincoln*. Chicago: Follet, 1961.

Martin, Patricia Miles. *Abraham Lincoln*. New York: H. W. Wilson, 1964.

McGovern, Ann. *If You Grew Up with Abraham Lincoln*. New York: Four Winds, 1966.

Richards, Dorothy Fay. *Abe Lincoln Made It Right*. Chicago: The Child's World, 1978.

ACTIVITIES

1. The most familiar coin to many students is the Lincoln penny. Share some pennies with your students and discuss the various parts of the penny, with particular references to Lincoln's portrait. Have students create different versions of a Lincoln penny using events, characters, or incidents from Lincoln's life. These new coins can be created from modeling clay or drawn on paper.

2. Invite students to conduct additional research on some of the events in Lincoln's life mentioned in the book. Have them put together their information in the form of a newspaper on the life and times of Abraham Lincoln. The newspaper can be prepared several weeks in advance of Lincoln's birthday and distributed throughout the school for all to enjoy.

3. Obtain a large map of the midwest. Have students plot the various places Lincoln lived during his life (Kentucky, Indiana, Illinois, Washington, D.C.). Ask students to measure the distances between all these points and plot those distances on a bulletin-board display.

4. Have students write to the tourist offices of each of the states (and the national capitol) in which Lincoln lived to obtain brochures and other appropriate travel/tourist information. Here are the addresses: Kentucky Department of Tourism, 2200 Capital Plaza Tower, Frankfort, KY 40601 (800-225-8747 or 502-564-4930); Indiana Department of Commerce, Tourism Development Division, One North Capital Street, Indianapolis, IN 46204 (800-292-6337 or 317-232-8860); Illinois Travel Information Center, 310 South Michigan Avenue, Chicago, IL 60604 (800-223-0121 or 312-793-2094); Convention and Visitors Association, 1575 I Street, NW, Suite 250, Washington, D.C. 20005 (800-544-1800 or 202-789-7000). When the information arrives, have students set up an attractive bulletin-board display.

5. Lincoln walked two miles to school and two miles home every day. Have students figure out how many times they would have to go around the high school track to cover four miles. On a volunteer basis, have students walk around the track and record the amount of time it takes them to cover two miles. Have them compute the time Lincoln would need to leave for school if school began at 8:00 a.m.

6. Lincoln used to walk great distances to obtain books to read. Take your class on a walking trip to the nearest public library. Encourage each student to select a book and read it while at the library. Upon your return to the classroom, have students write a journal entry on the trip and the books they selected.

7. Students may enjoy engaging in a classroom debate over an issue such as longer recesses, better lunch food, or less homework. Select two debate teams, each of which will defend one side of a selected issue. After the debate, encourage the audience members to discuss their reactions to the debate and whether they were influenced by the arguments presented.

8. The National Geographic Society has a series of three filmstrips entitled People of the American Civil War (No. 30789, 1991), which looks at the people involved in the issues and events of this period in American history. Also available is a series of sound filmstrips entitled Presidents of the United States Series (1979). Part IV (No. 04147) covers the lives of Abraham Lincoln, Andrew Johnson, and Ulysses S. Grant. Obtain copies of these and share them with your students.

9. Trains and train travel were an important part of life in the 1800s. Obtain one or more of the following books and share the magic of trains with your students: *Trains* by Byron Barton (New York: Crowell, 1986); *Trains* by Gail Gibbons (New York: Holiday House, 1987); *Death of the Iron Horse* by Paul Goble (New York: Bradbury, 1987); *The Train* by David McPhail (Boston: Little, 1977); *Casey Jones* by Glen Rounds (San Francisco, Calif.: Golden Gate, 1968); *The Polar Express* by Chris Van Allsburg (New York: Houghton Mifflin, 1985).

10. Ask students to locate the eleven southern states that formed the Confederate States of America. Provide students with an opportunity to do some library research on those states and set up a special bulletin-board display of the geographical features, traditions, regional recipes, customs, and traditions specific to that region of the country.

11. The years of some of the important events in Lincoln's life are listed in the back of Adler's book. Have students list each of those dates and compute Lincoln's age for each of the identified events. Students may wish to convert this information into a time line of Lincoln's life.

12. Divide the class into several pairs of students. Ask each pair to select one other U.S. president and create a comparison chart between the lives of that president and the life of Abraham Lincoln. What similarities do they note? What differences? Are there personality characteristics or historical events that lead one to become a president? Can you make any generalizations about future presidents?

13. Students may enjoy making some flatboats similar to the one Lincoln used to float down the Mississippi. Have students lay several round toothpicks on a sheet of paper and fasten them together with white glue (two layers may be appropriate). Have students float their flatboats in a pan of water. Encourage them to reflect on some of the sights and sounds they would see if they were to float down the Mississippi River. Have them record their impressions in personal journals.

14. Contact the local bar association and invite one or more lawyers to visit your class and discuss their jobs. Ask the lawyers to compare the type of work they do today to the type of work done by lawyers in the 1800s. How is it similar? How is it different? What kind of training did lawyers need to practice in the 1800s in comparison to the education needed today? (Note: it would be valuable to invite both male and female lawyers as classroom visitors.)

15. Students may wish to create their own models of a log cabin. Have them roll up squares of brown construction paper into log shapes. Provide students with bottles of white glue and ask them to put together several versions of Abraham Lincoln's log cabin (they may wish to use the illustrations in the book for reference).

16. Ask students to write an essay on "Abraham Lincoln was the best U.S. president because...." The finished essays can be collected into a scrapbook for classroom display.

17. Students may enjoy making their own quill pens like the ones used during Lincoln's time. Give each student a feather (feathers can be obtained from a local farmer, meat processing plant, large grocery store, or hobby shop). For each feather, strip off some of the feather from the fat end. Use a knife to cut the fat end in a slant to create a point. Clean the inside of the point with a paper clip. Carefully dip the point into fountain pen ink to fill the opening and begin writing (quills must be dipped several times).

18. Have students create a series of interview questions they would like to ask Abraham Lincoln if he were alive today. Ask one student to take on the role of Lincoln with other students directing questions to this individual for responses. This activity could also be conducted as a presidential press conference with student reporters asking "Abraham Lincoln" questions concerning events during the Civil War, for example.

19. Writing paper was a precious commodity when Abraham Lincoln was going to school. Your students may enjoy making their own recycled paper. Here is a simple recipe:

> newsprint or newspapers
> 1 cup of water
> ¼ cup laundry starch
> fiberglass or wire screen
> rolling pin

Have students tear the newsprint into small pieces no larger than one inch square. Mix 1 cup of the newsprint with the water and the laundry starch in a blender until smooth. Drain the mixture on the screening. Press it flat using hands and a rolling pin. Allow time to dry.

When each student has had an opportunity to create a piece of paper, encourage them all to write a maxim or slogan on their papers for posting in the classroom.

A Picture Book of Martin Luther King, Jr.
David A. Adler
(New York: Holiday House, 1989)

SUMMARY

This book is a biography of Martin Luther King, Jr., and his fight for civil rights. The book illustrates Dr. King's lifelong struggle with racism, with an emphasis on his childhood friends, the Atlanta bus protests, and his dream of freedom for all peoples.

SOCIAL STUDIES TOPIC AREAS

Political science, sociology, history

CONTENT-RELATED WORDS

protests, Atlanta, doctorate, boycott, prejudice, violence

CURRICULAR PERSPECTIVES

"I have a dream." While some youngsters today may not understand the significance of those words, for several generations of black Americans those four words had enormous potential and possibility. Those words signaled a desire and a need to change. They outlined a hope and promise of a better society, in which a person's skin color was not the primary criterion by which he or she was judged. It was a message that was long overdue and long needed.

Martin Luther King, Jr., did indeed have a dream—a dream of a better America, a dream of jobs and economic security, a dream of people working together for a common good. His dream was shared by many Americans who also saw years of injustice and decades of discrimination and prejudice. That dream had been around for a long time, but it needed a channel, a great orator, to make it heard above the din of oppression and racism. It was Martin Luther King, Jr., who took the dream of the common person and made it a dream of all people, black and white, rich and poor. For many the dream was possible; for others it was scary.

Although students may have some difficulties in understanding the political climate of the 1950s and 1960s, they can certainly appreciate the struggles of black Americans in their search for equality. Learning about the internal similarities that bind us together, rather than emphasizing the external differences that set us apart, is an important lesson within the pages of this book. As students read and discuss Martin Luther King, Jr.'s life, they learn to appreciate the ideals he stood for as well as the principles he advocated for all people.

This book is an important addition to any classroom library. It speaks to concerns that are still extant today, issues that this next generation of citizens will have to contend with in their lives. Dr. King knew there were no easy solutions, but he did know that violence and hatred were not the answer. Children will discover that his philosophy transcends race relations and is significant in any interaction with our fellow humans. That message is as important within the context of elementary social studies as it is in the larger world.

CRITICAL-THINKING QUESTIONS

1. Why do you think Martin Luther King, Jr. was killed?

2. Have you ever been discriminated against? If so, how did it feel? If not, how would you react if it happened?

3. Why is Dr. King considered a famous American?

4. How do you believe freedom for all people can be achieved in this country?

5. Why are equal rights so important for all people, no matter what their race?

6. Did Dr. King's dream ever come true? Why?

7. Why do you think Dr. King worked for freedom by using a nonviolent approach?

8. If you had one wish for your fellow human beings, what would it be?

RELATED BOOKS AND REFERENCES

Darby, Jean. *Martin Luther King, Jr.* Minneapolis, Minn.: Lerner, 1990.

Davidson, Margaret. *I Have a Dream*. New York: Scholastic, 1986.

DeKay, James T. *Meet Martin Luther King, Jr.* New York: Random House, 1989.

Greenfield, Eloise. *Daydreamers*. New York: Dial, 1981.

Haskins, James. *The Life and Death of Martin Luther King, Jr.* New York: Lothrop, Lee and Shepard, 1977.

Hughes, Langston. *The Dream Keeper*. New York: Knopf, 1985.

McKee, Don. *Martin Luther King, Jr.* New York: Putnam, 1969.

Smith, Kathie B. *Martin Luther King, Jr.* New York: Julian Messner, 1987.

ACTIVITIES

1. Ask a group of students to role play the incident in Martin Luther King, Jr.'s childhood when he was not allowed to play with his white friends. Have six students assume the roles of Martin, his friends, his friend's mother, and his parents. Direct students to write journal entries in response to the incident and encourage them to share their feelings.

2. Students may wish to begin a scrapbook about famous black Americans, such as Charles Drew, Harriet Tubman, Jackie Robinson, and Bill Cosby. Have students select individuals from the sports, political, medicine, and entertainment worlds. The class can be divided into small groups, with each group responsible for collecting data and research about individuals in one of the identified groups. A one-page biography, illustrations of significant events, a small collage, a time line, and a silhouette could all be included as part of each biographical sketch.

3. Students may enjoy hearing some traditional black poetry. Examples can be found in the following sources: *My Black Me: A Beginning Book of Black Poetry*, Arnold Adoff, ed. (New York: Dutton, 1974); *The Dream Keeper* by Langston Hughes (New York: Knopf, 1985); *Daydreamers* by Eloise Greenfield (New York: Dial, 1981); and *Bronzeville Boys and Girls* by Gwendolyn Brooks (New York: Harper & Row Junior Books, 1956).

4. Students can create an oral time line. Have a group of selected students each memorize an important date in Dr. King's life. Have these students line up chronologically. The first student steps forward and recites his or her information, then steps back. This process continues until all students in the line have completed their recitations. This oral time line can be presented to other classes, too.

5. The following segregation simulation could be used in your classroom. Randomly divide the class into two groups of students, a blue group and a green group. Pin colored pieces of construction paper to each child's shirt to denote his or her group. Tell the students that the blue group members will get all the advantages and privileges during the course of one day, such as going to lunch first, choosing where they want to sit, being the only ones allowed to go outside to recess, being the only ones allowed to drink from the water fountain, etc. On the following day, give all these privileges to members of the green group. On the third day, engage the class in a discussion about their feelings when they were members of the disadvantaged "minority" group. Journal entries should reflect their thoughts or reactions.

6. Ask students to create a two-part poster. On one half of the poster, record or illustrate the economic, social, or political conditions of black Americans in the 1950s and 1960s. On the other side of the poster, record conditions in the present. What differences are there? What similarities?

7. Have students imagine that the date is sometime in August 1963 and that Dr. King is coming to speak at their school. Have students plan an advertising campaign that would get their parents and other members of the local community to come hear the speech. Posters, bulletins, brochures, and other advertising literature may all be used.

8. Using the overhead projector and large sheets of paper, make a profile of each student. Project each student's image on the paper, trace, and cut it out. Direct students to write their names at the bottom of their profiles. Ask each student to exchange his or her profile with another student. Each student then writes something on the classmate's profile that the two of them have in common. Exchange profiles several times with other classmates, each of whom records a commonality. Discuss and display all the profiles.

9. Students may wish to create a newspaper accounting of the significant events in Dr. King's life. Students can be divided into reporting teams to conduct some library research and prepare appropriate articles for their newspaper. You may wish to provide students with a selection of headlines to get them started. Here are a few possibilities: *Close Friends Not Allowed to Play Together, Montgomery Buses to Be Integrated, Dr. King's Dream Excites Nation*, or *Nation Mourns Loss of Great Leader*. The finished newspaper can be duplicated and distributed throughout the school.

10. As part of the series People Behind Our Holidays, the National Geographic Society has a seventeen-minute sound filmstrip entitled *Martin Luther King, Jr.* (No. 30283, 1987). Obtain a copy and share it with your class. Students may wish to create their own homemade filmstrip about Dr. King's life. Have students draw individual illustrations on several index cards. Fasten the cards together by punching small holes in the top and bottom of each one and

looping a paper clip between the holes in two cards. Each series of index cards can be shown to the class and displayed by hanging them from the ceiling.

11. The book *Martin Luther King, Jr.: The Dream of the Peaceful Revolution* by Della Rowland (Englewood Cliffs, N.J.: Silver Burdett, 1990) contains Dr. King's speech "A Drum Major for Justice." Read the speech to the class and afterwards ask students to verbalize their opinions of the speech. Have students write reviews of the speech as if they were writing for a newspaper.

12. Most major urban areas have a Human Relations Commission. Contact the nearest one and ask whether they have a speaker who can address your class on civil rights or discrimination issues. Have students create a class invitation and design a series of appropriate questions to ask the speaker during the presentation.

13. Students may enjoy creating their own original picture books on the life of Dr. King. Direct small groups of students to select a period of time in Dr. King's life or a particular incident. Each of those events can then be turned into a series of picture books, all of which can be displayed in the school library. Such a display would be very appropriate as part of Black History Month.

14. Share the poem "No Difference" from *Where the Sidewalk Ends* by Shel Silverstein (New York: Harper and Row, 1974). Encourage students to discuss their interpretations of the poem, particularly in light of the efforts of Martin Luther King, Jr. toward racial equality. Students may enjoy creating some original poetry on their own for compilation into a collection of "no difference" poetry.

15. Encourage students to take a survey of the adults in their family or neighbors in their community on their perceptions of Dr. King. How influential do they think Dr. King was in terms of American politics or social issues? Students may wish to compile their data and present it in the form of a chart or graph in the classroom.

16. Although Dr. King's birthday is honored as a national holiday, there are some places in this country where it is not recognized. Ask students why this might be the case. Have students write to officials in those places (city, county, or state) and inquire as to reasons for the nonobservance of Dr. King's birthday.

The Star-Spangled Banner
Peter Spier
(New York: Doubleday, 1973)

SUMMARY

Many vivid and colorful illustrations are provided to accompany the words to the song "The Star-Spangled Banner." The pictures include events that led to Francis Scott Key's inspiration to write the song.

SOCIAL STUDIES TOPIC AREAS

History, sociology

CONTENT-RELATED WORDS

twilight, gleaming, perilous, ramparts, gallantly, foes, haughty, reposes, fitfully, conceals, desolation, preserv'd, triumph

CURRICULAR PERSPECTIVES

"The Star-Spangled Banner." Our national anthem. It is played at athletic events, during Fourth of July celebrations, at high school graduations, and even at car dealership openings. It is as much a part of the national fabric as mom and apple pie.

This anthem, conceived during a conflict that few of us recall from our U.S. history courses, is an important part of Americana. It taps the conscience of the country and incites a spirit of common beliefs and ideals that is much less evident in some other countries. It is a moving song that binds a nation together and celebrates the American spirit as do few other songs. Even though very few of us can remember all the words, most of us know the tune instantly and react to it immediately, even if we do not find it easy to sing.

Children are exposed early to "The Star-Spangled Banner." Although they may not understand all the historical events that led to the creation of the song, it can and should be an important part of their history lessons, not so much because it is sung at the ballpark but because it brings us all together for a common purpose. Children need to realize that "The Star-Spangled Banner" is as much their song as it is a song of the United States.

Teachers will discover a host of opportunities to make this song come alive for their students. History, music, art, reading, and science can all be involved in understanding and appreciating this tune. Students will begin to understand that this is more than a bunch of words and a bunch of notes strung together — rather, it is a symbol of patriotism and unification that has few comparisons and few equals. Young and old alike find a cohesive spirit within the bars of "The Star-Spangled Banner" that transcends generations and becomes a significant element in the lives of all Americans.

CRITICAL-THINKING QUESTIONS

1. If you were given the chance to change some words in "The Star-Spangled Banner," which words would you change? Why?

2. What is your favorite part of the song? Why?

3. Would you have enjoyed living during the time this song was written? Why?

4. Why are Americans so proud of "The Star-Spangled Banner"?

5. How would you feel if you were selected to write a song for the United States? What kind of song would you write?

6. Do you think that all Americans should know the words to this song? Do you think all Americans should know what the words mean?

7. Why do you think Francis Scott Key wrote this song?

RELATED BOOKS AND REFERENCES

America the Beautiful Sound Recording: A Musical Salute to the Statue of Liberty (compact disc). New York: Reader's Digest Association, 1986.

American Flag: Story of Old Glory (video). Chicago: Encyclopaedia Britannica Education Corp., 1988.

Botsford, Ward. *Sing Children's Songs: Songs of the United States of America*. New York: Columbia Studios, 1977.

Fradin, Dennis. *The Flag of the United States*. Chicago: Children's Press, 1989.

Lloyd, Michael. *Kid Songs Music Video Stories: Sing Out America* (video). Los Angeles, Calif.: Tap Video Production, Warner Bros., 1986.

Lyons, John Henry. *Stories of Our American Patriotic Songs*. New York: Doubleday, 1974.

Parish, Thomas. *The American Flag*. New York: Simon & Schuster, 1973.

Quackenbush, Robert M. *Pop! Goes the Weasel and Yankee Doodle*. New York: Harper, 1988.

ACTIVITIES

1. This country's first flag had thirteen stars to represent the states. Today, we have fifty stars on the flag. In small groups, have students research some of the changes that led to the addition of stars to the flag. Have students prepare a time line listing the ratification of states fourteen through fifty. This line can be illustrated on a large sheet of butcher paper and hung along one or more walls of the room.

2. Have students use mental imagery to imagine the time when Francis Scott Key got the inspiration to write "The Star-Spangled Banner." Direct students to close their eyes as you establish the setting for them (watching from another boat, early morning, the American flag flying in the field, cannons firing, etc.). After the setting has been given, instruct students to write journal entries as to how they feel about the situation. Can you relate to Francis Scott Key's song about the event? Why do you think he got the inspiration to write the song? How is the song related to the event at Fort McHenry?

3. Have students write a series of newspaper articles about the events surrounding the writing of "The Star-Spangled Banner." Ask students to assemble their articles into a class newspaper for publication and distribution throughout the school.

4. Invite a military person to your class to discuss the weapons used during the War of 1812 in comparison to the weapons used today. How effective are the weapons? What can modern weapons do that weapons of 150 years ago could not? Later, students may wish to create a pictograph of weapons from the past and weapons of the present.

5. Direct individual students to research one of the important people of the War of 1812, for example, Major George Armistead, James Madison, Francis Scott Key, or Colonel John S. Skinner. Students can create costumes for each of the individuals researched. Stations can be set up around the room, with selected students (in costume) taking on the role of each of the historical figures to explain some of their actions during that time period.

6. Direct students to make a tape recording of "The Star-Spangled Banner" to present to the school library. Students may wish to add selected sound effects (cannons firing, soldiers marching, waves pounding, etc.) for added interest.

7. Some students may enjoy doing some library research on the kind of medical treatment available during the War of 1812. How does that treatment compare with the type of health care available today? Ask small groups of students to prepare a health brochure describing health benefits for the soldiers fighting in the War of 1812. Ask other students to prepare a similar brochure outlining the health services available for soldiers today.

8. Direct students to create a bulletin board of some of the symbols that represent the United States, for example, the Statue of Liberty, "The Star-Spangled Banner," the flag, the Washington Monument, and the bald eagle. Have students write a short description of each of the symbols posted.

9. Direct students to design a cover for a compact disc (CD) recording of "The Star-Spangled Banner." Students can use poster board (in the shape of a CD box), tempera paints, markers, crayons, and other art materials to design the cover. Be sure these covers/boxes are displayed in an appropriate location.

10. In small groups, challenge students to rewrite the words to "The Star-Spangled Banner." After some time, ask each group to sing its version of the song and explain the lyrics chosen.

11. Direct students to create a fashion magazine for the 1800s. Students can design illustrations (using colored pencils and construction paper), write appropriate fashion articles, and design selected advertisements. Some library research may be necessary to discover what men and women wore during this time period.

12. Direct students to create a series of history cards (similar to baseball cards) about some of the events surrounding the War of 1812. Using 4" x 6" index cards, students can design illustrations for the upper half of each card. On the bottom half of each card, students can record selected facts about the event or person portrayed.

13. Sailors during the early 1800s did not have a large variety of foods to eat. Here is a recipe for Tavern Biscuits, a popular food of the day because they could be made and stored quite easily.

> 4 cups of flour
> 1 cup of sugar
> 1½ cups of warm water
> 2 tablespoons of shortening
> 2 teaspoons of salt

> Mix all the ingredients together and place a spoonful at a time on a baking sheet. Bake for 15 to 20 minutes at 400 degrees.

14. Develop a classroom stamp collection. Direct each student to create a stamp that symbolizes what America means to him or her. The stamps can be made larger than life size on construction paper using crayons, markers, or colored pencils to create the stamps. After students have designed their stamps, place them in a photo album for permanent display.

15. Direct students to create a time line of events that occurred during the 1800s. The time line can include other events that were happening around the world at the time of the War of 1812.

16. Challenge students to create a new name for "The Star-Spangled Banner." Explain to them that Francis Scott Key had problems coming up with a title for his song (he first called it the "Gallant Defense of Fort McHenry"). Have students pretend to be Francis Scott Key's assistant in charge of creating a title for the song. After students have generated some titles, have them explain the reasoning behind the choices and the appropriateness of each title.

17. Have students write to Fort McHenry (Attention: Superintendent, National Monument and Historic Shrine, Baltimore, MD 21230 [301] 962-4299) and request sample brochures and other information about the fort. Have them create a scrapbook detailing all the data they gather.

Those People in Washington
David Flitner
(Chicago: Children's Press, 1973)

SUMMARY

The author weaves an interesting tale of the history of United States government and the laws that have evolved over the years. How people govern and how they are governed is the focus of this book.

SOCIAL STUDIES TOPIC AREAS

History, political science, sociology

CONTENT-RELATED WORDS

continent, colonize, declaration, independence, revolutionary, confederation, constitution, federal, amendments, Congress, judicial, legislative, Senate, districts, law, bill, cabinet, election, political, Democratic party, Republican party, conventions, delegates

CURRICULAR PERSPECTIVES

Government and politics can be confusing for many children. With a host of terms and special vocabulary, the very thought of government can be daunting for most youngsters, as it is for many adults. Trying to explain the working of our federal system of government is not an easy task, but one that is necessary for children to gain an appreciation of how their country runs as well as their responsibilities as citizens of that country.

The author provides young readers with a thorough and complete guide to the process of U.S. government. He discusses the roles and responsibilities of senators and congresspeople, the president, and the president's cabinet. How laws are made and how people are voted into office are also described in simple yet effective language. Political parties and their influence on the American system of politics are also described.

Students will discover that, although our system of government may seem perplexing and complicated at first, it is logical, systematic, and straightforward. It is much more than several hundred people sitting in Washington, D.C. deciding the fate of people all over the country. It is a continuous process of advice and consent, decisions and deliberations, and checks and balances. Students will learn that they, as participating citizens, have much to say about the way this country is run and will discover how it was able to meet the challenges of colonial times just as well as it is able to meet the challenges of modern times.

Teachers will find this to be a most appropriate introduction to politics and the political system. One note of caution is in order, however: the author has a tendency to overuse masculine pronouns. Teachers should encourage classroom discussions that focus on equal opportunities to decide and govern regardless of gender. Despite this shortcoming, the book will enhance textual presentations in a language children can understand and enjoy.

CRITICAL-THINKING QUESTIONS

1. What does it mean to you to be a citizen of the United States?

2. How have the laws our forefathers created affected you or your family?

3. Why do you think laws are created?

4. How will staying in school benefit you as an adult?

5. What would you like to put in a class constitution?

6. If you were a congressperson, what would you change? What would you fight for? What would you try to preserve?

7. Do you think the press has the right to broadcast all the news concerning the government? Why?

RELATED BOOKS AND REFERENCES

Berey, Jay. *Every Kid's Guide to Laws that Relate to School and Work*. Chicago: Children's Press, 1987.

Breslow, Aaron. *Happy Birthday, America*. New Canaan, Conn.: Happy History, 1976.

A Child's History of America by America's children. Boston: Little, Brown, 1975.

Coen, Rena Neumann. *American History in Art*. Minneapolis, Minn.: Lerner, 1966.

Hopple, Cheryl. *As I Saw It: Women Who Lived the American Adventure*. New York: Dial, 1978.

Patriotic and Historical Plays for Young People. Boston: Boston Plays, 1975.

Rosh, William. *Fabulous Facts about the Fifty States*. New York: Scholastic, 1981.

Tower, Samuel. *A Stamp Collector's History of the United States*. New York: Messner, 1975.

Wright, Louis B., and Elaine W. Fowler. *Everyday Life in the New Nation*. New York: Putnam, 1972.

ACTIVITIES

1. Designate each student in the class as president of the United States. Ask students to design their own letterhead (stationery) for this high office. Encourage them to use typography or illustrations that reflect their interests and/or lifestyles.

2. Have students write a letter to their local congressperson requesting a flag that has flown over the White House (these are free for the asking). Have children indicate reasons why they want a flag for their classroom and what makes it special to them.

3. Brainstorm with students all the rules they must obey at school. Discuss how these rules are related to rules for the general public, either at the local or national level.

4. Have students select a law that affects them personally and write journal entries on why and how it affects them.

5. Have students generate a list of laws they would like to see improved. Ask them to describe the shortcomings of some of these laws and the suggestions they would make to their representatives for the improvements.

6. Encourage students to construct a classroom "Bill of Rights." What laws or regulations would they like to have in terms of classroom behavior, teacher responsibilities, and individual rights? How does their Bill of Rights compare with the one in the U.S. Constitution?

7. Invite a local congressperson to your classroom to explain the nature of his or her job. What responsibilities does that person have to each constituent in the district, including children? Students may wish to set up a panel discussion and videotape the proceedings for presentation to the entire school.

8. Establish a "Pursuit of Happiness" time during the day. Develop learning centers to allow students to investigate art, music, free reading, and other cultural activities apppropriate to everyday life.

9. Have students set up a special classroom journal for freedom of expression. Each day allow several students to record and reflect on ideas, events, and statements with which they do not agree. These can include cafeteria food, math homework, reading materials, and the like. Ask students to express their displeasure as well as offer solutions or alternatives to the undesirable situation(s).

10. Have students construct a letter of welcome for immigrants to this country. How would they like to welcome these persons? What would they like to share about the new country? How can they help new immigrants become part of the mainstream?

11. Have students try to invent a new flag for the United States. What changes or modifications in the current flag do they feel are appropriate? Provide them with opportunities to explain their decisions.

12. Ask students to design tombstones for famous American leaders. What data or information should be placed on each tombstone? Is there an outstanding quote or historical event that should be remembered for each individual? Students may wish to construct a historical tombstone display on a bulletin board or create a model cemetery or tombstones carved from clay.

13. Have students vote for two class senators to represent the class and sit in on monthly P.T.O. meetings. Be sure the senators take the concerns, grievances, or issues of the class to each scheduled P.T.O. meeting. The senators should report their findings to the class.

14. Designate yourself as president of the class. Assemble a cabinet designating students (on a rotating basis) for specific roles. For example:

Secretary of Transportation	Makes sure students get to the buses on time each day.
Secretary of Labor	Designates students for various classroom jobs.
Secretary of Treasury	Counts the lunch money each day.
Secretary of State	Shares classroom discoveries with students in other classes.
Attorney General	Makes sure the rules of the classroom are adhered to by all.

15. Set up a classroom supreme court. Have students participate in the court on a rotating basis. The responsibility of the supreme court will be to determine the appropriateness of classroom laws and rules for all individuals.

16. Have students set up a time capsule that includes the class constitution, rules for behavior, and other laws. Bury this at the beginning of the school year and dig it up at the end of the year. Have students discuss whether any changes need to be made or have already been made since the original drafting of those regulations.

17. Encourage students to discuss **reasons why not all laws and rules need to be recorded.** Rules such as no spitting, no biting, and the like may be suggested as examples of nonrecorded rules.

18. Have students write a letter to the editor of the local newspaper expressing their observations or concerns about local issues. These can be written individually or as a class project. Students may be surprised at how many of these letters are printed in the newspaper. After several have been published, create a special scrapbook or bulletin-board display.

11—World

All in a Day
Mitsumasa Anno et al.
(New York: Philomel, 1986)

SUMMARY

In all the countries of the world, people are doing different things all at the same time. While some children are having lunch, other children in a distant land are asleep and others are just beginning their days. In spite of the time differences, everyone is still very much the same—inhabitants of the same planet.

SOCIAL STUDIES TOPIC AREAS

Geography, anthropology, sociology

CONTENT-RELATED WORDS

uninhabited, International Date Line, shuttlecock

CURRICULAR PERSPECTIVES

Students are always delighted to discover what children are doing in other countries. Are they the same as we are? How are they different? What things do they do that we do not? These are the kinds of questions typically asked by youngsters as they seek information on their peers across the sea or in a distant land.

This book is a celebration of the similarities among children of the world. Even though we live in different countries in different time zones, our activities are similar and universal. We get up in the morning, eat breakfast, go to school, play and interact with our families and friends, and go to bed. Our customs and traditions may differ, but we all share some common goals and events in our lives.

Through this book, students learn about the twenty-four time zones, why they were created, and why time changes as one moves around the world. They also discover the fact that while it is summer in one country it can be winter in another. This book is as much a science book as it is a social studies book. It demonstrates for children the mystical element we call *time*, and how time influences what we do as well as when we do it.

Children will delight in the layout of the eight completely different illustrations on each two-page spread. Done by some of the world's foremost children's illustrators, the pictures represent the simplicity and complexity of our lives in a variety of ways. The illustrations portray children in a host of settings and activities, once again demonstrating the similarities we share, no matter what our country of origin.

CRITICAL-THINKING QUESTIONS

1. Which country would you most like to visit? Why?

2. How would you feel if we switched to a twenty-four hour clock? Would it be easier or more difficult to tell time or plan activities?

3. What would you do if you were the one shipwrecked on Uninhabited Island? How would you try to get help?

4. How do you think we should take care of our planet?

5. Would you like to live in a place that was hot year-round? In a place that was cold year-round? Why?

6. Would you enjoy doing a lot of traveling around the world? What difficulties do you think you would encounter?

7. How is the United States similar to some Asian or European countries? How is it different?

8. How can people learn to live in peace with each other?

9. Which character from the book would you like to be friends with? Why?

RELATED BOOKS AND REFERENCES

Branley, Franklyn. *What Makes Night and Day*. New York: Crowell, 1961.

Breiter, Herta. *Time and Clocks*. Milwaukee, Wis.: Raintree, 1979.

Chwast, Seymour. *Tall City, Wide Country*. New York: Viking, 1983.

Domanska, Janina. *What Do You See?* New York: Macmillan, 1974.

Hautzig, Esther. *At Home: A Visit in Four Languages*. New York: Macmillan, 1968.

Millen, Nina. *Children's Festivals from Many Lands*. New York: Friendship, 1964.

Nordqvist, Sven. *Willie in the Big World*. New York: Morrow, 1986.

ACTIVITIES

1. Have students pretend they are correspondents for an international newspaper. Have them decide on a single topic, such as Christmas, the beginning of the school year, New Year's, etc. Have students, in eight different teams, write stories and draw illustrations telling how the eight countries mentioned in the book celebrate that day.

2. Let students imagine that they are travel agents and that they must prepare travel plans for any two of the following:

    A trip for four to the Bahamas
    A trip across five U.S. states
    A trip to three different European countries
    A trip across six time zones
    A trip over the North Pole
    A trip on a houseboat, yacht; in a kayak or canoe

Make sure students include information on how they will travel, what they might see and do, what they will pack, and how long each trip will take.

3. Work with your school's music teacher or local librarian to locate songs from each of the eight countries mentioned in the book. (Note: Write to Folkways Records, 43 West 61st Street, New York, NY 10023 and ask for their latest catalog.) Have students put together a song scrapbook of selected music from these countries. Have the music teacher teach your class a song from one of the countries.

4. Instruct the class on the use of the twenty-four-hour clock. Then, for a week, conduct the entire class on a twenty-four-hour schedule. Have students set up the activities and lessons according to the twenty-four-hour clock. At the end of the week, discuss with them the difficulties or advantages they discovered while using this form of time-telling.

5. Schedule a series of New Year's Eve parties for eight separate days, one day for each of the eight countries. Have students design costumes, plan a menu, and design decorations for each of the eight celebrations. Some library research may be necessary, or students could gather information from relatives or other adults who have traveled to one or more of the countries.

6. Have students go through the book and identify all the activities children are doing throughout the world on New Year's Eve. Set up a "We Are All Alike" bulletin board and ask students to cut out pictures from old magazines that depict some or all of the illustrated activities. The pictures can be turned into a collage and posted on the bulletin board. Children should feel free to add additional activities not represented in the book.

7. Students may wish to select magazine pictures that depict life in a foreign country. Have students paste their selected pictures on sheets of oaktag and cut them into postcard shapes. Have students write messages on the back of each postcard about how they are enjoying an imaginary visit to that country. Students may wish to send their postcards to students in other classrooms.

8. Divide the class into small groups of students. Assign each group one of the countries mentioned in the book. Direct each group to cut a piece of posterboard into the shape of the assigned country. Group members must then collect pictures and provide illustrations of activities typically done by children in the assigned country. These illustrations can be pasted inside the shape of the designated country and the poster hung on a classroom wall.

9. Have students make an eight-month calendar, designating one month for each of the countries mentioned in the book. After some library research, students can note the celebrations and holidays of each country on the dates of its appropriate month.

10. An excellent resource for the classroom is the Our World series of filmstrips produced by the National Geographic Society. Part III (No. 30513) in the series offers two sound filmstrips, one entitled *Countries* and showing a journey through the different countries of the world and the other titled *Earth*, an exploration of where people live and how they interact with their environment.

11. Students may be interested in creating a sports book on the sports of another country. Have student groups each select one of the countries mentioned in the book and construct a listing (including illustrations) of the popular sports played in that country. Your school's physical education teacher may be able to help by demonstrating selected sports to your students. These demonstrations could be photographed and included in the sports book.

12. Have students plot trips to each of the eight countries. Tell them that they can travel by car, airplane, or ship. Is it possible to use just one mode of transportation to get from their home town to a designated country? If so, what is the most direct route? Must two or more modes of transportation be used? If so, which ones? How long will each trip take?

13. Have students create a series of diary entries as though they were stranded on Uninhabited Island. What would a typical day consist of in terms of daily chores and responsibilities? Students may want to create a month-long diary, imagining themselves stranded for an extended period of time.

14. Invite students to select favorite scenes or illustrations from the book. Ask them to create dioramas of their selections. They may wish to create original drawings and use clay, construction paper, pipe cleaners, and wire to construct three-dimensional objects to be placed in the diorama. Each diorama should be prominently displayed in the classroom.

15. Have students select a particular time of the school day. Have them speculate on what children in other countries around the world are doing at that time. Provide small groups of students with an opportunity to develop appropriate illustrations and diary entries from children in selected countries. What was that child doing at the designated time in the United States?

16. Provide students with opportunities to act out selected pages of the book. Divide the class into eight groups, one for each country. Have a narrator read the events on a page as each group mimes the appropriate actions.

17. On one day, have students locate the weather report for each of the eight countries (in your local newspaper). Direct students to prepare illustrations of the weather for each country, along with accompanying descriptions.

The Great Kapok Tree
Lynne Cheery
(New York: Gulliver, 1990)

SUMMARY

A young man enters the rain forest to cut down a Kapok tree, but before he knows it the heat makes him tired and weak. The man sits down to rest and falls asleep. While he sleeps, the animals of the forest whisper in his ear not to cut down the Kapok tree. Each animals has a different reason. Upon awakening, the man realizes the importance of the Kapok tree.

SOCIAL STUDIES TOPIC AREAS

Geography, anthropology, political science

CONTENT-RELATED WORDS

squawking, Kapok, Yanomamo tribe

CURRICULAR PERSPECTIVES

Whether one considers the environment a political issue, a social issue, or a personal issue, there is certainly no question that it is an issue for our times. Each day the media bombards us with the facts and figures of how the environment is changing or being altered by humans. Stories on the depletion of the ozone layer, the defoliation of rain forests, and overburdened waste disposal systems are frequently in newspapers and television newscasts. We can hardly escape the fact that our planet is in peril and that some tough questions need to be asked and long-range solutions reached.

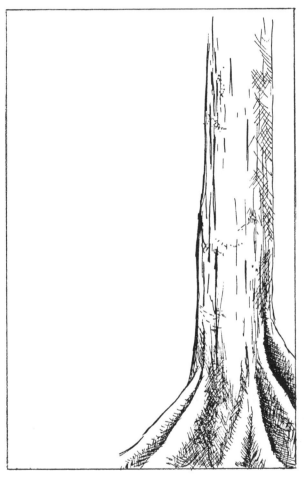

The tropical rain forests of the world provide the arena for one of the most pressing environmental issues of our times. The eradication of hundreds of thousands of acres of forest is a problem with far-reaching effects. Some scientists suggest that we may experience climatic changes as a result of the burning of Amazonian rain forests. Many others point to the fact that whole species of plant and animal life may be eliminated completely, because, even though rain forests cover a relatively small portion of the earth's surface, they are home to more than half the plant and animal species in the world. Whatever the consequences, it is inescapable that humankind has a significant impact on the flora and fauna of our world.

This book provides young readers with a marvelous introduction to environmental issues. A well-told tale full of colorful creatures and dynamic illustrations, this book makes an important case for a harmonious relationship between humans and the plants and animals they live with in the forest. Beyond that, it is a book that can be enjoyed by both adults and children while it provides a way to begin discussing the impact humans have on their world and everyone's responsibility for preserving that world.

CRITICAL-THINKING QUESTIONS

1. If you could be one of the animals in the forest, which one would you be? Why?

2. How do trees affect your life?

3. What do you think would happen if all the rain forests were eliminated?

4. What can children do to protect the rain forests?

5. Would you enjoy visiting a rain forest? What would you like to see there?

6. Why do some people do things which are harmful to the environment, such as littering?

7. Why do you think the author decided to write a book about the Amazon rain forest?

RELATED BOOKS AND REFERENCES

Amazonia: A Celebration of Life (video). New York: Andrew L. Young, 1989.

Baker, Jeannie. *Where the Forest Meets the Sea*. New York: Greenwillow, 1987.

Bramwell, Martin. *Planet Earth*. New York: Watts, 1987.

Burton, John. *Close to Extinction*. New York: Watts, 1988.

Conservation Activities for the Classroom (booklet). Silver Springs, Md.: Conservation and Renewable Energy Inquiry and Referral Service, P.O. Box 8900, Silver Springs, MD 20907.

Dorros, Arthur. *Rain Forest Secrets*. New York: Scholastic, 1990.

Earthworks Group. *50 Simple Things Kids Can Do to Save the Earth*. Kansas City, Kans.: Andrews and McMeel, 1990.

Elkington, John. *Going Green: A Kid's Handbook to Saving the Planet*. New York: Puffin, 1990.

George, Jean C. *One Day in the Tropical Rainforest*. New York: Crowell, 1990.

A Kid's Guide to Protecting the Environment (free comic-strip tabloid). New York: Natural Resources Defense Council, Department ER, 40 West 20th Street, New York, NY 10011.

Landau, Elaine. *Tropical Rain Forests*. New York: Watts, 1990.

Living Planet—A Portrait of the Earth: Jungle (16-mm film). London, England: BBC Bristol Natural History Unit, 1984.

Peet, Bill. *The Wump World*. Boston: Houghton Mifflin, 1970.

Rain Forest (16-mm film). Washington, D.C.: National Geographic Society, 1983.

Silverstein, Shel. *The Giving Tree*. New York: Harper & Row, 1964.

ACTIVITIES

1. Have students make a collage of all the animals listed in the book.

2. Create a cardboard Kapok tree. Tie a bag around the trunk of the tree. Place pencils, erasers, crayons, and scissors in the bag. Invite students to go to the tree and borrow supplies from the tree's bag whenever they are needed. Then one day tie the tree's bag closed and tell the students they are not allowed to borrow from the tree. Encourage the students to discuss their feelings about this sudden decision.

3. Compare heights of the Kapok trees in the rain forest with the heights of trees commonly found in your community. Encourage students to create a chart or graph listing any significant differences.

4. Visit a local paper recycling center. Be sure to explain to students that recycling can save millions of trees (students may be interested in learning that 60,000 trees are needed for just one run of the Sunday *New York Times*). Students may wish to create a campaign for their families on how they can recycle.

5. Provide students with blank maps and ask them to color or shade in the areas of the world that have rain forests.

6. Obtain names of companies that make and/or produce life jackets (this information may be obtained from your local public library or from the local Coast Guard Auxiliary). Have students write to these companies asking for information on how life jackets are manufactured.

7. Have students create a large map of Brazil on a bulletin board or on a sheet of newsprint that has been taped to the wall. Direct them to color in the areas of Brazil that are rain forests. Let each student select one of the animals illustrated on the inside jacket of the book, draw and color it with colored pencils, and attach it to the rain forest area of the map.

8. Have students rewrite the ending of the story and tell what would have happened if the man *had* cut down the tree. This can be done in the form of letters written by the animals that used to live in the tree. Students can tell what happens to the animals now that their home is gone.

9. Create a rain-forest environment in the classroom. Cover the walls with paper and let students paint scenes of the rain forest, using vibrant colors. Individual animals can be painted directly on the paper, or created out of papier-mâché or cardboard and suspended from the ceiling with strings. Make some of the trees and plants in relief by constructing them out of cardboard and attaching them so they stand out from the wall. Use *The Art of Paper Mâché* by Carla and John B. Kenny (Radnor, Penn.: Chilton, 1968) as a guide for making papier-mâché animals.

10. Have students imagine that they are one of the creatures in the story. Ask them to create posters that say "Save Our Home." They should include a full-color drawing of their creature and write a convincing ad for saving the Kapok tree.

11. Have each student assume the role of one of the creatures in the story and write a thank-you note to the man for sparing the tree.

12. Bring in a cross section of a tree trunk. Show students how to count rings in order to tell the age of the tree. Let students count the rings to come up with an approximate date for the tree's "birthday." Students can then write a biography of the tree describing its contributions to the world during its lifetime.

13. Have students write to the National Wildlife Federation (Educational Publications, 1400 16th Street, NW, Washington, D.C. 20036) and request a free copy of "You Can Do It!," a sixteen-page pamphlet giving tips on how children can help clean up the environment.

14. Have students plant terrariums, using an old mayonnaise jar or other wide-mouthed jar, to observe a mini-rain-forest environment. Place a layer of clean gravel on the bottom of the jar, followed by a layer of charcoal and a layer of potting soil. Have students bring in small plant cuttings to plant in their terrariums (try to include slow-growing plants and mosses). Students may also wish to collect some tools for their terrariums, such as tweezers, chopsticks, cotton swabs, long-handled spoons, and meat basters. For helpful hints, consult *The Terrarium Book* by Charles M. Evans (New York: Random House, 1973).

15. The whole class may wish to adopt an animal. Contact the American Association of Zoological Parks and Aquariums (4550 Montgomery Avenue, Suite 940N, Bethesda, MD 20814). Allow the class to decide on the type of animal to adopt and draw pictures of the adoptee to display in the room.

16. For a $10 donation, CARE will plant thirty trees in a rural community in Latin America and teach farmers there the best planting techniques. To raise money for this, you may wish to have your class create a play dramatizing an environmental issue. Invite parents and other community members and ask for donations for the cause.

17. Get permission to plant a tree on the school grounds. Take a field trip to a local nursery to learn about the types of trees available for your area. Have students help with the planting and care of the tree. They can keep a class journal, writing about the planting, care, and growth of the tree and how the tree changes through the seasons. They may also want to develop a tree "baby book," taking pictures of its first year of growth and describing its first spring, its first leaf, the first picnic under the tree, etc.

18. Share the poems "The Creation" by Cecil Frances Alexander and "Be Different to Trees" by Mary Carolyn Davies from *Favorite Poems Old and New* (Garden City, N.Y.: Doubleday, 1957). Have students generate lists of the importance of trees and other plants to our cultural and environmental heritage.

19. Create an "Ecology Club." Interested students can initiate school and community projects aimed at improving the environment. See *50 Simple Things Kids Can Do to Save the Earth* by the Earthworks Group (Kansas City, Kans.: Andrews & McMeel, 1990) for ideas. Invite local senior citizens to join the club and help out with the projects.

Jafta and the Wedding
Hugh Lewin
(Minneapolis, Minn.: Carolrhoda, 1983)

SUMMARY

Jafta, an African boy, describes the week-long village festival in celebration of his sister's wedding. He is caught up in the excitement of the wedding and all the traditions associated with the special day.

SOCIAL STUDIES TOPIC AREAS

Anthropology, sociology

CONTENT-RELATED WORDS

festival, wedding, feast, songololo dance, sakabula birds

CURRICULAR PERSPECTIVES

Every culture, religion, and country has its own traditions for celebrating weddings. Some are elaborate, lasting for several days; others are small, intimate affairs. No matter what the place or who the guests, there is always something special about a wedding. More than an affirmation of a new life together, it is also a time when people join together to dance, sing, and celebrate life.

This story tells of a traditional African wedding with its many days of preparation, the infectious dancing and drinking, and the predominating rituals. Told from the perspective of a young boy watching his older sister, it is a wonderfully woven tale of awe and surprise, wonder and delight, and joy and anticipation. The narrator is not unlike any child watching an older sibling get married—he is overcome by both joy and sadness.

Students will find much to like about this book. If they have ever participated in a wedding or read accounts of traditional church weddings in this country, they will discover many similarities. So, too, they will discover several differences between an African wedding and the ones they may be used to. This book provides a wonderful opportunity to share the differences and similarities we have with other cultures and countries and a chance to compare and contrast lifestyles and traditions.

Teachers will want to explore the variety of customs that surround traditional events in other countries as well as the United States. In so doing, students will get a sense that there is much to celebrate in life, whether those celebrations take the form of a wedding or another ritualistic event. Teachers are encouraged to share the other Jafta books with their students to help broaden their understanding of the African tradition.

CRITICAL-THINKING QUESTIONS

1. Would you like to live where Jafta lives? Why?

2. How would you feel if a brother or sister left home?

3. Do you think Jafta would enjoy visiting your home? Why?

4. When was the last time you were so excited about a coming family event that you could not sleep?

5. Would you like to be a guest at Nomsa's wedding?

6. If you were a guest, what do you think would be an appropriate present to bring for the bride and groom?

7. What are some differences between the wedding in the story and the types of weddings we celebrate in this country? What are some similarities?

8. What kinds of things would you like to talk about with Jafta?

RELATED BOOKS AND REFERENCES

Aardema, Verna. *Bringing the Rain to Kapiti Plain*. New York: Dial, 1981.

Bleeker, Sonia. *Zulu of South Africa*. New York: Morrow, 1970.

Darbois, Dominique. *Agossou, Boy of Africa*. New York: Follett, 1962.

Dayrell, Elphinstone. *Why the Sun and the Moon Live in the Sky*. Boston: Houghton Mifflin, 1968.

Feelings, Muriel. *Jambo Means Hello*. New York: Dial, 1974.

Lewin, Hugh. *Jafta*. Minneapolis, Minn.: Carolrhoda, 1983.

_____. *Jafta's Father*. Minneapolis, Minn.: Carolrhoda, 1983.

_____. *Jafta's Mother*. Minneapolis, Minn.: Carolrhoda, 1983.

Why Mosquitoes Buzz in People's Ears (16-mm, ten-minute sound filmstrip). Weston Woods, Conn.: Weston Woods Studios, 1976.

ACTIVITIES

1. Weddings are typically filled with great food and lots of feasting. Although your students may never be able to attend an African wedding, they can enjoy a typical food from Africa. Following is a recipe for *kanya*, a popular sweetmeat in many West African countries.

   Thoroughly mix ½ cup smooth peanut butter and ½ cup superfine sugar in a large bowl. Press any granules of sugar against the side of the bowl with a wooden spoon until they are completely crushed and mixed with the peanut butter. Slowly add ⅔ cup of uncooked Cream of Rice and continue stirring until the mixture is completely and thoroughly blended. Spread the mixture in a loaf pan and press down with your hands until it is evenly spread. Cover the pan with plastic wrap and refrigerate for two to three hours until firm. Cut into small bars with a knife and enjoy!

2. Have students make a list of the customs of the Zulu family surrounding the wedding. Have them make another list of customs surrounding a typical American wedding. Discuss any similarities or differences.

3. Have students attempt to create a menu for Nomsa's wedding using the foods listed in the book. Have students research several cookbooks for recipes for the food items on their menus. They may wish to put together an original "African Wedding Cookbook."

4. Students can make their own version of oxtail soup. Here is a recipe:

    Boil oxtails in a large pot until the meat falls off the bones. This may require simmering for several hours (if oxtails are not available at a local butcher shop, use beef bones). Have students bring in vegetables of their choice. Put the vegetables in the pot along with the oxtails and 3 to 4 quarts of water. Season to taste and simmer for another hour. Have a student recorder keep a list of the ingredients used in the soup and develop it into an original recipe. Send the recipe home or invite parents to come in and enjoy the soup with your class.

    Note: Other ingredients, such as beans, rice, or macaroni, can also be added to the soup.

5. Have students write a story about why they would or would not like to have a goat or a pig for a pet, like Jafta's friends do. Have them compare a goat or pig to any pets they have at home. What are the advantages of owning a goat or pig? What are the disadvantages?

6. Have students write invitations to people from different countries or cultures who live in your community. Have students ask those people to come to the classroom to discuss wedding customs in their countries.

7. Ask students to tape record an interview with their grandparents about their wedding. Next, have them tape an interview with their parents on the same topic. Have students make comparisons between the two. This activity may have to be altered for children with special family considerations. For example, if grandparents are not living or if parents are divorced, students might like to interview an older friend or neighbor.

8. Have students make a time line showing the sequence of events leading up to Nomsa's wedding. This can be written and illustrated on a large roll of butcher paper and hung across one or two walls of the classroom. Talk about the planning that leads up to an event of this type. Next, have students plan for a birthday party or similar event. Have them make a comparable time line to be hung in proximity to Nomsa's wedding time line. Talk about any differences.

9. Have students make mosaics of Sakabula birds. Instruct them to use various kinds of seeds, beans, split peas, rice, macaroni, and spices to create their mosaics. These can be painted with water colors and hung throughout the room.

10. Ask students to suppose that they had been invited to Nomsa's wedding. Have them research the forms of transportation they could use to get to South Africa, how much it would cost, and how long it would take them to get there. Have them locate South Africa on a map and trace the route they would follow for each form of transportation considered. Invite a local travel agent to discuss the advantages of different forms of transportation in terms of pleasure, cost, efficiency, etc.

11. Jafta does not wear shoes. Set up buckets or tubs filled with various substances. Allow students to stand barefoot in the tubs. Assign a partner for each student to record the words the student uses to describe how each substance feels on his or her feet. Use mud, sand, gelatin, oats, cotton, sawdust, leaves, or anything else the students might think of.

12.   Have students read three other Jafta books (also by Hugh Lewin and published by Carolrhoda Books). These include *Jafta, Jafta's Father*, and *Jafta's Mother*. Ask students to write an original story about themselves and pretend that a young Zulu boy or girl would be the reader.

13.   Students may enjoy creating a tabletop model of a Zulu village. Cardboard cutouts of animals can be combined with pipe-cleaner people and toothpick houses to create the village. Blue cellophane can be crinkled and used to represent the river. Have students label the various parts of their village.

14.   Students may enjoy writing a letter to a U.S. embassy in one or more African countries. The addresses of specific embassies can be obtained from the U.S. Department of State (2201 C Street, NW, Washington, D.C. 20520). Students should decide on the type of information they would like to receive from a specific embassy (brochures, agriculture facts, type of government, etc.) before drafting their letters. As information is received, it can be posted on a collective bulletin board and reviewed throughout the year.

15.   Divide the class into two groups. Assign one group the task of writing a prequel to the story; the other group gets the task of writing a sequel to the story. Encourage students to discuss the various types of events and actions they could include in their additions.

Jambo Means Hello
Muriel Feelings
(New York: Dial, 1974)

SUMMARY

This book is an introduction to some basic words in Swahili, a language spoken by approximately forty-five million Africans. Words are followed by the correct pronunciation, a definition, and a descriptive illustration.

SOCIAL STUDIES TOPIC AREAS

Sociology, anthropology, history

CONTENT-RELATED WORDS

Swahili, environment, continental, Kiswahili, proverb, homestead, Muslim, savannah, courteous, prey, hartebeest, fetching, utensils, gourds, xylophone

CURRICULAR PERSPECTIVES

As varied as its terrain, Africa has a plethora of different peoples, tribes, and cultures. Each is distinctive. Together, they combine to form one of the most fascinating continents on earth. Separately, they stand as important markers for the diversity of life in this rich and multifaceted land.

This book provides readers with a brief glimpse into the lives and customs of Swahili people. Using each letter of the English alphabet, the author takes us on a journey through the traditions and heritage of the twelve African countries in which Kiswahili is spoken. The trip is a marvelous one, for it illustrates both the flavor and features of these people in a way that is engaging and full of surprises.

Students are given a rich cultural vision of people and places they may never see in real life yet can still marvel at. Each letter, each celebration, and each greeting illustrated in this book is filled with wonderful customs and traditions that expand our consciousness of this vast continent. Readers are actively engaged in discovering how the Kiswahili of Africa live, play, and work.

An excellent book that can be woven into any aspect of world geography or cultural awareness, this dictionary provides youngsters with insights and journeys into both the differences among peoples and their similarities. A Caldecott Medal Book, the book opens up new vistas and stimulates imaginations about people who, though an ocean away, are as close as the letters of the alphabet.

CRITICAL-THINKING QUESTIONS

1. What would you enjoy most about living in Africa?

2. How is your life similar to that of an African youngster? How is it different?

3. How do you feel about the roles men and women have in African society?

4. What was your favorite Swahili word in the book? Why?

5. How are our schools different from African schools?

6. If you had an African pen pal, what would you like to tell him or her about your life?

7. What would be the most difficult thing about learning Swahili?

8. If you were asked to create an A-to-Z book about your neighborhood or community, what words would you use?

RELATED BOOKS AND REFERENCES

Aardema, Verna. *Bringing the Rain to Kapiti Plain*. New York: Dial, 1981.

Bernheim, Marc, and Evelyne Bernheim. *In Africa*. New York: Atheneum, 1975.

Blanch, Lesley. *Around the World in Eighty Dishes*. New York: Harper, 1955.

Bond, Jean Carey. *A Is for Africa*. New York: Watts, 1969.

Brown, Marcial. *Shadow*. New York: Scribner's, 1982.

Georges, D. V. *Africa*. Chicago: Children's Press, 1986.

Haskins, James. *Count Your Way through Africa Game*. Minneapolis, Minn.: Carolrhoda, 1989.

McKenna, Nancy Durrell. *A Zulu Family*. New York: Lerner, 1986.

Musgrove, Margaret. *Ashanti to Zulu: African Traditions*. New York: Dial, 1976.

Russell, Joan. *Creative Dance in the Primary School*. New York: Praeger, 1968.

Steptoe, John. *Mufaro's Beautiful Daughters*. New York: Lothrop, Lee and Shepard, 1987.

Sutherland, Efua. *The African Way*. New York: Atheneum, 1962.

Williams, Brian, and Brenda Williams. *The Book of Facts and Records*. New York: Derrydale, 1989.

ACTIVITIES

1. Students may enjoy creating their own *gudulia*. Provide each pupil with some modeling clay and some sharp pencils. Ask students to create a clay pot similar to the illustration in the book. Have them use the pencils to trace designs into the sides of their pots. Encourage students to write descriptive paragraphs about the history of their pots or the meanings of the characters on the sides.

2. Have students create their own A-to-Z book about events, landmarks, traditions, and customs within their own neighborhood or community. Students from the same area of the local community may enjoy working together to develop an appropriate alphabet book.

3. Bring in a collection of varied alphabet books (check with your school or public librarian). Ask students to develop a chart listing the similarities between the books as well as the differences. Ask students to explain why alphabet books are so popular.

4. The National Geographic Society has a variety of videos that would offer your students an intriguing look into the richness and vastness of the African continent. Try to obtain one or more of the following: *Africa* (No. 51440), *Journey to the Forgotten River* (No. 51461), *Serengeti Diary* (No. 51388), *African Odyssey* (No. 51336), *Bushmen of the Kalahari* (No. 51027), *African Wildlife* (No. 50509), *Africa's Stolen River* (No. 51373), and *Lions of the African Night* (No. 51331).

5. Many children have never tasted mangos. Check to see whether your local grocery store carries mangos. If not, ask the grocer if he or she can order them. If that is not possible, you can have the students sample some mango preserves or jam. Ask them to compare the taste of mangos to other fruits that are more familiar to them.

6. "Hello" is a familiar greeting in almost every language. Students may wish to do some library research to create a dictionary of the various ways "hello" is said in different languages. They may also be interested in creating a dictionary of the various ways we have of greeting each other in this country (including slang words).

7. Students may enjoy setting up a small garden on the school grounds. Encourage them to plant several different varieties of vegetables and tend them according to directions on the seed packets. After the harvest, have students make a class salad for all to enjoy.

8. Classes in Africa are typically held outdoors. Conduct a day's worth of lessons outside on the school grounds. Afterwards, have students reflect on the differences experienced between outdoor education and indoor education. How would they feel about having all their classes outdoors? What difficulties would they encounter? What modifications in the current program would have to be made?

9. Obtain some simple musical instruments from the school's music teacher or at the local high school. Instruments such as bongo drums, sticks, claves, recorders, or xylophones would all be appropriate. Encourage students to practice with several instruments and develop their own beats, rhythms, or songs to share with the class.

10. Have each student create a diary of some of the things he or she does with a best friend. What kinds of games do they play together? What jobs do they do together? How do they help each other? How do the things they do together compare with the chores Swahili children do together?

11. Peanut soup is a very popular dish in many African countries, partly because Africa is one of the world's largest suppliers of peanuts. Here is a recipe you and your students may enjoy preparing and sharing:

> 2 celery sticks
> 2 carrots
> 2 onions
> 2 potatoes
> 2 tomatoes
> 4 cups of water
> 2 bouillon cubes (any flavor)
> 2 teaspoons salt
> 1 teaspoon pepper

> 1 cup chunky peanut butter
> 1 cup milk
> 2 tablespoons brown sugar
> 6 tablespoons rice

> Cut all the vegetables into small pieces and place in a large saucepan. Add the water, bouillon cubes, salt, and pepper and boil gently for about 20 minutes, stirring occasionally. Blend the peanut butter, milk, and brown sugar together in a mixing bowl and add to the saucepan. Stir in the rice and allow all the ingredients to simmer at low heat for about 30 minutes. Ladle into bowls and enjoy!

12. Have students put together a book of all the games they play outdoors. Their book may include organized sports activities as well as pick-up games. Students may wish to include pictures or illustrations of selected activities. Have them discuss comparisons between their games and African games.

13. Students may enjoy putting together a book of elephant facts. Have them research several books and resources in the school or public library on elephants and their habits. The information can be collected into a book constructed in the shape of an elephant (two pieces of cardboard and several sheets of paper, all cut into large elephant shapes and bound together). Here are some facts to get students started:

> A full-grown male elephant has nearly one ton of skin covering his body.

> Elephants often communicate by stomach rumbles.

> Elephants must consume nineteen to twenty-four gallons of water every day.

> You can tell where an elephant comes from by the size of its ears: large-eared elephants come from Africa, small-eared elephants from India.

14. Ask students to create a list of the various ways in which they show respect to older people (including their parents). What are some customs that everyone follows? What are some optional customs? Why is it important to demonstrate respect for older people?

15. Many hobby stores have broom straw for sale. Obtain some straw and a roll of thin wire. Have students cut the broom straw into lengths of about two feet each. Each student should then select a quantity of straws and bind them together at one end, using the wire, to create hand brooms. Provide students with opportunities to sweep the floor using their brooms, as in the illustration in the book.

Maps and Globes
Jack Knowlton
(New York: Crowell, 1985)

SUMMARY

Maps have been around since the dawn of recorded history. This Reading Rainbow selection explores the history of maps and globes, their various uses, and their importance to people around the world.

SOCIAL STUDIES TOPIC AREAS

Geography, history, sociology, anthropology

CONTENT-RELATED WORDS

Babylonian, civilization, Magellan, sphere, hemisphere, longitude, latitude, elevation, physical and political maps

CURRICULAR PERSPECTIVES

The shape of the earth, the location of distant lands, contours, depths, heights, and other geographical features of our world have long been a fascination for humans. Ever since humans traveled from one place to another and back again, maps have become part of our heritage. They have ranged from the most primitive ones scratched on clay tablets, to unusual ones woven by Pacific Islanders from twigs and sticks, to sophisticated globes. Yet, whatever format a map takes, it provides people with a record of physical features in their own neighborhoods as well as around the corner, down the street, or in some far-distant land.

Maps are also a fascination for youngsters. This book provides students with some eye-opening facts about the world around them and how humans have charted that world for thousands of years. Although the earliest maps were quite primitive, they nevertheless served as important references for anyone wishing to travel. As we explored more and more of our planet, our map-making skills became more sophisticated. Explorers and discoverers helped to make map-making both a skill and an art, because what they learned about our world had to be translated into codes, symbols, and representations that could be understood by all.

This book is an excellent introduction to the nature of maps and how they have become significant information sources for all humans. The wide variety of information that can be obtained from maps is explained and described in language that children can easily understand. The author is careful to use vocabulary easily understood by most children, but does not talk down to them. Important points are highlighted and emphasized without confusion.

This book is a welcome introduction to maps and globes and complements any social studies curriculum. Teachers will find this book a perfect starting point for presenting mapping skills to their students in a nonthreatening format. Concepts are carefully spelled out and plenty of examples are given throughout the text. The simple illustrations enhance the textual discussions.

CRITICAL-THINKING QUESTIONS

1. What might be some disadvantages of using maps made from sand, clay, or sticks and shells?

2. What are some of the most important parts of a map?

3. Why did people believe the world to be flat?

4. Besides maps, what other ways do we have of locating distant places?

5. Why are flat maps less accurate than globes?

6. What are some symbols that should be included on all maps?

7. Why is it important for people to learn how to use maps?

8. As civilization expanded, why was there a need for better maps?

RELATED BOOKS AND REFERENCES

Atlas of the World. 6th ed. Washington, D.C.: National Geographic Society, 1990.

Basic Map Skills (filmstrip). Boulder, Colo.: Learning Tree Filmstrips, 1977.

Cartwright, Sally. *What's in a Map?* New York: Coward, McCann & Geoghegan, 1976.

Colby, Charles-Carlyle. *Successful Teaching with Maps—World and Continental Geography.* Washington, D.C.: Geographical Research Institute, 1961.

Estep, Irene. *Good Times with Maps.* Chicago: Melmont, 1962.

Fredericks, Anthony D. *The Whole Earth Geography Book.* Glenview, Ill.: Scott, Foresman, 1990.

Music and You. New York: Macmillan, 1988 (pp. 22-23 contain the song, "Little Blue Top").

Stanek, Muriel. *How We Use Maps and Globes.* Chicago: Benefic, 1968.

ACTIVITIES

1. Provide students with opportunities to create personal and individual maps. Some students may wish to create simple maps of their bedrooms at home. Others may want to create maps of their homes or immediate neighborhood or community. Some students may want to attempt to create specialized maps of their town, such as a map of all the shopping areas, a map of all the entertainment areas (playgrounds, theaters, etc.), or a map of all the community helpers (police, fire station, etc.).

2. Provide students with cookie sheets and some wet sand. Direct students to spread the wet sand on the cookie sheet and trace a route from the school to their house. Discuss with them the difficulties these types of maps had for early people. How might those problems be solved?

3. Groups of students may enjoy developing a scale model of the school. Provide them with balsa wood, white glue, and sheets of construction paper. Ask them to determine an appropriate scale for their model (such as 1 inch = 10 feet) and to design and build a corresponding model. (Note: Students should not cut the wood. This should be done by the teacher using an X-Acto™ knife or coping saw.)

4. Have students bring in several examples of road maps. Discuss with them the similarities and/or differences among all the maps. Which map is easiest to use? Why? Which map is most difficult to use? Why? Which map would students want to use to get from their town to a place 500 miles away? 1,500 miles away?

5. Have students create their own globes. Provide them with round balloons, newspapers torn into strips, some liquid starch, and water. Have students blow up their balloons, dip strips of newspaper into the starch, and wrap them around the balloons (two to three layers should be used). When the balloons are completely covered, allow them to dry for a day or two. When completely dry, each balloon can be painted with tempera paints.

6. If possible, invite a sailor or boating enthusiast into your classroom to explain the use of sea charts. Ask the individual to bring in several charts of a port, channel, or ocean area. Encourage students to investigate the differences between those charts and land maps. Why are depths indicated on the charts?

7. Obtain several compasses and take students on a walking tour of the school grounds. Encourage students to plot locations of various sites and their positions. Have the class create a map of the school grounds.

8. Have students (with their parents) each visit one or two travel agencies. Ask them to obtain brochures and other descriptive literature about foreign countries and other vacation spots. Have students bring this material into class and organize it into several categories, such as places northeast of the school, places more than 500 miles from the school, places a ship cannot travel to, etc. Students may wish to make several posters or collages about their findings.

9. Students may want to try creating altitude maps of their local area. Show them the examples of altitude maps in the book and encourage them to create similar maps on their own. You may wish to obtain geological maps from a local college (check with the geography department) to help students create their own.

10. Many communities have local and regional historical societies. Contact one of these organizations and ask if they have speakers who can bring some historical maps into your classroom as part of a presentation.

11. Students may want to create a play or skit about some of the famous explorers and their use of maps. Magellan, Balboa, de Gama, and Columbus could all be role played by students, each of whom would describe their trials and tribulations with the maps of their day.

12. Create a treasure hunt (on school grounds) for students, using map directions to locate the various items. Directions could be written in scale (such as 1 inch = 5 feet) and use cardinal directions ("Your first spot, mates, is seven inches to the north of the jungle gym").

13. Have students bring in weather maps from the local newspaper. Examine the symbols used and their various meanings. Later, students may wish to create their own weather maps based on the past week's weather patterns. Encourage them to create new weather symbols (for example, a symbol for high humidity).

14. Have students create a large poster devoted exclusively to map legends. Have them collect several different examples of legends from a variety of maps and paste them or redraw them on the poster. Explanations should be provided for each of the legends or groups of legends.

15. Students may want to create body maps. Have a student lie down on a large sheet of butcher paper or newsprint. Have other students trace his or her outline on the paper. Afterwards, have each student cut out his or her individual outline and fill in the "map" with the correct body parts and features. These maps can then be posted around the classroom.

16. An excellent video on maps and their symbols is *From Here to There* (No. 51080) (Washington, D.C.: National Geographic Society, 1981). This sixteen-minute color film is a wonderful introduction to the uses and importance of maps.

17. Provide students with opportunities to create their own three-dimensional maps of the local community or geographical area. Following is a recipe for edible spreadable clay which can be used to construct various landforms and then eaten when the activity is completed:

> Mix two parts peanut butter with one part honey. Add three parts dry milk (a little at a time) until a stiff mixture forms. The mixture should be thoroughly kneaded with hands. Refrigerate overnight and use the next day.

Mufaro's Beautiful Daughters
John Steptoe
(New York: Lothrop, Lee and Shepard, 1987)

SUMMARY

Mufaro lived in a small village in Africa with his two beautiful daughters, Nyasha and Manyara. Nyasha was kind and considerate, while Manyara was selfish and spoiled. When the king announced that he was looking for the most beautiful woman in the land to be his wife, Manyara was determined to reach the city before her sister. The ending is a lesson for us all, as kindness prevails over greed.

SOCIAL STUDIES TOPIC AREAS

Anthropology, political science, geography

CONTENT-RELATED WORDS

temper, bountiful, worthy, silhouetted, acknowledges, destination, transfixed, piercing, proclaimed

CURRICULAR PERSPECTIVES

"Pride goeth before a fall." This familiar maxim has survived centuries of storytellers from earliest times to the present. It is part of many cultures and the oral history of many lands. Stories and folktales have been created from it and have endured through hundreds of years as part of the literature and heritage of peoples around the world. From Aesop to modern novelists, the story of a character brought down by his or her own self-aggrandizement is a most popular theme.

This story concerns the different personalities of two daughters, one thoughtful and caring, the other self-indulgent and brash. While the tale concerns the search for an appropriate wife for the king, the author weaves a beautifully told moral into all threads of the story: Can desire win out over patience? Will deceit triumph over affection? Will evil predominate over good? While the answers to these questions are certain, the author has provided the reader with a distinctive and illustrative look into a host of answers.

Through this story children become aware not only of the reasons for sharing and caring, but also of some of the rich traditions of African peoples. The flora and fauna of Africa are marvelously depicted in the colorful and insightful illustrations (the book is a Caldecott Honor Book).

155

Children also become sensitized to the vast tapestry of African cultures and customs that created this magnificent folktale.

This book can be effectively used as part of a world cultures unit, an exploration of the oral traditions of many lands, the unique heritage of African people, and the wonder of storytelling. Teachers will discover that this book is more than a moral tale—it is a celebration of tradition and history through the years and across countries.

CRITICAL-THINKING QUESTIONS

1. Do you know any other stories that are similar in plot and theme? What are they and how are they like this story?

2. How was Manyara deceptive? Do you think Mufaro would have approved of her behavior? Why?

3. Why was Nyasha not afraid of the snake, Nyoka, the first time she saw him?

4. Would you like to visit Mufaro's Africa? Why?

5. Which daughter would you like to have for a friend?

6. How did the illustrations add to the story?

7. What was your favorite part of the story? Which part did you like least?

8. What do you think the king meant when he said that Nyasha was "the most worthy and most beautiful daughter in the land"?

9. Could this story take place in today's world? Why?

10. In what ways is the daily life in the village in this story different from yours? In what ways is it alike?

RELATED BOOKS AND REFERENCES

Aardema, Verna. *Bringing the Rain to Kapiti Plain*. New York: Dial, 1981.

Ashanti Market Women (fifty-two-minute video). New York: Filmmakers Library, 1982.

Atlas of the World. 6th ed. Washington, D.C.: National Geographic Society, 1990.

Bernheim, Marc, and Evelyne Bernheim. *In Africa*. New York: Atheneum, 1975.

Coen, Rena Neumann. *The Black Man in Art*. Minneapolis, Minn.: Lerner, 1970.

Georges, D. V. *Africa*. Chicago: Children's Press, 1986.

Gray, Nigel. *A Country Far Away*. New York: Orchard, 1989.

The Heritage of Africa (map). Washington, D.C.: National Geographic Society, 1971.

Holy, Ladislav. *The Art of Africa: Masks and Figures from East and South Africa*. London: Paul Hamlyn, 1967.

Maren, M. *The Land and People of Kenya*. New York: Lippincott, 1989.

Musgrove, Margaret. *Ashanti to Zulu: African Traditions*. New York: Dial, 1976.

Tracey, Hugh. *The Music of Africa Series: Uganda 1* (LP recording). Washington, D.C.: Traditional Music Documentation Project, 1972.

ACTIVITIES

1. Read the introductory page of the story to the students, explaining the meanings of the names of the characters in the story. Allow students to use a name dictionary and look up the meaning of their own names. Have students write their names on small pieces of poster board, decorate each with illustrations of things they enjoy doing, and write the meanings of their names underneath. Hang these throughout the classroom.

2. Have students study several maps of Africa and create an outline of the continent on the classroom floor, using colored tape. Let students stand around the edges of the outline, holding hands if necessary, to "become" the shape of Africa. Have students sit down in place and sing "Kumbaya," a traditional African folksong (see Nancy Cassidy and John Cassidy's *Book of Kidsongs* [Palo Alto, Calif.: Klutz, 1986]).

3. Have students create puppets of the story characters by decorating old socks with markers, colored paper, bits of yarn, or other scraps. Divide the class into small groups and assign one scene from the story to each group. Let each group paint a background for its scene on butcher paper or an old bed sheet. Hang the background on a bulletin board or use a table turned on its side for the puppet theater. For puppet ideas, consult *Children's Crafts* (San Francisco, Calif.: Lane, 1976).

4. Provide students with old white bed sheets and fabric scraps. Using the book as a guide, have students create costumes like the ones worn by the characters in the story. Students can then dramatize their favorite parts of the story.

5. Use the book *Jambo Means Hello* by Muriel Feelings (New York: Dial, 1974) to introduce one or two new Swahili words each day. Write a continuing class story about life in Africa, incorporating the new words each day.

6. Listen to the recording *Musical Instruments 3: Drums, The Music of Africa Series*, by Hugh Tracey (Washington, D.C.: Traditional Music Documentation Project, 1972). Discuss the different rhythms produced and the types of drums used. Have students construct African drums by stretching pieces of vinyl or rubber across the tops of empty coffee cans which have both ends removed. Lace the edges of the vinyl together with shoestrings or other string. Let students develop a code and send messages back and forth to each other.

7. Read the poem "African Dance" by Langston Hughes aloud to the class. Read it again and let students keep a steady beat with the rhythm of the poem by beating homemade drums, clapping hands, or using other rhythm instruments.

8. Have an African foods celebration. Bring in a variety of foods native to Africa: honey, dates, coffee, cloves (try clove gum), yams, sunflower seeds, peanuts, grapes, and olives. Have students each write a paragraph describing their reactions to the foods. Have students pick their favorite foods.

9. Hang a large world map on one wall of the room. Let each student plot a travel route to Africa by making a cardboard ship and marking the trip (on the map) with yarn. Attach the ships so that they can travel freely along the string from the United States to Africa. Students should write stories describing their feelings as they begin their trips to Africa, including what they expect to see or do along the way.

10. Working in groups, have students construct models of one of the houses found in Africa: thatched-roof huts, apartment houses, houses on stilts, adobe houses, or nomadic tents. Refer to *In Africa* by Marc and Evelyne Bernheim (New York: Atheneum, 1975) for ideas.

11. Plant sunflower seeds in empty margarine tubs. Keep the lids on until the seeds have sprouted. Then remove the lids and place the tubs in a sunny window. Have students generate a list of all the products that are made from sunflowers. Plant the seedlings on the school grounds. Students can tend the plants until they are ready to be harvested.

12. Read the poem "The Lion" by Jack Prelutsky (found in *Random House Book of Poetry for Children* [New York: Random House, 1983]). Let each child choose one of the animals native to Africa and write a poem about it. Have students draw their animals on construction paper and attach their poems to the bodies of the animals.

13. Encourage students to write to African pen pals through the Afro-Asian Center (P.O. Box 337, Saugerties, NY 12477; [914] 246-7828).

14. Use the book *The Dance of Africa: An Introduction* by Haris Petie (New York: Prentice-Hall, 1972) to teach students a traditional African dance. *The Dance, Art and Ritual of Africa* by Michel Huet (New York: Pantheon, 1978) will provide pictures to refer to so that students can construct dance costumes.

15. Give students an opportunity to sing in an African language by using *Call and Response Rhythmic Group Singing*, a recording by Ella Jenkins (New York: Folkways Records, 1957). This record is designed so that students repeat the words in rhythm and thus experience the language and music of Africa firsthand.

16. Teach students to give the African hand signals for the numbers one through nine as shown in *Africa Counts* by Claudia Zaslavsky (Boston: Prindle, Weber and Schmidt, 1973). Let students practice signing simple addition and subtraction problems to each other.

17. Select and celebrate some holidays from around the world. Use *The Book of Holidays around the World* by Alice van Straalen (New York: Dutton, 1986) or *The Whole Earth Holiday Book* by Linda Polon and Aileen Cantwell (Glenview, Ill.: Scott, Foresman, 1983) as a resource for this activity. Let students make costumes and foods for each celebration.

18. Read the book *Why Mosquitoes Buzz in People's Ears* by Verna Aardema (New York: Dial, 1975). Explain to students that this is an African folktale, as is *Mufaro's Beautiful Daughters*. Ask students to compare the two stories and work with a partner to generate a list of similarities and differences between the two stories.

19. Have students write a sequel to the story, entitled "How Manyara Learned Kindness."

My Sister Says
Betty Baker
(New York: Macmillan, 1984)

SUMMARY

Two sisters take a walk to the ship docks to wait for the return of their father. They discuss the ships in the water and the places they travel to and imagine what gifts their father will bring back for them from the faraway lands.

SOCIAL STUDIES TOPIC AREAS

Geography, history, anthropology, political science

CONTENT-RELATED WORDS

tomahawk, tom-tom

CURRICULAR PERSPECTIVES

Distant lands. Distant cities. Distant ports. Humans have always been fascinated with the adventures and possibilities of

faraway places. What lies over the horizon or at the other end of the ocean is a question sailors and adventurers have been asking for centuries. Even in the space era we still ask that same question as we seek out new planets, stars, and galaxies beyond our own world.

This story is about the discussions two sisters have as they wait for their father's return from a distant place. It is a tale of anticipation as much as a story about the wonders that lie beyond the horizon. It is also a story about families and the emotions shared—emotions that are more significant and certainly more important than any gold or riches brought back from a long journey.

This story not only helps children appreciate the vastness and mystery of lands and countries beyond the sea, but also emphasizes the relationships that are a necessary part of everyday life. Traveling to a far-off country is exciting and magical, but being part of a family certainly holds more significance in one's everyday life. This story is two stories in one. It is about travel and it is about relationships. Although they may appear to be separate entities, the author has woven them together in an intriguing tale.

This book can be slotted into many places within the social studies curriculum. It underscores the value of the family unit, it illustrates the wonder of travel, it embraces the differences among individuals, and it promotes discussion on the differences and similarities we all share. Teachers will find this book a powerful adjunct to many parts of their curriculum.

CRITICAL-THINKING QUESTIONS

1. Would you like to have a dragon for a pet? Why?

2. How do you think the father feels about being away from his family for long periods of time? Would you feel the same way? Why?

3. Would you like to travel to California or India or China by boat? Why?

4. Why do you think the sisters would enjoy the dragon?

5. What part of a sailor's life would you enjoy most? What part would you enjoy least?

6. If you have a brother or sister, what do you enjoy talking about together? If you do not, what would you want to share with a brother or sister?

7. Would your friends enjoy this story? Why?

RELATED BOOKS AND REFERENCES

Auster, Benjamin. *I Like It When*. Milwaukee, Wis.: Raintree, 1990.

Burt, Denise. *Our Family Vacation*. Milwaukee, Wis.: G. Stevens, 1985.

Carlson, Nancy. *Louanne Pig in the Perfect Family*. Minneapolis, Minn.: Carolrhoda, 1985.

Domanska, Janina. *A Scythe, a Rooster, and a Cat*. New York: Greenwillow, 1981.

Henkes, Kevin. *Grandpa and Bo*. New York: Greenwillow, 1986.

Oxenburg, Helen. *Family*. New York: Wanderer, 1981.

Rius, Maria. *Grandparents*. New York: Barron's, 1987.

Spier, Peter. *People*. New York: Doubleday, 1980.

Tigwell, Tony. *A Family in India*. Minneapolis, Minn.: Lerner, 1985.

ACTIVITIES

1. Set up a Big Brother or Big Sister program with students in a class younger than yours. The students in your classroom can act as older friends, tutors, or guides for the younger students. Time can be set aside each week for the two classes to get together and share.

2. Discuss the different kinds of relations there are in families. Introduce cousins, aunts, grandparents, and other types of relatives to your students. Create a large "tree" on a bulletin board to illustrate how family members are related to each other.

3. Have students interview their parents or guardians on the kinds of relationships they had with their siblings. Students can create individual journals of those memories and include family photographs for illustrative purposes.

4. Bring in an old throw rug (or obtain one at a yard or garage sale). Turn it into a "magic carpet" and invite students to sit on it and pretend they are flying over several distant countries. Have students make journal entries on the places they visited and the sights they saw during their journeys.

5. Obtain an old clothing catalog (the town or college librarian may be able to help). If one is not available, have students create their own, using illustrations from the book. Ask students to price some of the items in their catalog and discuss the differences between clothing of long ago and clothing of today. Students may want to bring in a current clothing catalog (such as Sears, Penney's, or L.L. Bean) and compare and contrast clothing of years gone by with current styles and prices.

6. Have students create a transportation bulletin board. Have them cut out pictures from old magazines that depict transportation of 100 years ago. These pictures can be assembled into a collage and posted on the bulletin board. Have students do the same with pictures of modern-day transportation. Discuss any similarities and/or differences.

7. Have students create a class scrapbook entitled "My Family Says." Students can bring in photographs of family members and affix them in the scrapbook. A caption should be included with each photo using a saying or quotation from the appropriate family member. These should be shared on a regular basis.

8. Invite a local antique dealer to your classroom. Ask him or her to bring in items related to the objects mentioned in the book.

9. Pair off students and have each pair make up a mock dialogue between siblings. Have each pair argue a problem or situation in front of the whole class. Encourage the class to arrive at a mutually agreeable solution for each discussion.

10. Students may wish to construct tom-toms from empty oatmeal boxes. Have students paint their drums with tempera paint. Groups of students may then want to create some war dances to share with the entire class.

11. Explain to students that rice is the most important crop in China (in fact, more than one-third of the people in the world use rice as a staple food). Students may enjoy making a typical Chinese breakfast known as *congee*.

    Put one cup of rice (not instant) and eight cups of water in a pot and put on the top loosely. Bring the water to a boil, turn the heat to low, and cover the pan completely with the lid. Cook for about 40 minutes, until the rice has absorbed all the liquid and become very soft. Serve plain or with little bits of cooked chicken or vegetables sprinkled on top.

12. Rice cakes can be purchased at most larger grocery stores. Purchase some and have your students eat them. Discuss how they would feel if a major portion of their daily diet consisted of these cakes.

13. Explain to the class that India has three major seasons: cold, hot, and rainy. Provide the class with an oversize map of India and ask them to color in sections of that country according to the predominant weather conditions.

14. Students may enjoy creating "honor feathers" like those mentioned in the book. Obtain some feathers from a local farm or nearby hobby store and distribute them to the class. Students' honor feathers can be designed to stand for "Good Work," "Most Improved," "Best Behavior," and/or "Superior Homework."

15. Have students create a fantasy list of gifts they would like to receive from distant places. Have each student make a list of gifts from California, India, and China that they would enjoy receiving. Which gift would be most meaningful?

16. Have the students design and create an oversize "Welcome Home" card for the father in the story. Discuss an appropriate cover illustration and the caption for the inside of the card.

17. Students may enjoy playing a variation of "Simon Says" entitled "My Sister Says."

18. Here is a recipe for oriental fried rice which your students will enjoy:

> 1 small onion, chopped
> 2 tablespoons chopped green pepper
> 2 tablespoons vegetable oil
> 2 cups cooked rice
> 1 can water chestnuts, thinly sliced
> 1 can mushroom stems and pieces
> 2 tablespoons soy sauce
> 3 eggs, beaten

    Cook and stir green pepper and onion in oil in a skillet for about 3 minutes. Stir in rice, water chestnuts, mushrooms, and soy sauce. Cook over low heat, stirring frequently, for about 5 to 7 minutes. Stir in eggs. Cook and stir 4 to 5 minutes longer. Makes 4 to 5 servings.

    After the rice is made, hand out some chopsticks and demonstrate how to use them. Take one stick between the thumb and first finger. Trap the base of the other in the pouch of the thumb and rest the tip against the third finger. Only the upper chopstick is moved. Allow students to experiment eating the rice with chopsticks.

19. The National Geographic Society produces a three-part series of sound filmstrips on the People's Republic of China (No. 04638, 1983). The three parts include *Introducing China Today, Living and Working in China*, and *Chinese Arts and Culture*. Obtain a copy of this series and share it with your students.

20. Students may be interested in learning about the variety of periodicals and books available about China or written in Chinese. Have them write for a catalog to: U.S. Distributor, China Books and Periodicals, 2929 24th Street, San Francisco, CA 94110.

Appendix A
An Annotated Bibliography of Children's Literature

The number of books available in social studies is limitless. My own investigations led me to hundreds of literature possibilities, many of which could easily be integrated into all aspects of the social studies curriculum. Obviously, no book this size is able to do justice to the scores of literature selections you can choose for your program. Thus, I have tried to provide a variety of possibilities: some old favorites, some classics, and some new and fascinating books for every part of your social studies program. In short, there is something for everyone.

This appendix contains two annotated bibliographies. The first is a collection of books organized according to the seven basic topics of all social studies curricula (self, family, community, city, state, nation, world). The second bibliography is a selection of books arranged according to the six major disciplines of social studies (geography, anthropology, sociology, political science, economics, history). Any one book may, of course, encompass more than one topic as well as more than one discipline. There are also many more books in your school library or community library than appear in these lists. In other words, the organization of books within each of the two bibliographies is somewhat arbitrary and is certainly arguable. Nevertheless, it is hoped that these selections offer a plethora of potential literature selections for *all* areas of your social studies curriculum, no matter what its scope, sequence, or instructional emphasis.

The Topics of Social Studies

SELF

Baehr, Patricia. **School Isn't Fair**. New York: Four Winds, 1989.
  A four-year-old's self-concept and esteem are low until he is recognized for a particularly useful skill.

Hewett, Joan. **Hector Lives in the United States Now: The Story of a Mexican-American Child**. New York: Lippincott, 1990.
  As a recent immigrant to Los Angeles, Hector experiences many things in his new country. What he learns and how he deals with life in the United States is beautifully told.

Kellogg, Stephen. **Won't Somebody Play with Me?** New York: Dial, 1972.
  It is Kim's birthday, but none of her friends can play with her. She gets angry, but learns how to deal with it.

Levin, Ellen. **I Hate English!** New York: Scholastic, 1989.
  A caring teacher helps a young girl from Hong Kong learn to speak English.

Lionni, Leo. **It's Mine**. New York: Knopf, 1986.

Three frogs, who continually argue and disagree, eventually learn how to resolve their differences.

Mendez, Phil. **The Black Snowman**. New York: Scholastic, 1989.

A black snowman and a magic cloth help a young boy appreciate his ethnicity and own self-worth.

Waber, Bernard. **Ira Sleeps Over**. New York: Houghton Mifflin, 1972.

Young Ira has a tough decision to make when he goes to sleep over at his friend's house for the first time.

Waddell, Martin. **Once There Were Giants**. New York: Delacorte, 1989.

Full of illustrations, this book depicts the growth of a girl from infancy through adolescence to adulthood.

Wilhelm, Hans. **Let's Be Friends Again**. New York: Crown, 1986.

A big brother gets very angry at his little sister, but learns the importance of forgiving.

FAMILIES

Bennett, Olivia. **A Family in Brazil**. New York: Lerner, 1986.

The daily life of a Brazilian family is wonderfully told through colorful photographs. Other books in this series include *A Zulu Family, A Family in Morocco, A Family in Chile, A Family in Singapore*, and *A Family in Ireland*.

Browne, Anthony. **Piggybook**. New York: Knopf, 1986.

Mom takes on all the household responsibilities until one day she decides to leave. Things are different after that.

Flournoy, Valerie. **The Patchwork Quilt**. New York: Dial, 1985.

Family members are brought together as they involve themselves in the construction of a patchwork quilt.

Haseley, David. **Kite Flyer**. New York: Four Winds, 1986.

A story about the love between a father and his son, the importance of kite flying, and a longing to see the world.

Johnson, Angela. **Tell Me a Story, Mama**. New York: Orchard, 1989.

A young girl and her mother share stories about the mother's childhood.

Le Tord, Bijou. **Joseph and Nellie**. New York: Bradbury, 1986.

A fishing family and the daily responsibilities of family members are dramatized in this tale.

Nelson, Vaunda M. **Always Gramma**. New York: Putnam, 1988.

When a grandmother gets old and must be sent off to a nursing home, her granddaughter remembers all their special times together.

Pomerantz, Charlotte. **The Chalk Doll**. New York: Lippincott, 1989.
When her daughter is sick, a mother shares stories of childhood in Jamaica.

Ray, Deborah K. **My Daddy Was a Soldier: A World War II Story**. New York: Holiday House, 1990.
While their husband and father is off to war, a wife and daughter must work to keep the family together during some trying times.

Tsutsui, Yoriko. **Anna in Charge**. New York: Viking, 1989.
This story profiles a young Japanese girl and how she must take care of her younger sister.

COMMUNITIES

DeArmond, Dale (adapter). **The Seal Oil Lamp**. New York: Sierra Club/Little, Brown, 1988.
An adaptation of an Eskimo folktale about a blind boy left to die in the wilderness. Filled with wonderful black-and-white woodcuts.

Grifalconi, Ann. **The Village of Round and Square Houses**. New York: Little, Brown, 1986.
In the village of Tos in the Cameroons, the women and children live in round houses and the men live in square houses.

McCurdy, Michael. **Hannah's Farm: The Seasons on an Early American Homestead**. New York: Holiday House, 1988.
Rural life and the changing of the seasons dominate this tale of a farm family in the 1800s.

Rice, Melanie, and Chris Rice. **All about Things People Do**. New York: Doubleday, 1989.
This book provides a fascinating look into the occupations and jobs that keep a community running.

Schotter, Roni. **Efan the Great**. New York: Lothrop, 1986.
The story of how a ten-year-old boy gives a special gift to his New York community one Christmas season.

Sewell, Marcia. **The House on Maple Street**. New York: Morrow, 1987.
Number 107 Maple Street is a special place because of all the people who have passed by or lived there over the course of several years.

Shelby, Anne. **We Keep a Store**. New York: Orchard, 1990.
Describes how a young black girl and her family operate a country store.

Waters, Kate, and Madeline Lovenz-Low. **Lion Dancer: Ernie Wan's Chinese New Year**. New York: Scholastic, 1989.
Describes the preparation a Chinese-American boy undertakes for the annual Chinese New Year parade.

CITIES

Climo, Shirley. **City! San Francisco**. New York: Macmillan, 1990.
  A wonderful introduction to a city many adults feel is the most intriguing of any in the United States.

Coats, Laura J. **Mr. Jordan in the Park**. New York: Macmillan, 1989.
  The story of a man, his activities in an urban park, and the passage of time.

Craft, Ruth. **The Day of the Rainbow**. New York: Viking, 1989.
  A big city, a hot summer day, sounds and smells, and lots of people are all combined in this story of urban life on one particular day.

Kopper, Lisa. **Jafta: The Town**. Minneapolis, Minn.: Carolrhoda, 1983.
  Jafta, a South African boy, travels with his mother to the busy, bustling city where his father works.

Smucker, Anna E. **No Star Nights**. New York: Knopf, 1989.
  A child looks back at how life was in a small mill town.

Spier, Peter. **The Legend of New Amsterdam**. Garden City, N.Y.: Doubleday, 1979.
  Bright illustrations enhance this description and history of the founding of New York City. A delightful introduction to the evolution of cities.

STATES AND REGIONS

Aylesworth, Thomas G., and Virginia L. Aylesworth. **Western Great Lakes**. New York: Chelsea House, 1987.
  A wonderful and intriguing look at the people, places, and facts about Illinois, Iowa, Minnesota, and Wisconsin. Part of a series of seventeen books on various regions of the United States.

Cooney, Barbara. **Island Boy**. New York: Viking, 1988.
  Several generations of the Tibbetts family are traced in this eloquent portrayal of New England culture and history.

Glubok, Shirley. **The Art of the Old West**. New York: Macmillan, 1971.
  A wonderful collection of western art, with biographical sketches of the artists and historical conditions surrounding each painting. A definite must for the classroom.

Grant, Matthew. **Lewis and Clark: Western Trailblazers**. Mankato, Minn.: Creative Education, 1974.
  This wonderfully illustrated text describes the travels of Lewis and Clark as they explored a great uncharted region of our country.

Little, Lessie Jones. **Children of Long Ago**. New York: Philomel, 1988.
  A collection of poems that describe growing up in the rural South.

Monjo, N. **The Drinking Gourd**. New York: Harper & Row, 1970.
 The story of, and the adventures associated with, the Underground Railroad.

Precek, Katherine. **Penny in the Road**. New York: Macmillan, 1989.
 A superb book comparing Pennsylvania life in 1913 with that in 1793.

Rice, James. **Texas Alphabet**. Gretna, La.: Pelican, 1988.
 The author selects a key word for each letter of the alphabet covering the history and geography of Texas.

Sandin, Joan. **The Long Way Westward**. New York: Harper, 1989.
 Describes the journey of Carl Erik and his family from New York City to relatives in Minnesota.

Siebert, Diane. **Heartland**. New York: Crowell, 1989.
 An extended poem that paints a beautiful picture of life in the American Midwest.

Thompson, Kathleen. **Arkansas**. Milwaukee, Wis.: Raintree, 1988.
 Everything from history, farming, education, historical events, places to visit, maps, and other valuable data is included in this book (part of the Portrait of America series on U.S. states).

Turner, Ann. **Grasshopper Summer**. New York: Macmillan, 1989.
 The trials, tribulations, misery, and discoveries made by a young boy as he travels from Kentucky to the Dakota Territory.

NATION

Asch, Frank, and Vladimir Vagin. **Here Comes the Cat**. New York: Scholastic, 1989.
 Two author/illustrators, one American and one Soviet, collaborated on this tale of a group of mice who anticipate the arrival of a cat.

Glubock, Shirley. **The Art of the North American Indians**. New York: Harper & Row (varying
 dates).
 Children sometimes have a limited view of the arts and crafts of Native Americans. This book provides a panorama of artifacts, masks, clothing, pottery, and other artistic items created by Native Americans.

Gray, Nigel. **A Country Far Away**. New York: Orchard, 1989.
 A city boy from the west and a rural boy from Africa are compared and contrasted. Marvelous illustrations.

Harvey, Brett. **Cassie's Journey: Going West in the 1860s**. New York: Holiday House, 1988.
 Heading for California in a covered wagon, Cassie tells of the sights and adventures encountered during a memorable journey.

Jacobs, William Jay. **Ellis Island: A New Hope in a New Land**. New York: Scribner's, 1990.
    A thorough and enlightening history of the entry point for many Americans from early days to its present status as a historical museum.

Purviance, Susan, and Marcia O'Shell. **Alphabet Annie Announces an All-American Album**. Boston: Houghton Mifflin, 1988.
    An alphabet book of alliterative sentences about U.S. cities and descriptive traits of each city.

Williams, Vera, and Jennifer Williams. **Stringbean's Trip to the Shining Sea**. New York: Scholastic, 1988.
    Stringbean Coe and his brother take a trip from Kansas to the Pacific Ocean. Their travel story is told through postcards and photographs.

WORLD

Baer, Edith. **This Is the Way We Go to School: A Book about Children around the World**. New York: Scholastic, 1990.
    Readers have an opportunity to see how children their own ages from many different countries start their school days.

Delacre, Lulu. **Arroz con Leche**. New York: Scholastic, 1989.
    A fascinating book, in both English and Spanish, of the songs and rhythms of Mexico, Puerto Rico, and Argentina.

Demi. **Dragon Kites and Dragonflies: A Collection of Chinese Nursery Rhymes**. San Diego, Calif.: Harcourt, 1986.
    Chinese rhymes and Chinese illustrations highlight this interesting look into the traditions of China.

Elkin, Judith. **A Family in Japan**. New York: Lerner, 1987.
    Bright, colorful photographs depict the life of a twelve-year-old Japanese boy and his family. Part of the Families the World Over series.

Kandoian, Ellen. **Is Anybody Up?** New York: Putnam, 1989.
    The early morning experiences of one girl and several other persons who occupy the same time zone from Baffin Bay to Antarctica.

Mangurian, David. **Children of the Incas**. New York: Macmillan, 1979.
    A series of photographs and simple text describe a boy growing up in Peru.

Morris, Ann. **Bread, Bread, Bread**. New York: Lothrop, 1989.
    Lots of colorful photographs show how people from different parts of the world make, eat, and share bread.

Raynor, Dorka. **My Friends Live in Many Places**. Chicago: Whitman, 1980.
    Different nationalities of children from around the world are wonderfully portrayed in this collection of black-and-white photographs.

Rutland, Jonathan. **Take a Trip to Spain**. New York: Watts, 1980.
A variety of color photographs illustrate the people and culture of Spain.

Ryan, P. **Explorers and Mapmakers**. New York: Lodestar, 1990.
A vivid description of how various explorers discovered and charted the world from early history to present day.

Shalant, Phyllis. **What We've Brought You from Vietnam**. New York: Messner, 1988.
The recipes, stories, games, and crafts of Vietnam are presented in a well-illustrated format.

St. John, Jetty. **A Family in Bolivia**. Minneapolis, Minn.: Lerner Publications, 1986.
Superb photos enhance this description of life in a South American country. Part of a series of twenty-four books entitled Families the World Over.

The Disciplines of Social Studies

GEOGRAPHY

Aardema, Verna. **Bringing the Rain to Kapiti Plain**. New York: Dial, 1981.
The story of the effects of a terrible drought on a region of Africa that lives and dies according to the amount of rainfall it receives.

Allen, Thomas B. **Where Children Live**. Englewood Cliffs, N.J.: Prentice-Hall, 1980.
Stories about thirteen different children from different parts of the world fill this book about where people live.

Bellamy, David. **The River**. New York: Clarkson Potter, 1988.
Life on a small river and its perils highlight this wonderfully illustrated book.

Hendershot, Judith. **In Coal Country**. New York: Knopf, 1987.
A richly illustrated story about life in a coal-mining community in middle America.

Knowlton, Jack. **Maps and Globes**. New York: Crowell, 1985.
A fascinating look into mapmaking, cartography, and global measurements via some exciting illustrations and graphics.

Siebert, Diana. **Mojave**. New York: Crowell, 1988.
The beauty and vastness of the Mojave Desert are wonderfully illustrated in this book about the United States' best-known desert.

ANTHROPOLOGY

Aliki. **Corn Is Maize: The Gift of the Indians**. New York: Crowell, 1976.
All about corn: its history, how it grows, and its many uses.

Cawthorne, W. A. **Who Killed Cockatoo?** New York: Farrar, Straus & Giroux, 1989.
The aboriginal culture of Australia is delightfully described and illustrated through a traditional children's rhyme.

Climo, Shirley. **The Egyptian Cinderella**. New York: Crowell, 1989.
The age of the pharaohs is dramatically brought to life in this blend of fact and fiction about a sixth-century Cinderella.

dePaola, Tomie. **The Legend of Bluebonnet**. New York: Putnam, 1983.
The story of a Comanche girl who brings rain to her people and also brings them the bluebonnet flower.

Dunrea, Olivier. **Skara Brae: The Story of a Prehistoric Village**. New York: Holiday House, 1986.
The excavation of a four-thousand-year-old archaeological site on the Orkney Islands is described in this intriguing look into the past.

Feelings, Muriel. **Jambo Means Hello: Swahili Alphabet Book**. New York: Dial, 1974.
The culture and tradition of East African life is beautifully illustrated in this alphabet book for all ages.

Hou-tien, Cheng. **Six Chinese Brothers**. New York: Holt, 1979.
A tale of six look-alike brothers and their plot to outwit the king's executioner.

Hoyt-Goldsmith, Diane. **Totem Pole**. New York: Holiday House, 1990.
A Tsimshian Indian boy watches his father carve a new totem pole.

Lester, Julius. **How Many Spots Does a Leopard Have?** New York: Scholastic, 1989.
A collection of engaging folktales reflecting both African and Jewish traditions.

Musgrove, Margaret. **Ashanti to Zulu: African Traditions**. New York: Dial, 1976.
Introduces and describes a collection of African peoples, one for each letter of the alphabet. Wonderful illustrations.

Siberell, Anne. **Whale in the Sky**. New York: Dutton, 1982.
A Northwest Indian story about how Thunderbird saves the salmon from Whale.

SOCIOLOGY

Allen, Thomas B. **On Granddaddy's Farm**. New York: Knopf, 1989.
A child recalls summers growing up on a Tennessee farm during the 1930s.

Anderson, Joan. **Christmas on the Prairie**. New York: Clarion, 1985.
Offers some delightful information on present-day Christmas traditions that began during the early 1800s.

Desbarats, Peter. **Gabrielle and Selena**. San Diego, Calif.: Harcourt Brace Jovanovich, 1968.
Two girls, one white and one black, develop a close friendship.

Gray, Nigel. **A Country Far Away**. New York: Orchard, 1989.
An African boy and a boy from a Western country have more similarities than differences.

Kandoian, Ellen. **Is Anybody Up?** New York: Putnam, 1989.
A look at some persons who live in the same time zone and how they begin their days.

Kroll, Steven. **The Hokey-Pokey Man**. New York: Holiday House, 1989.
A sensitive recounting of immigrant life in New York City around the turn of the century that provides readers with a realistic portrayal of the trials and tribulations of life at that time.

Levinson, Riki. **Watch the Stars Come Out**. New York: Dutton, 1985.
The fears and adjustments of immigrating to the United States in the late 1800s as seen through the eyes of a child.

Maruki, Toshi. **Hiroshima No Pika**. New York: Lothrop, Lee and Shepard, 1980.
A moving and dramatically illustrated story of one family and the aftermath of the atomic bomb dropped on Hiroshima.

Morey, Janet, and Wendy Dunn. **Famous Mexican Americans**. New York: Cobblehill, 1989.
Includes biographical sketches of fourteen well-known Mexican-Americans.

Sandin, Joan. **The Long Way Westward**. New York: Harper & Row, 1989.
A Swedish family, seeking a new life, moves from Sweden to New York and then to the Midwest.

Young, Ed, translator. **Lon Po Po: A Red-Riding Hood Story from China**. New York: Philomel, 1989.
An inventive Chinese version of a familiar tale. This particular folk story is believed to be more than a thousand years old.

POLITICAL SCIENCE

Ables, Harriette S. **Future Government**. Mankato, Minn.: Crestwood House, 1980.
This book describes how government serves people, how technology becomes a part of the governmental process, and the importance of people working together for the common good.

Adler, David A. **Martin Luther King, Jr.: Free at Last**. New York: Holiday House, 1986.
A brief yet important biography of one of America's most influential political figures.

Adler, David A. **A Picture Book of Benjamin Franklin**. New York: Holiday House, 1990.
A straightforward biography of one of the most influential individuals in early U.S. history.

Fisher, Leonard Everett. **Leonard Everett Fisher's Liberty Book**. Garden City, N.Y.: Doubleday, 1976.
A collection of sayings, notices, proclamations, poetry, songs, and letters honoring this country's bicentennial.

Fradin, Dennis. **Voting and Elections**. Chicago: Children's Press, 1985.

All about voting, elections, counting votes, the importance of voting, and other relevant information on the electoral process.

Fritz, Jean. **The Great Little Madison**. New York: Putnam, 1989.

An engrossing biography of one of the most important leaders in early U.S. politics.

Johnson, Linda. **Patriotism**. New York: Rosen Publishing, 1990.

Describes what patriotism is, the symbols of patriotism, what a patriot is, and devotion to country. Uses examples from many different countries.

Krementz, Jill. **A Visit to Washington, D.C.** New York: Scholastic, 1987.

Highlights and landmarks of one family's visit to the nation's capital.

Maestro, Betsy, and Giulio Maestro. **A More Perfect Union: The Story of Our Constitution**. New York: Lothrop, Lee and Shepard, 1987.

A colorful and descriptive account of the events that preceded the creation of the U.S. Constitution, as well as its writing and ratification.

Richards, Norman. **The Story of the Mayflower Compact**. Chicago: Children's Press, 1967.

The events and social conditions leading to the creation of a significant political document in U.S. history.

ECONOMICS

Cowcher, Helen. **Rain Forest**. New York: Farrar, Straus & Giroux, 1988.

The onslaught of man and machines on the rain forest is vividly described in this straightforward book.

Field, Rachel. **General Store**. New York: Greenwillow, 1988.

Merchandising during the early years of the twentieth century is vividly portrayed in this well-crafted poem.

Lobel, Arnold. **On Market Street**. New York: Greenwillow, 1981.

A young child finds a number of fascinating gifts along Market Street, each beginning with a different letter of the alphabet.

Mitgutsch, Ali. **From Gold to Money**. Minneapolis, Minn.: Carolrhoda, 1984.

Provides an interesting glimpse into the development and uses of different forms of money throughout history.

Schwartz, David M. **If You Made a Million**. New York: Lothrop, 1989.

Various sums of money from one cent to $1 million are explained, along with checking and savings accounts and bank loans.

Ziefert, Harriet. **A New Coat for Anna**. New York: Knopf, 1986.

Anna obtains a much-needed winter coat from her mother, although there is no money to spend.

HISTORY

Adler, David. **A Picture Book of Thomas Jefferson**. New York: Holiday House, 1990.
An interesting look into the life and times of one of America's most prominent statesmen.

Behrens, June, and Pauline Brower. **Colonial Farm**. Chicago: Children's Press, 1976.
The activities, chores, and lives of a typical colonial family are depicted in this book filled with colorful photographs.

DeKay, James T. **Meet Martin Luther King, Jr.** New York: Random House, 1969.
An informative and engaging insight into Martin Luther King, Jr.'s life and the causes he fought for.

Fisher, Leonard E. **The Great Wall of China**. New York: Macmillan, 1986.
The trials and tribulations associated with the building of one of the greatest architectural wonders of all time.

Gibbons, Gail. **Trains**. New York: Holiday House, 1987.
Exciting graphics and colorful words outline the history of trains and their influence in America.

Jassem, Kate. **Sacajawea, Wilderness Guide**. Mahwah, N.J.: Troll Associates, 1979.
The story of the Indian woman who was invaluable during the Lewis and Clark expedition.

Lobel, Arnold. **On the Day Peter Stuyvesant Sailed into Town**. New York: Harper & Row, 1971.
This book offers some interesting perspectives and observations about humanity's relationship to the environment, circa 1647.

Rappaport, Doreen. **The Boston Coffee Party**. New York: Harper, 1988.
A Boston merchant during the time of the American Revolution raises the ire of a group of women and children.

Sanders, Scott R. **Aurora Means Dawn**. New York: Bradbury, 1989.
A family arrives in the Ohio Territory during the early 1800s and begins to settle on the land and deal with all the attendant hardships of frontier life.

Scarry, Hugh. **On Wheels**. New York: Philomel, 1980.
Traces the evolution of the wheel from earliest times to the "horseless carriage." Precise and descriptive illustrations.

Waters, Kate. **Sarah Morton's Day: A Day in the Life of a Pilgrim Girl**. New York: Scholastic, 1989.
Taken from the diary of a child who lived in Plimouth Plantation in 1627, this book illustrates the similarities and differences between children then and today.

Weisgard, Leonard. **The Plymouth Thanksgiving**. Garden City, N.Y.: Doubleday, 1967.
The story of the Pilgrims, presented in easy-to-read prose. A good introduction to the way of life of early settlers.

Appendix B
Social Studies Resources

Social Studies Activity Books

Abruscato, Joseph, and Jack Hassard. **The Earthpeople Activity Book: People, Places, Pleasures and Other Delights**. Glenview, Ill.: Scott, Foresman, 1978.
Although currently out of print, this is an excellent resource book, full of ideas, games, biographies, music, puzzles, and projects in every dimension of social studies.

Barchers, Suzanne. **Wise Women: Folk and Fairy Tales from around the World**. Englewood, Colo.: Libraries Unlimited, 1990.
A wonderful collection of original tellings and retold tales about women from around the world.

Cheyney, Arnold B., and Donald L. Capone. **The Map Corner**. Glenview, Ill.: Scott, Foresman, 1980.
Includes seventy-two activities, six complete lesson plans, ten explorer stories, twenty-three activity quizzes, and fifty reproducible outline maps.

Elder, Pamela, and Mary Ann Carr. **Worldways: Bringing the World into the Classroom**. Reading, Mass.: Addison-Wesley, 1980.
A collection of seventy-five activities, resources, blackline masters, and an extensive resource list to help students understand their place in global society.

Fredericks, Anthony D. **The Whole Earth Geography Book**. Glenview, Ill.: Scott, Foresman, 1990.
Provides over two hundred daily reinforcement activities in U.S. and world geography, as well as map and globe skills. Uses a problem-solving approach to geography.

Heltshe, Mary Ann, and Audrey B. Kirchner. **Multicultural Explorations: Joyous Journeys with Books**. Englewood, Colo.: Libraries Unlimited, 1990.
Offers integrated units of study on six areas of the world: Japan, Italy, Hawaii, Australia, Kenya, and Brazil.

Kellman, Jerold L., and Nancy L. Kellman. **Birthday Bonanza**. Glenview, Ill.: Scott, Foresman, 1984.
Includes short biographies of seventy well-known individuals with activities to use throughout the school year.

Lenning, Lorene R. **More than Money**. Glenview, Ill.: Scott, Foresman, 1986.
Incorporates problem-solving, cooperative learning, and bulletin-board ideas to involve students in economic concepts and activities.

McElmeel, Sharron L. **Adventures with Social Studies (through Literature)**. Englewood, Colo.: Libraries Unlimited, 1991.

Supplies a variety of theme-based units focusing on topics such as heroes, folklore, and history. Includes activities to stimulate creative thinking and writing skills.

Michaelis, John U., and Haig A. Rushdoony. **Elementary Social Studies Handbook**. San Diego, Calif.: Harcourt Brace Jovanovich, 1987.

Contains a variety of useful activities and prepared lesson plans for implementation into a social studies curriculum.

Morris-Lipsman, Arlene. **Notable Women**. Glenview, Ill.: Scott, Foresman, 1987.

Offers the life stories of twenty-three notable women (such as Benazir Bhutto, Sally Ride, and Wilma Rudolph) along with follow-up activities and projects.

National Geographic Society. **Directions in Geography: A Guide for Teachers**. Washington, D.C.: National Geographic Society, 1991.

A handbook based on geographic themes; includes lesson plans and a host of intriguing maps.

National Geographic Society. **National Geographic Picture Atlas of Our World**. Washington, D.C.: National Geographic Society, 1990.

A compendium of 120 maps, this book offers students an inviting look into more than 170 countries plus the oceans and polar regions.

Skeel, Dorothy J. **Small-Size Economics**. Glenview, Ill.: Scott, Foresman, 1985.

A variety of lessons, procedures, and reproducibles to be integrated into a social studies curriculum.

Sources for Children's Literature in Social Studies

Arbuthnot, May Hill. **Children's Books Too Good to Miss**. 8th ed. Cleveland, Ohio: Press of Case Western Reserve University, 1989.

Children's Books: Awards and Prizes. Compiled by the Children's Book Council (revised periodically).

The Children's Catalog. New York: H. W. Wilson, n.d.

Children's Choices. Newark, Del.: International Reading Association (issued each year).

A compilation of the best books published each year, as selected by teachers and librarians.

Cranciolo, Patricia. **Picture Books for Children**. Chicago: American Library Association, 1973.

Eakin, Mary. **Subject Index to Books for Primary Grades**. 3d ed. Chicago: American Library Association, 1967.

The Elementary School Library Collection. 15th ed. Williamsport, Pa.: Brodart, 1986.

Gillespie, John. **Elementary School Paperback Collection**. Chicago: American Library Association, 1985.

Gillespie, John, and Christine Gilbert. **Best Books for Children: Preschool through the Middle Grades**. 3d ed. New York: R. R. Bowker, 1985.

Hirschfelder, Arlene. **American Indian Stereotypes in the World of Children: A Reader and Bibliography**. New York: Scarecrow, 1982.

Jett-Simpson, Mary. **Adventuring with Books: A Booklist for Pre-K-Grade 6**. Urbana, Ill.: National Council of Teachers of English, 1989.

Kobrin, Beverly. **Eyeopeners! How to Choose and Use Children's Books about Real People, Places, and Things**. New York: Viking, 1988.
A thorough annotated bibliography of nonfiction books. Includes a variety of books in various topics along with a potpourri of extending activities and projects for selected books.

Kuipers, Barbara. **American Indian Reference Books for Children and Young Adults**. Englewood, Colo.: Libraries Unlimited, 1991.
Lists more than two hundred recommended reference books on the American Indian for grades 3-12.

Lima, Carol, and John A. Lima. **A to Zoo: Subject Access to Children's Picture Books**. 3d ed. New York: R. R. Bowker, 1989.
An all-inclusive listing of more than twelve thousand titles catalogued under seven hundred subjects. This is the authoritative, comprehensive collection of picture-book titles.

The New York Times Parent's Guide to the Best Books for Children. New York: Times Books, 1988.

Norton, Donna E. **Through the Eyes of a Child: An Introduction to Children's Literature**. New York: Merrill, 1991.
A marvelous introduction to children's literature, its different genres, and ways to use it productively in the classroom. Contains hundreds of annotated listings of social studies literature.

Pilla, Marianne L. **The Best: High/Low Books for Reluctant Readers**. Englewood, Colo.: Libraries Unlimited, 1990.
A carefully researched bibliography of high-interest, low-vocabulary books for students in grades 3-12. Includes books from many subject areas.

A Reference Guide to Historical Fiction for Children and Young Adults. New York: Greenwood, 1987.

Schon, Isabel. **A Hispanic Heritage: A Guide to Juvenile Books about Hispanic People and Cultures**. New York: Scarecrow, 1980.

Stensland, Anna Lee. **Literature by and about the American Indian: An Annotated Bibliography**. 2d ed. Urbana, Ill.: National Council of Teachers of English, 1979.

Trelease, Jim. **The Read Aloud Handbook**. New York: Penguin, 1985.
Wonderful ideas and suggestions for making reading a natural and normal part of children's lives. Includes an extensive listing of quality literature in all subject areas.

VanMeter, Vandelia. **American History for Children and Young Adults: An Annotated Bibliographic Index**. Englewood, Colo.: Libraries Unlimited, 1990.
Provides annotations for more than two thousand books about historical people and events in American history.

Whole Language Resource Books

Barrs, M. **Primary Language Record**. Portsmouth, N.H.: Heinemann, 1990.

Butler, Andrea, and Jan Turbill. **Towards a Reading-Writing Classroom**. Portsmouth, N.H.: Heinemann, 1984.

Calkins, Lucy. **The Art of Teaching Writing**. Portsmouth, N.H.: Heinemann, 1986.

Cambourne, Brian. **The Whole Story**. New York: Scholastic, 1988.

Eggleton, J. **Whole Language Evaluation: Reading, Writing, and Speaking**. San Diego, Calif.: Wright, 1990.

Goodman, Ken. **What's Whole in Whole Language**. Portsmouth, N.H.: Heinemann, 1986.

Goodman, Ken, Yetta Goodman, and W. Hood. **Whole Language Evaluation Book**. Portsmouth, N.H.: Heinemann, 1989.

Graves, Donald. **Build a Literate Classroom**. Portsmouth, N.H.: Heinemann, 1990.

Holdaway, Don. **The Foundations of Literacy**. Portsmouth, N.H.: Heinemann, 1979.

Mooney, M. **Reading to, with, and by Children**. Katonah, N.Y.: Richard Owen, 1990.

Pappas, C., B. Keifer, and L. Levstik. **An Integrated Language Perspective in the Elementary School: Theory into Action**. New York: Longman, 1990.

Routman, Reggie. **Transitions: From Literature to Literacy**. Portsmouth, N.H.: Heinemann, 1988.

Strickland, Dorothy, and Leslie Morrow. **Emerging Literacy: Young Children Learn to Read and Write**. Newark, Del.: International Reading Association, 1989.

Weaver, Constance. **Understanding Whole Language: From Principles to Practice**. Portsmouth, N.H.: Heinemann, 1990.

Periodicals for Teachers

Booklist. American Library Association, Chicago, Ill.

Book Review Digest. Wilson, New York, N.Y.

The Bulletin of the Center for Children's Books. Graduate Library School, University of Chicago, Chicago, Ill.

Children's Literature Association Quarterly. Children's Literature Association, Purdue University Press, West Lafayette, Ind.

The Horn Book. Horn Book Inc., 14 Beacon Street, Boston, Mass. 02108.

Instructor. Scholastic, Inc., P.O. Box 2039, Mahopac, N.J. 10541.

Language Arts. National Council of Teachers of English, Urbana, Ill.

Learning. P.O. Box 51593, Boulder, Colo. 80321-1593.
Periodically carries a section called "Reader Exchange"—a way to contact teachers from many different places. In a recent issue, one teacher was looking for picture postcards from different U.S. communities, another teacher from Canada wanted her students to correspond with students from different states, and yet another teacher was looking for ideas for celebrating Women's History Month.

National Geographic. National Geographic Society, Washington, D.C.

The Reading Teacher. International Reading Association, Newark, Del.

School Library Journal. R. R. Bowker, New York, N.Y.

Social Education. National Council for the Social Studies, 3501 Newark Street, NW, Washington, D.C. 20016.

The Social Studies. Heldref Publications, 4000 Albemarle Street, NW, Washington, D.C. 20016.

Teacher. P.O. Box 2091, Marion, Ohio 43305-2091.

Teaching K-8. 40 Richards Avenue, Norwalk, Conn. 06845. P.O. Box 54808, Boulder, Colo. 80322-4808 for subscriptions only.
Publishes a monthly rundown of exciting and new books, many dealing with social studies issues. Look for Carol Hurst's column in each issue.

The Web. Center for Language, Literature, and Reading, Ohio State University, Columbus, Ohio.

Periodicals for Children

Calliope. 30 Grove Street, Peterborough, N.H. 03458.

Cobblestone. 30 Grove Street, Peterborough, N.H. 03458.

Cricket: The Magazine for Children. Open Court, Boulder, Colo.

Faces. 30 Grove Street, Peterborough, N.H. 03458.

Highlights for Children. 2300 W. 5th Avenue, Columbus, Ohio 43272.

National Geographic World. National Geographic Society, Washington, D.C.

Ranger Rick. National Wildlife Foundation, Vienna, Va.

Miscellaneous

Consumer Information Center, Pueblo, Colo. 81009.
    Write for a copy of the all-purpose catalog listing more than two hundred federal publications, many of which are free.

Corporation for Public Broadcasting, Department of Education, P.O. Box 549, Alexandria, Va. 22313.
    Will provide a listing of resource people in your local area who can help you use public television as a social studies resource.

The Council on Interracial Books for Children, 1841 Broadway, New York, N.Y. 10023.
    Has a variety of pamphlets on selecting sexually and racially unbiased books for children.

Educators Progress Service, Inc., 214 Center Street, Randolph, Wis. 53956.
    Publishes an annual edition of *Educators Guide to Free Social Studies Materials*.

I Can Be a … (Children's Press, Chicago).
    This is a series of children's books about different occupations. Included are books about computer operators, doctors, firefighters, teachers, musicians, television camera operators, and truck drivers.

National Council for the Social Studies, 3501 Newark Street, NW, Washington, D.C. 20016.
    Write for their publications catalog and membership opportunities. Also, inquire about their quarterly journal, *Social Studies and the Young Learner*, as well as their informative document, *Preparing for the 21st Century, NCSS Task Force Report on Early Childhood Elementary Social Studies*.

National Geographic Society, 17th and M Streets, NW, Washington, D.C. 20036.
    Their catalog, *National Geographic Educational Services Catalog*, is an invaluable resource that is also fun to read.

New True Books. (Children's Press, Chicago).

This series of children's books offers varied and informative insights into a host of topics. Included in the social studies series are books about Japan, Mexico, North America, Congress, money, the Incas, and newspapers, to name a few. Lots of descriptive photographs highlight each book.

Scott, Foresman and Co., 1900 East Lake Avenue, Glenview, Ill. 60025.

Has four Social Studies Classroom Libraries, one each for kindergarten, grade 1, grade 2, and grade 3. Each library contains from thirteen to seventeen books encompassing all social studies areas.

Social Studies School Service, 1000 Culver Boulevard, Culver City, Calif. 90230.

A fantastic source of historical photographs and pictures. Write for information.

Society for Visual Education, 1345 Diversey Parkway, Chicago, Ill. 60614.

Write for information on the films and videos in their Black Heroes series.

Take a Trip to ... (Franklin Watts, New York).

Simple yet informative text distinguishes this series of books about various countries throughout the world.

Index

About the Author

Anthony D. Fredericks

Anthony D. Fredericks received his bachelor of arts degree in history from the University of Arizona, his master's degree in reading from Kutztown State College in Pennsylvania, and his doctor of education degree in reading from Lehigh University.

Tony has been a classroom teacher and reading specialist in public and private schools for more than fifteen years. He is a frequent presenter and storyteller at conferences, reading councils, schools, and inservice meetings through the United States and Canada. The author or coauthor of more than two hundred articles and fourteen books, he has written for *The Reading Teacher, Reading Today*, and *Teaching K-8*. He is the recipient of many education awards, including the Innovative Teaching Award from the Pennsylvania State Education Association.

Tony currently resides in Glen Rock, Pennsylvania, with his wife, Phyllis, two children, Rebecca and Jonathan, and four cats. He is an Assistant Professor of Education at York College, York, Pennsylvania, where he teaches methods courses in reading, language arts, science, and social studies.

from **Teacher Ideas Press**

U.S. HISTORY THROUGH CHILDREN'S LITERATURE
From the Colonial Period to World War II
Wanda J. Miller

Enhance the study of U.S. history with historical fiction and nonfiction. Stepping back in time to experience a character's dilemmas, thoughts, feelings, and actions helps students more easily grasp and retain a true understanding of an era. Here is all the material you need to begin a literature-based history program. **Grades 4–8**.
xiv, 229p. 8½x11 paper ISBN 1-56308-440-6

TEACHING U.S. HISTORY THROUGH CHILDREN'S LITERATURE
Post World War II
Wanda J. Miller

Following the format of Miller's book, mentioned above, this one contains great resources to help you combine recommended children's literature with actual events in U.S. History from World War II to the present. **Grades 4–8**.
xiii, 229p. 8½x11 paper ISBN 1-56308-581-X

MATH THROUGH CHILDREN'S LITERATURE
Making the NCTM Standards Come Alive
Kathryn L. Braddon, Nancy J. Hall, and Dale Taylor

Launch children into the world of mathematical literacy with books that give them the opportunity to experience the joy of math through their **own** understanding. Following the NCTM Standards, these literature activities are designed around an integrated reading process that captures a child's interest and brings math to life. **Grades 1–6**.
xviii, 218p. 8½x11 paper ISBN 0-87287-932-1

MORE SCIENCE THROUGH CHILDREN'S LITERATURE
An Integrated Approach
Carol M. Butzow and John W. Butzow

Back by popular demand! The Butzows have collected more fascinating thematic units of instruction that make science more understandable and enjoyable to young learners. Hands-on and inquiry-based topics, games, puzzles, word searches, and more accompany 30 quality works of children's literature. **Grades K–3**.
xviii, 245p. 8½x11 paper ISBN 1-56308-266-7

SCIENCE ADVENTURES WITH CHILDREN'S LITERATURE
A Thematic Approach
Anthony D. Fredericks

A must for all elementary science teachers! Focusing on the new National Science Teaching Standards, this activity-centered resource uses a variety of children's literature to integrate science across the elementary curriculum. **Grades K–3**.
xi, 233p. 8½x11 paper ISBN 1-56308-417-1

For a FREE catalog or to place an order, please contact:

Teacher Ideas Press
Dept. B94 · P.O. Box 6633 · Englewood, CO 80155-6633
1-800-237-6124, ext. 1 · Fax: 303-220-8843 · E-mail: lu-books@lu.com

 Check out our TIP Web site!
www.lu.com/tip